SOCIAL SERVICES IN SCOTLAND

SOCIAL SERVICES IN SCOTLAND

Edited by
JOHN ENGLISH

THE MERCAT PRESS
EDINBURGH

First published by Scottish Academic Press 1988.
Reprinted 1992 by Mercat Press, James Thin,
53 South Bridge, Edinburgh EH1 1YS

ISBN 1873644086

Printed and bound in Great Britain by
Antony Rowe Limited, Chippenham, Wiltshire

CONTENTS

INTRODUCTION

The aim of this book is to provide an introduction to social services in Scotland and the context in which they operate. It is concerned not only with describing the services but also with needs and problems in each field and current policy issues. Although social services in Scotland, with the notable exception of the children's hearings system, are broadly similar to their counterparts south of the border, there are many important differences. Social conditions also differ but the situation in Scotland is more or less ignored by most social policy textbooks.

A broad view of the social services has been taken: there are chapters on social security, health services, mental health services, housing, the personal social services, children's hearings and services for the elderly and physically handicapped. In addition the book covers central and local government in Scotland, employment services and urban social policy. At the end of each chapter there are suggestions for further reading which should be useful to those who want to know more about a particular topic or service.

Social Services in Scotland was first published in 1979 and it is now in its third edition. The late Fred Martin, whose death in 1985 was so widely regretted by his friends and colleagues, was joint editor of the first and second editions. The structure of the book is unchanged since the last edition except for a new chapter on urban social policy. The other chapters have, however, either been extensively revised or rewritten. Those on central and local government, health services and education are by new authors. Two chapters, on mental health services and the personal social services, are based on those written by Fred Martin for the previous edition of the book.

The editor would like to acknowledge the help of Madhu Satsangi who compiled the index and of Sheena Butler who prepared the word processor disks.

1
CENTRAL AND LOCAL GOVERNMENT

The government of Scotland differs from the rest of Britain in a number of ways: the Scottish Office, headed by the Secretary of State for Scotland, is responsible for many aspects of domestic policy and administration, there is often separate legislation for Scotland, and the local government system is rather different. In this chapter the origins of these arrangements are traced, their working is outlined and the extent of Scottish autonomy is considered. An historical dimension is crucial to an understanding of the arrangements which have been developed incrementally, that is in an *ad hoc* manner as a response to pressures and to meet perceived needs. An historical section, therefore, introduces Scottish central and local government. In the section on Scottish central government the Scottish Office's responsibilities are described and this is followed by a discussion of the limits on and opportunities for policy innovation by a territorial department. The section on local government describes its structure and origins. Local government is then considered under the four headings which the Royal Commission on Local Government in Scotland (the Wheatley report) of 1961[1] considered important: powers, effectiveness, local democracy and local involvement. In discussing local authority powers the increasingly fraught relations between central and local government are examined.

British government operates in a fluid constitutional framework, yet it has remained more stable than most of its European neighbours with their written and entrenched constitutions. However, change does occur frequently in Britain, though it tends to be gradual and almost unnoticed; during the past two decades much change has been evident in Scotland and more appears likely. Local government has altered dramatically but new institutions are also to be seen at central government level.

THE HISTORICAL BACKGROUND

Scotland is in a unique constitutional position. It has a separate legal system, a separate structure of local government and a territorial department of state at central government level. The reasons for these arrangements are to be found in Scottish history, and the consequences can be seen in the provision of public services and the existence of what one political scientist has called a 'Scottish political system'.[2] Before the advent of the modern welfare state, rudimentary provision of education, poor relief, prisons and other features of the nightwatchman state were administered in a highly unsystematic, localised fashion. No two areas provided for their school children, their poor and sick and their criminals in exactly the same way.

The emergence of the welfare state brought with it a greater degree of centralisation and consistency in service provision throughout Scotland and indeed Britain. In the Scottish context, what is most striking is the extent to which distinct forms of provision, however superficial the effect of the differences, continue to exist. In particular, the administrative apparatus and governmental machinery stand out in this respect. As elsewhere in Europe, the church – which meant the Church of Scotland – was once responsible for much of such administration as was carried on. The transition from church to state did not, however, mean the demise of Scottish national distinctiveness.

The Disruption of 1843, when the Church of Scotland split, was a crucial watershed in Scottish history, marking not simply an ecclesiastical controversy in the narrow theological sense, but also a dispute affecting education and poor relief. Though the 'presbyterian inheritance' remains, the Disruption facilitated the already evident movement of the secular state towards taking a more direct involvement in social welfare provision. The divided church was no longer in a position to provide parochial relief and other services. Two years after the Disruption, the Poor Law Amendment (Scotland) Act, 1845 was passed which set up parochial boards, statutory bodies for the administration of the poor law in each parish.

At the level of central government, by the late nineteenth century a number of boards based in Edinburgh, and largely manned by lawyers, had been set up to administer poor relief, fisheries, lunatic asylums and prisons. There was also a Scotch Education Department. The Scottish Office was established in 1885, headed by the Secretary for Scotland who assumed responsibility for the education department and the boards. But not all functions of the emerging welfare state were allotted to the Scottish Secretary; the main examples of where this did not happen were in the field of social security benefits when these developed in the early twentieth century (see chapter 2).

THE ORGANISATION OF BRITISH GOVERNMENT

The basis of the organisation of British government is essentially functional rather than territorial; that is, there is generally a department with responsibility for education and another for defence rather than departments for the Midlands and for Wales. Scotland, however, stands out in that for many functions it and not Britain is the unit of administration; but not all functions come under the Scottish Office's jurisdiction. This somewhat untidy arrangement has continued throughout the present century. The origins of the distinct form of territorial government in Scotland are to be found in an historical evolution which owes much to *ad hoc* developments and little to rational and coherent organisational change.

The structure of British government is continuously changing; departments appear, disappear and re-appear over time. Trade and industry have sometimes been organised together in one department while at other times they have been separate. Before the creation of the Department of Health and Social Security (DHSS) in 1968 there was a Ministry of Health and a Ministry of Social Security. In 1988 the DHSS was split into the Department of Health and Department of Social Security (DSS).

Within the informal departmental pecking order, the Treasury with its role of controlling public expenditure is undeniably at the top. Though a small department, the Treasury has staff who are concerned with the financial and economic implications of the work of all other departments, and any proposed policy changes with public expenditure implications have to be cleared with it. The highest spending department is the DSS. In the government's public expenditure white paper the projected expenditure on social security benefits for 1987-88 amounted to 31 per cent of the total (excluding debt interest)[3]. The DSS also has a huge staff, largely because it is responsible for dealing with claims for social security benefits throughout Britain. Some three-quarters of DSS staff are situated in the regional and local offices of the department. This example of extensive 'field administration' does not, of course, mean that the DSS is decentralised in any meaningful sense. Local discretion is minimal and central control makes the DSS an example of deconcentration rather than decentralisation. Most other departments have offices throughout Britain. Even the Foreign and Commonwealth Office has a small outpost in Scotland, and the Overseas Development Administration (ODA) has its base in East Kilbride. It is important to distinguish between the *deconcentration* of administration, as in the case of the DSS with its regional and local offices throughout Britain, *dispersal* (from London) of administration, for example the ODA; and *decentralisation* of administration, as represented by the Scottish Office.

The entry into the European Community of the United Kingdom in 1973 has had considerable repercussions on government and public administration. In essence, there is no longer a British agricultural policy but rather a European Common Agricultural Policy. Europe has, however, been slow in developing common policies in the sphere of social and regional affairs. Nevertheless, certain projects are funded, wholly or partly, through the European Social Fund, and Scottish local authorities have been particularly successful in gaining such support.

British central government does not consist entirely of departments of state. A very substantial element of work is conducted by semi-autonomous and, indeed, wholly autonomous bodies. *Quangos* – quasi-autonomous national (or non-) governmental organisations – have been variously defined. The original academic definition focused on those bodies which are non-governmental but are allocated resources by government to perform certain functions. They include such organisations as the Scottish Council for Voluntary Service. The initial concern was with the accountability of independent bodies but more recently the term has come to include essentially governmental institutions such as the Scottish Development Agency and the Highlands and Islands Development Board. Questions of accountability are still important but in these latter bodies a government minister appoints the organisations' members and is responsible to parliament for their actions.

The total number of quangos is difficult to assess and, despite the stated intention of the present Conservative government to reduce it dramatically, little change has occurred. Though a few fringe bodies whose work was negligible have been wound up, the problem arises of who should take over their responsibilities. The rather excited debates of the late 1970s and early 1980s distracted attention from important questions of accountability. The accountability of government bodies is a matter of importance which transcends the debate on quangos. The parliamentary time which is available for the detailed examination of government activities is limited. Question time in the House of Commons, when ministers have to answer for the work of their departments and allied bodies, functions more as a party political jousting match than as an effective means of making the government accountable.

The select committee system of the Commons was reformed in 1979 and consists of some 14 committees; each has between nine and 13 members and is concerned with a government department. One of them is the Scottish Affairs Committee (though it had not been reappointed a year after the 1987 general election); its remit extends beyond the Scottish Office to include other government departments with responsibilities north of the border. The committees have power to call witnesses and examine in detail the work of departments. They are, however, weakened by the fact that front-bench spokesmen do not serve on them so that their membership consists of relatively junior MPs (though they do include some ex-ministers). The committees also have a habit of dividing along party lines and their findings and recommendations are often simply ignored by the government. In addition to these select committees, the Public Accounts Committee has been in existence since 1861. It is the most important parliamentary committee and is chaired by a senior back-bench opposition MP. The committee is serviced by the office of the Comptroller and Auditor General, who is responsible solely to parliament through the committee. This is, inevitably, a limited form of accountability as the committee can only be concerned with a very small part of government activity each year.

SCOTTISH CENTRAL GOVERNMENT

The Scottish Office

Pressure from within Scotland resulted in the establishment of the Scottish Office, and from the point of view of the British government it was mainly intended to appease the Scots who felt that their distinct ways, supposedly guaranteed in the Act of Union of 1707, were under threat. Although the Secretary for Scotland normally sat in the cabinet, he did not become a secretary of state (really a matter of prestige) until 1926. Over the half century from its foundation in 1885 to the outbreak of the second world war the Scottish Office built up a substantial role. It had responsibility for most of the emerging social services (notably education, public health and poor relief), nearly all of which were administered by the system of boards based in Edinburgh. In 1928 most of the boards were replaced by departments headed by civil servants though they remained legally separate bodies. The Scottish Office in its modern form dates from 1939 when the departments were abolished except as administrative divisions of a single organisation.

Education, through the Scotch (from 1918 Scottish) Education Department, was the principal responsibility of the Scottish Office in 1885 but its functions expanded as the state's role increased. Housing and health became major concerns of government following the first world war and ensured that the Scottish Office was a firmly established part of the Whitehall network. In 1939 the opening of St. Andrew's House brought together most of the civil servants working for it in Edinburgh under one roof. But over the years St. Andrew's House became inadequate, and in 1975 New St. Andrew's House was opened as the headquarters of the Scottish Office.

Scottish Office functions and responsibilities have increased further and it now has responsibility for the equivalent of some 11 functional Whitehall departments.[4] This is an approximate figure as the functional departments' responsibilities are not neatly delimited territorially. For example, the Scottish office is, in many ways, Scotland's Home Office but immigration, nationality and broadcasting in Scotland are the responsibility of the latter department. Another example is in the field of education. The Department of Education and Science has responsibility for universities throughout the United Kingdom though all other aspects of education in Scotland come under the Scottish Education Department within the Scottish Office. This truncated form of administration has consequences for education policy, and proposals to improve the situation appeared in the short-lived Scottish Tertiary Education Advisory Council's review of higher education in Scotland.[5] The proposal for a Scottish Higher Education Planning and Funding Council under the Scottish Office was, however, rejected by the government.

Fears that lower standards would follow Scottish Office jurisdiction have not been uncommon during the century of its existence. In the debate preceding the establishment of the Scottish Board of Agriculture in 1912, concern was expressed that devolving responsibility for animal health to it would lead to lower standards and consequently disease would spread over the border into England. The transfer was not made until 1955.

With the growth in the functions of the Scottish Office there have been a number of reorganisations during its existence. The Scottish Office departments have a separate public identity, unlike the divisions of most other ministries, reflecting the wide range of functions covered. In 1988 there are five departments:

Department of Agriculture and Fisheries for Scotland (DAFS).

Scottish Education Department (SED): education (except the universities). The personal social services are the responsibility of the *Social Work Services Group* (SWSG) within the SED.

Scottish Development Department (SDD): housing, local government, planning, roads and transport.

Industry Department for Scotland (IDS): regional economic and industrial development, the Scottish Development Agency, new town development and electricity.

Scottish Home and Health Department (SHHD): police, prisons and crime, and the national health service.

In January 1986 there were some 9,900 civil servants in the Scottish Office, representing less than two per cent of the total civil service manpower in the United Kingdom. Of course, there are many more civil servants in Scotland than simply those serving the Scottish Office. A total of about 62,000 civil servants are based in Scotland; of these 8,400 work for the Department of Social Security, 6,900 for the Ministry of Defence, 6,800 for the Inland Revenue, and 5,500 for the employment group of government bodies (the Department of Employment, the Training Commission and the Health and Safety Executive). By far the largest concentration of civil servants is in the London conurbation with some 112,000; Newcastle which has many DSS staff follows with 13,000 and Edinburgh is behind that with 12,000.[6]

The ministerial team serving the Scottish Office comprised, following changes after the 1987 election, the Secretary of State with a seat in the cabinet, two ministers of state (one of whom was a member of the House of Lords), and two parliamentary under-secretaries of state. The ministers of state and under-secretaries have specific responsibilities, such as industry and local government, and home affairs and the environment. Apart from these responsibilities, the Secretary of State for Scotland and his junior ministers have other political functions not dissimilar to those of appeasing the Scots which were present at the establishment of the office. A major inquiry into Scottish administration published in 1937 noted that the Secretary of State was

> popularly regarded as 'Scotland's Minister'; and our evidence shows that there is an increasing tendency to appeal to him on all matters which have a Scottish aspect, even if on a strict view they are outside the province of his duties as statutorily defined ... even apart from his multifarious duties, there is a wide and undefined area in which he is expected to be the mouthpiece of Scottish opinion in the Cabinet and elsewhere.[7]

This governor-general type role, added to the heterogeneous assortment of territorially delimited functions, has seemed particularly anachronistic when, as has been the case since 1979, the party in power in Westminster has been in a minority in Scotland. The legitimacy of the Scottish Office is inevitably called into question at such times, and its continued existence clearly demonstrates that it is not about decentralisation of power to the Scottish people. The Scottish Office involves rather the decentralisation of administration to a specific government minister and his civil servants. Despite the claims made for it as a case of devolution, the Scottish Office represents a very limited form of administrative devolution and one which is not related to democratic principles. As a consequence, demands for a Scottish legislature as a means of providing accountability and democratic legitimacy have been most pronounced when the government does not enjoy majority political support in Scotland.

The Lord Advocate

The Lord Advocate is the government's chief law officer for Scotland and a minister in the United Kingdom government. Unlike the Secretary of State for Scotland, the Lord Advocate has had a continuous existence since before the Union of 1707, a clear indication of the importance of Scots law for Scottish administration. Today the Lord Advocate has two main functions. Assisted by the Solicitor General for Scotland and the Crown Office, he is in overall charge of public prosecutions. In the more serious cases prosecutions are undertaken directly by the Lord Advocate and in others by local procurators fiscal.

The other function of the Lord Advocate is to advise government ministers about legislation affecting Scotland and other legal matters. The Lord Advocate's Department which undertakes this function also includes the Scottish parliamentary draftsmen. Law reform, the appointment of judges, sheriffs and justices of the peace, arrangements for the provision of legal aid, and the relationship of the government with the legal profession are all effectively in the hands of the Lord Advocate, although the Secretary of State, as a cabinet minister, also deals with many of them.

Innovation and Policy Leadership

A small number of Scottish Office civil servants do not work from Edinburgh; these are the officials stationed at Dover House in Whitehall. Other officials spend periods of time in London, for example when Scottish legislation for which they are responsible is before parliament. Dover House remains the interface between the administrative apparatus in Edinburgh and the political decision-making centre of London. The Secretary of State for Scotland works mainly from Dover House and normally spends from Tuesday to Thursday of each week in London. This is because parliament, the cabinet and other departments of state including the Treasury are all situated there. Major decisions of policy and finance are thereby necessarily made far from the main body of officials who serve the Scottish Office.

Many decisions are obviously made in St. Andrew's House and New St. Andrew's House. There is nothing unusual in bureaucrats taking decisions without the direct involvement of ministers, except perhaps the extent to which this must occur in the Scottish office given the wide range of its responsibilities and the physical distance which often exists between them.

An elaborate complex of cabinet meetings, cabinet committees, official committees, informal bargaining and negotiation constitutes the Whitehall-Westminster network of decision-making. The pre-eminence of the

Treasury is the most notable feature of the process. An interesting, but difficult to determine, set of questions concerns the extent of freedom of action afforded to the Scottish Office in this network. In what circumstances can it operate autonomously and innovatively? The answer will be determined by a variety of factors:

(1) whether distinctive Scottish circumstances already prevail;
(2) whether there will be any consequences south of the border;
(3) the extent of pressure exerted by the 'Scottish political community'; and
(4) whether additional public expenditure is involved.

Examples may provide a clearer understanding.

The Social Work (Scotland) Act, 1968 which introduced children's hearings, is an example, though a rare one, of a distinct and innovative Scottish social policy (see chapter 7). The existing judicial procedure for the trial of juveniles was perceived to be inadequate. However, the innovation was only implemented in Scotland – and has not been replicated in England – because of the distinct basis offered by the Scottish legal system and strong advocacy on the part of the junior minister responsible at the Scottish Office, Judith Hart. Another example relates to the proposals to reform Scottish licensing laws made by the Clayson Committee in 1973[8] which were followed by legislation, though a parallel inquiry in England did not lead to government action until a bill was introduced in 1987. It might seem that the scope for distinctive Scottish policies which would have no consequences in England is wide, but account must always be taken of the need for what might be called ideological harmony throughout Britain. Whereas a different policy can be applied in Scotland, as with licensing reform, if party political commitments are not affected, in most cases policies will inevitably be similar to those in England. The introduction of the right to buy public sector houses in 1980 is one of many examples of a policy which was a matter of party commitment being applied throughout Britain. The Scottish Office's freedom in policy innovation is thus severely limited.

The establishment of the Scottish Development Agency (SDA) in 1975 and the more recent proposals for rates reform are examples of policy inovation as a consequence of political pressure from Scotland. The SDA had been promised in the Labour Party's Scottish manifesto in October 1974 as the 'main instrument for the regeneration of the Scottish economy'.[9] It was, together with Labour's promise to establish a Scottish Assembly, that party's response to the Nationalist threat. A more recent example of pressure from Scotland is the forthcoming abolition of domestic rates and their replacement with a 'community charge', which came about as a result of a revolt against the rates revaluation of 1985 by middle class people who were formerly seen as staunch supporters of the Conservative Party. The precarious position of the party in Scotland encouraged the government to press ahead with a reform which only two years earlier the Secretary of State had opposed.[10]

Public Expenditure and the Scottish Office

As with all government departments, the greatest constraint facing the Scottish Office is financial. The negotiations involved in the determination of public expenditure for each financial year take place over a period of months. The details of the Scottish Office's involvement have never been very clear. In 1980 it became known that a formula had been adopted in the calculation of marginal changes in the public expenditure of the Scottish Office. Marginal changes are increases or decreases in public expenditure from the previous year's total; they do not, therefore, concern total levels of expenditure. This formula has since been named the 'Barnett formula' after the Chief Secretary to the Treasury from 1974 to 1979, Joel Barnett, though he maintains that it was a 'fairly long standing formula that has been used over many years and indeed before I became Chief Secretary to the Treasury'.[11]

The arrangements were explained by the Principal Finance Office of the Scottish Office in June 1982:

> What happens is that changes to the Secretary of State's programme are determined by reference to changes in comparable programmes in England or, as the case may be, in England and Wales... The government does not reach a decision on a total change for a particular programme covering the whole of Great Britain and then apportion it as between England, Scotland and Wales. The decision is taken in relation to England, or as the case may be England and Wales. The Scottish ... consequences of that are thereafter followed through by applying the 10/85ths or 10/90ths and formula [to changes in comparable English or English and Welsh spending programmes respectively].[12]

In other words, changes in Scottish expenditure are determined without any reference to specific Scottish needs or circumstances. If the Secretary of State for Education and Science, for instance, is a weak minister who is unable to fight the Treasury then the Scottish Office budget also suffers. Within the resultant total the Secretary of State is free to allocate resources to specific services according to his own priorities (see below).

Some two-thirds of Scottish Office expenditure is covered by the formula: the whole of the housing, tourism, and health and personal social services programmes, and substantial items in the transport, law and order, education and science, environmental services programmes. Expenditure which is not covered includes the agriculture budget, for example, which is determined by the European Community's Common Agricultural Policy.

For historical reasons, partly because it used to contain a larger proportion of Britain's population, public expenditure per head in Scotland is greater than in England and Wales. The Barnett formula is intended to reflect the current population balance and means that Scotland receives a lower proportion of expenditure increases than its share of existing expenditure. Nevertheless, it would be a long time before changes at the margin made by the formula could bring expenditure in the different parts of Britain into line.

Furthermore, if public expenditure on a programme decreases, Scotland loses proportionately less than England and Wales, thus increasing differences in expenditure per head.

The Scottish Office receives a block grant from the Treasury but the Secretary of State's powers of virement mean that he is not obliged to alter the amount spent on each comparable programme by the same percentage as changes south of the border. In other words, changes to expenditure on specific programmes in England and Wales merely affect the size of the block grant. In 1982, for example, George Younger told the Scottish Select Committee that, compared with the changes in the comparable programmes of his cabinet colleagues, he had allocated less to housing and transport and more to education and law and order.[13] The amounts of money involved in such shifts in priority are not known; to reveal them would raise, as the Scottish Select Committee's specialist adviser noted in a memorandum in 1983, sensitive issues concerning the Scottish Office's relationship with the Treasury.[14] Specifically Scottish policy changes and priorities which require additional expenditure are not impossible, but they can only be achieved at the expense of lower spending on other services in Scotland. Furthermore, substantially different priorities may have political repercussions on both sides of the border.

A comparison of expenditure *per capita* in each of the constituent nations of the United Kingdom is sometimes claimed to favour Scotland. That Scots somehow get a better deal certainly appears to be the case at first sight; but a more careful examination of public expenditure makes the conclusion less clear. First, figures are available only for 'identifiable expenditure' which excludes almost 20 per cent of total public expenditure. Furthermore, departmental running costs amount to £13 billion in 1987-88 and, although not all ministries are based in London, much of this benefits the home counties in the form of civil servants' salaries and government purchases. Second, 'tax expenditures' (or tax reliefs) are not included in public expenditure. In 1985-86 Scotland appeared to spend twice as much as England on a *per capita* basis on housing; but this figure excludes the substantial amounts involved in tax relief on mortgage interest which benefits homebuyers who are, proportionately, more numerous in England. Third, needs differ: for example, the fact that services cost more to provide in sparsely populated areas, that unemployment is higher in Scotland and that levels of deprivation are greater can make such comparisons misleading. It would be wrong to infer, therefore, that Scotland is necessarily treated more favourably than other parts of the United Kingdom.

LOCAL GOVERNMENT

Nineteenth century welfare provision in Scotland has been described as having had three distinctive features: a lack of overt central control, the individualistic ethos of welfare administrators, and their preference for voluntary rather than rate-financed aid to the needy.[15] The rapidly changing circumstances during the course of the century resulted in the enactment of a number of important administrative changes. The development of social rights and the concomitant need for arrangements for the administration of services brought about a change in the features mentioned above. Over time, more overt central control developed, the individualistic ethos gave way to more collectivist thinking and public services largely replaced voluntary assistance.

All of this was reflected in local government. The century to 1935 was the 'era of *ad hoc* administration, with a trend in favour of amalgamation of duties in a single body for a particular area'[16] in Scotland. As the state's functions grew, so did the need for a more coherent system of local government. The Local Government (Scotland) Act, 1929 established or reconstituted 33 county councils, 24 town councils of large burghs, 171 town councils of small burghs, and 199 district councils in counties (so-called landward areas). The plethora of local *ad hoc* bodies in each locality – parish councils responsible for poor relief, district boards of control responsible for mental hospitals, and education authorities – were concentrated into a single body, the town or county council.

This structure of local government lasted, with some amendment, until 1975, when it was reformed by the Local Government (Scotland) Act, 1973. This legislation was based on the findings of the Royal Commission on Local Government in Scotland chaired by Lord Wheatley which reported in 1969. Wheatley stated that the reform should have four basic objectives: local government should be enabled to play a more important, responsible and positive part in the running of the country; it should be equipped to provide services in the most satisfactory manner; it should constitute a system in which power is exercised through the elected representatives of the people; and it should bring the people into the process of reaching decisions as much as possible.[17] Consideration of the development of local government since the 1973 act under these headings will follow a description of the new structure created by the legislation.

The Structure of Local Government

Wheatley recommended a two-tier system with seven regional authorities and 37 district authorities together with provision for the establishment of community councils. In the event, the new structure consisted of three all-purpose islands authorities and a two-tier system of nine regional councils and 53 district councils (Figure 1.1). The population of the authorities varies widely: that of regions from Strathclyde with well over two million to Borders with some 100,000, and of districts from Glasgow with about 730,000 to Badenoch and Strathspey with little more than 10,000 (Table 1.1).

Additionally, Wheatley recommended that community councils should be created. These are not a third tier of local government: they have no statutory powers and are set up by the district and islands councils. Over 1,000 community councils exist in Scotland with a variety of compositions and activities. Their principal function is to speak and act, representatively, for the

FIGURE 1.1 Local Government Areas in Scotland

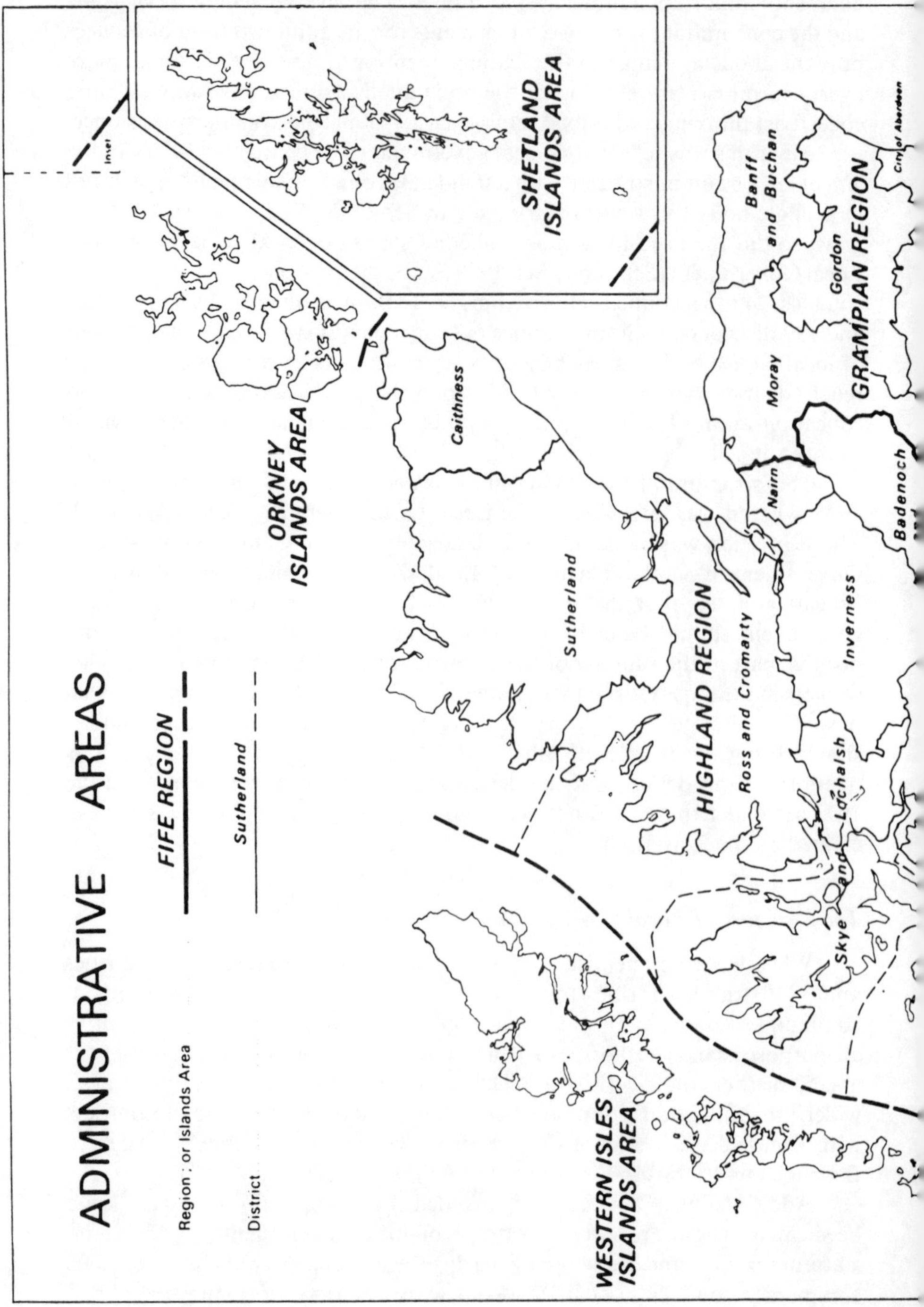

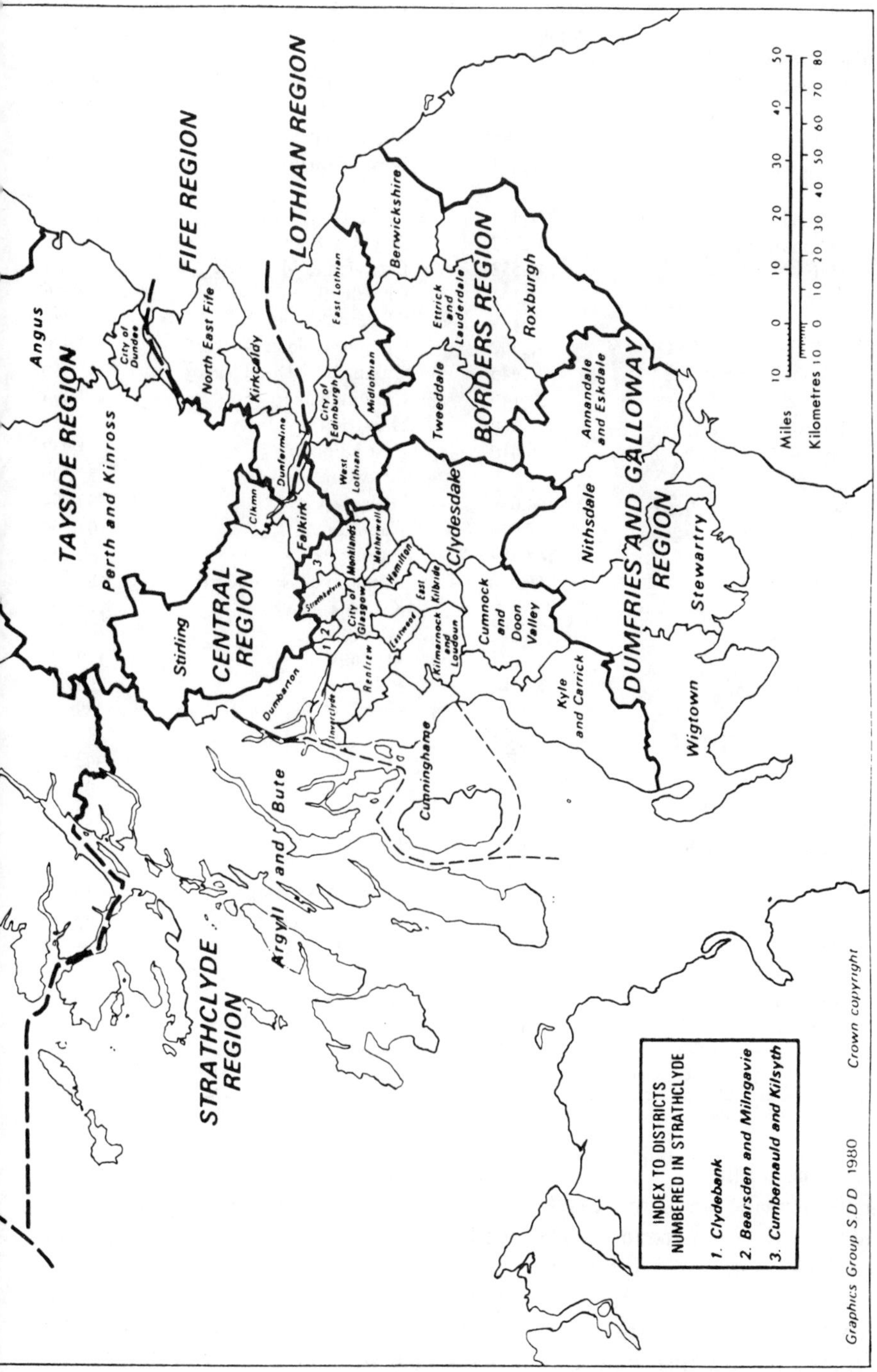
TAYSIDE REGION
Angus
City of Dundee
Perth and Kinross
FIFE REGION
North East Fife
Kirkcaldy
Dunfermline
Clkmn
LOTHIAN REGION
East Lothian
City of Edinburgh
Midlothian
West Lothian
CENTRAL REGION
Stirling
Falkirk
BORDERS REGION
Berwickshire
Ettrick and Lauderdale
Roxburgh
Tweeddale
DUMFRIES AND GALLOWAY REGION
Annandale and Eskdale
Nithsdale
Stewartry
Wigtown
STRATHCLYDE REGION
Argyll and Bute
Dumbarton
Inverclyde
Renfrew
Strathkelvin
City of Glasgow
Monklands
Motherwell
Hamilton
East Kilbride
Eastwood
Kilmarnock and Loudoun
Cumnock and Doon Valley
Kyle and Carrick
Cunninghame
Clydesdale
Miles 10 0 10 20 30 40 50
Kilometres 10 0 10 20 30 40 50 60 70 80
INDEX TO DISTRICTS NUMBERED IN STRATHCLYDE
1. Clydebank
2. Bearsden and Milngavie
3. Cumbernauld and Kilsyth
Graphics Group S D D 1980
Crown copyright

TABLE 1.1: Population of Regional, District and Islands Council Areas, 1985

	Population		Population
BORDERS	101,705	LOTHIAN	745,229
Berwickshire	18,602	East Lothian	82,160
Ettrick & Lauderdale	33,296	Edinburgh	439,672
Roxburgh	35,294	Midlothian	81,453
Tweeddale	14,513	West Lothian	141,944
CENTRAL	272,426	STRATHCLYDE	2,358,727
Clackmannan	47,747	Argyll & Bute	65,873
Falkirk	143,532	Bearsden & Milngavie	40,154
Stirling	81,147	Clydebank	49,966
		Clydesdale	58,246
DUMFRIES & GALLOWAY	146,562	Cumbernauld & Kilsyth	62,970
Annandale & Eskdale	35,945	Cumnock & Doon Valley	43,750
Nithsdale	57,149	Cunninghame	137,094
Stewartry	23,058	Dumbarton	79,385
Wigtown	30,410	East Kilbride	81,952
		Eastwood	55,530
FIFE	344,019	Glasgow City	733,794
Dunfermline	129,115	Hamilton	107,569
Kirkcaldy	148,894	Inverclyde	97,932
North-East Fife	66,010	Kilmarnock & Loudon	81,078
		Kyle & Carrick	113,290
GRAMPIAN	500,566	Monklands	108,155
Aberdeen City	215,246	Motherwell	149,185
Banff & Buchan	83,341	Renfrew	203,447
Gordon	70,170	Strathkelvin	89,537
Kincardine & Deeside	46,788		
Moray	85,021	TAYSIDE	394,322
		Angus	94,288
HIGHLAND	198,617	Dundee City	177,674
Badenoch & Strathspey	10,442	Perth & Kinross	122,360
Caithness	27,302		
Inverness	58,849	ORKNEY ISLANDS	19,351
Lochaber	19,409	SHETLAND ISLANDS	23,440
Nairn	10,180	WESTERN ISLES	31,545
Ross & Cromarty	47,889		
Skye & Lochalsh	11,308	SCOTLAND	5,136,509
Sutherland	13,238		

Source: Registrar General Scotland, *Annual Report 1985*, HMSO, 1986.

local community. Community councils raise money through voluntary activities and in some cases the local authority provides financial and administrative assistance. The method of election and appointment of members is determined by the district or islands council.

Reorganisation also brought about changes in the collective representation of Scottish local authorities. Previously there were four bodies representing Scottish local authorities – the Convention of Royal Burghs, the Association of County Councils in Scotland, the Scottish Counties of Cities

Association and the District Councils' Association of Scotland. Though two tiers were created on reorganisation, only one representative body, the Convention of Scottish Local Authorities (COSLA), was set up. COSLA represents Scottish local government in negotiations with central government in financial and other matters, acts as a discussion forum and provides services, such as training and information facilities, for local authorities. It is funded by the local authorities themselves.

Local Government Functions

Since reorganisation there have been minor changes in the functions of the tiers of local government. In 1980 the Secretary of State appointed a committee under Anthony Stodart to review the working relations between the new authorities, and recommend whether any transfer or rationalisation of functions between them was desirable and consistent with fully maintaining the viability of the existing two-tier structure. In particular, the vexed question of concurrent functions where both regional and district councils had powers was considered by the committee.[18]

Some of Stodart's recommendations were enacted in the Local Government and Planning (Scotland) Act, 1982. This tidying-up exercise reallocated certain functions. Leisure, recreation and tourism became district functions and industrial development became a regional function, though the districts retained some powers in this area.

Regional Council Functions: education, careers service, social work, police, fire, civil defence, water and sewerage, flood prevention, coast protection, strategic planning, industrial promotion, industrial development (concurrently with districts), roads and road safety, public transport, highways lighting, airports, ferries, harbours, consumer protection, weights and measures, diseases of animals, valuation and rating, electoral registration, registration of births, deaths and marriages.

District Council Functions: local planning*, development control*, urban development*, industrial development (concurrently with regions), listed buildings and ancient monuments*, conservation areas*, housing, building control*, libraries*, tourism, countryside†, nature conservation, leisure and recreation, parks, museums and art galleries, environmental health, cleansing, refuse collection and disposal, public conveniences, employment of young persons, administration of district courts, licensing of dogs, betting and gaming, theatres and cinemas, taxis and liquor, community centres‡, caravan sites, war memorials, burials and cremation, markets, slaughterhouses, allotments, shops hours, food hygiene, standards and labelling, health and safety at work.

* Except in Borders, Dumfries and Galloway, and Highland where the functions are regional.
† Regions also have a role in the countryside.
‡ Regions can also provide community centres depending on their purpose.

Local Government Powers

The functions of local government are not the same as its powers. For each function the local authority will be constrained in its actions in a number of ways. First, the doctrine of *ultra vires* limits the scope of local government. As 'creatures of statute' local authorities have no entrenched rights or powers. In Britain, local authorities have no recourse to a written constitution or other sovereign authority should parliament decide to limit their powers or, indeed, to abolish them. Local authorities are obliged by law to act within their statutorily defined powers.

Second, central government often sets minimum standards of service provision. However desirable it may be to have minimum standards, these limit local autonomy, especially given the limited resources available to local authorities. Third, policies of ideological importance to the government, which may have featured in a parliamentary election campaign, will also limit local autonomy. For the Labour Party an example has been the policy of comprehensive education; for the Conservatives the sale of council houses.

Fourth, the most important limitation placed on local government, as with central government, is financial. Wheatley noted that local government expenditure had increased over the years at a remarkable rate, far more than could be accounted for by the effects of inflation. New responsibilities, increased demand for existing services and higher standards had all contributed to this. The turning point came in 1975 when Anthony Crosland, Labour's Environment Secretary, told local authorities that the 'party's over'. This heralded a new era: expenditure constraints were introduced which were imposed with even greater determination by the Conservative government which came to power in 1979.

Local authority expenditure accounts for over a quarter of all public expenditure in Britain and 11 per cent of gross national product. In Scotland, the regions account for almost 80 per cent of local government expenditure, the districts for just under 20 per cent and the islands authorities for about three per cent. Local authority expenditure is split into two parts: capital expenditure on projects such as building schools, roads and houses; and revenue (or current) expenditure on salaries, maintenance of buildings and other recurrent costs. The means by which these forms of expenditure are financed are quite distinct. Capital expenditure is met through loans, largely from the Public Works Loan Board which is controlled by the Treasury. Central government informs local authorities of the maximum capital expenditure which they are permitted, whereas revenue expenditure is not directly limited.

The most important sources of income for local government current expenditure are central government grants, local rates, and income from charges. The proportion met from government grants in Scotland was 58 per cent in 1985-86 (49 per cent in England and 67 per cent in Wales). This represents a substantial decrease in the proportion of income funded through central grants from 69 per cent in 1980-81. Of course, if Scotland was compared with an area of England with a similar socio-economic composition then the disparities in the proportions of expenditure met by central government subventions might well disappear as an assessment of differing needs is crucial to the assessment of Rate Support Grant (RSG). That is, the relatively high level of RSG paid to Scottish local authorities as a whole reflects high levels of need. Similar high levels of grant are awarded to relatively depressed areas of England, and within Scotland better-off areas receive much less grant than do poorer ones.

Wheatley called for a 'real shift of power from central to local government'[19] and intended that local authorities should be able to raise more of their own finances. However, the amount local authorities can raise through rates has been severely limited by central government. Since 1981-82 the Secretary of State has been empowered to take selective action against individual authorities planning 'excessive and unreasonable' expenditure by reducing their RSG. These powers have dramatically altered the relationship between the Scottish Office and Scottish local government.

The Rating and Valuation (Amendment) (Scotland) Act, 1984 increased the Secretary of State's power and influence over local authority revenue spending in a number of ways. First, he was empowered to relate RSG penalties to the degree of spending over Scottish Office guidelines by individual local authorities. Thus the amount which has to be raised from rates where there is 'excessive' expenditure is further increased through loss of exchequer grant, with the intention of making the consequent rate burden politically unacceptable. Second, the Secretary of State was empowered to 'rate-cap' all local authorities by placing a general limit on the level of rates, but this power has not been used. Third, the act streamlined the existing power to limit the rates levied by specific local authorities. This power has been used on a number of occasions, notably in the case of Edinburgh district council; though there was talk of confrontation in some cases, councillors have always drawn back and reduced the rate to the level specified by the Secretary of State. Had they not done so, councillors who had voted for the illegal rate would have been liable to legal action. Fourth, the Secretary of State was empowered to limit the amount a local authority can contribute from its rate fund to the housing revenue account to subsidise council house rents (see chapter 5).

Provisions contained in the Abolition of Domestic Rates, Etc. (Scotland) Act, 1987 further altered the relationship in favour of central government. Domestic rates will be replaced by a 'community charge' in 1989 while increases in non-domestic rates (rates on industry and commerce) will be index-linked and ultimately standardised so that their level is outwith the control of local authorities. Under a fifth of their total income (that from the community charge) will therefore be under the control of local authorities. The community charge is a primitive flat-rate, and therefore regressive, tax; it is often referred to as the poll tax. Its introduction is intended to put pressure on high spending local authorities to reduce the amount of revenue which they raise locally. The argument is that because the community charge (unlike rates) will in principle be paid by almost all electors, people will be more likely to vote against candidates and parties advocating high levels of expenditure.

The Effectiveness of Local Government

Effective delivery of services and effective tackling of local problems were deemed by Wheatley to be important objectives for local authorities. Obviously, such objectives will be affected by the resources made available by central government. Nevertheless, an important criterion in assessing Scottish local government is the efficacy with which it performs these tasks.

The need for a co-ordinated and integrated approach to service delivery is important. Problems arise in relations between tiers of authorities and with other agencies, as well as within authorities. The division of responsibilities between housing and social work, in planning and the provision of leisure facilities have required co-ordination between tiers which has not always occurred. Professional jealousies and guarding of professional territory make for difficulties in co-ordination within authorities.

In 1967 the *Report of the Committee on the Management of Local Government* (the Maud report) criticised the specialised management, lack of co-ordination and profusion of committees and departments in local government.[20] Its recomendations included the creation of a management board of senior councillors, the appointment of a chief executive within each authority to co-ordinate the work of different departments, and simplified committee and departmental structures. Few changes occurred in Scottish local government along these lines compared with what happened in England between Maud reporting and reorganisation in 1975. Following reorganisation the Paterson committee issued its report, *New Scottish Local Authorities: Organisation and Management Structures*.[21] The Bains report dealt with similar issues to Paterson for England and Wales.[22]

The Paterson report urged authorities to appoint a chief executive as well as a team of officers who would act together to co-ordinate the work of departments. Paterson also urged councillors in each authority to establish a policy and resources committee charged with guiding the council in formulating its objectives and priorities, in addition to a committee structure related to departmental responsibilities. Changes in keeping with Paterson have certainly been more evident than responses to Maud. The situation differs from one authority to another but by 1978 almost all Scottish councils had a policy and resources committee and all had appointed a chief executive, though in some cases this official combines the post with heading a functional department. One consequence which the improved management techniques have arguably had has been to shift power away from the elected representatives into the hands of the officials.

Local Democracy

The need for local democracy was one of the prime objectives sought by Wheatley. Elections to Scottish local authorities are held every four years;

regional and islands authorities are elected at the same time and districts two years later. Candidates for election to the councils must be 21 years of age or over (though the voting age is 18), they must be electors within the local authority area or have lived or had their main workplace in the area during the year previous to the election, and they must not be an employee of the authority to which election is sought nor an undischarged bankrupt. Unlike elections for parliament there is thus a residential qualification in those for local authorities.

Apart from the formal provisions for local democracy in the legislation setting up the system, other factors affecting its extent should be noted. The degree of central control of local government, the existence of bodies which are not accountable to locally-elected representatives, and the resources available to councillors to fulfil their duties all have a bearing on the nature and extent of local democracy.

Central control of local government clearly removes power from locally-elected representatives, though responsibility may often still be seen by the electorate as remaining with them. This places councillors in the invidious position of appearing to be unwilling to respond to local demands and may well further weaken local democracy. Any gap which exists between the electorate's perception of local government's powers and responsibilities and its actual powers and responsibilities can only be detrimental to local democracy.

As far as the national health service is concerned, accountability to the public at the local level is provided for in a more limited and indirect way than in the case of local government. Fifteen health boards are responsible to the Secretary of State for Scotland. The chairmen and members of the boards are appointed by the Secretary of State, the latter after consultation with local authorities and other bodies. In addition there are 48 local health councils which were established in 1975 following the reorganisation of the health service. They have no executive powers and have been compared with community councils, both having largely advisory roles.[23]

Local councillors, as basically unpaid representatives, are limited in the amount of time they can devote to their duties. A survey of Scottish councillors in 1983 found that 41 per cent were full-time employees and an additional 21 per cent were self-employed. Despite this, councillors in 1983 were spending an average of 31 hours a week on council business[24] for which they receive limited payment in the form of attendance allowances. In 1977 the Robinson committee published their report on the *Remuneration of Councillors* [25]. The committee was critical of attendance allowances but opposed salaried councillors as these, it was felt, would undermine the voluntary principle. Instead, the committee proposed a lump sum for all councillors, a financial loss allowance, and additional allowances for senior councillors with more onerous responsibilities. The Stodart Committee which, as noted earlier, was appointed in 1980 to review the structure of Scottish local government, gave support to the idea of full-time salaried councillors. However, this proposal was rejected by the government.

Local democracy requires elected representatives who can devote much time and attention to their duties. Councillors also require research, secretarial and support services. Since local government reorganisation there have been improvements in these areas, strengthening local democracy, though the position varies from one authority to another.

Local Involvement

Participation has been described by a leading theorist of decentralisation as one of the values which should be inherent in local government,[26] and local involvement was also seen as an objective of the reformed structure by Wheatley. Turnout at elections, the composition of local councils and the limited means of wider public involvement do not suggest great success in the achievement of this objective.

The proportion of the electorate which turns out to vote at local authority elections is notoriously low. Turnout at elections has averaged 46 per cent since reorganisation, the highest being 51 per cent at the immediate post reform elections in 1974 when districts, regions and islands all held elections. At the regional elections in 1986 the turnout was 45 per cent.

A survey of Scottish councillors in 1983[27] demonstrated that the proportion of women councillors had hardly changed from a previous survey conducted in 1965. In 1983 only 13 per cent of councillors were women compared with ten per cent in 1965. The 21-34 age group was strongly under-represented and the 45-64 group over-represented when compared with the adult population as a whole. Though councillors were younger in 1983 than in 1965 the change was small. Other groups which were over-represented when compared with the population as a whole were the retired and the self-employed. The unemployed were under-represented and others, mainly housewives, grossly under-represented. Those in employment were predominantly in managerial, professional and executive occupations with manual occupations being under-represented. The findings of the survey are not surprising. Councillors tend to be both middle class and middle aged, and the survey suggests that certain occupations are more compatible than others with serving on a local authority.

Decentralisation and community participation have been seen as possible means of increasing local involvement. In Glasgow district a structure consisting of nine area management committees was established following the local elections in 1980. As well as district and regional councillors and MPs, these committees include representatives from the local community councils, residents' and tenants' associations and similar bodies. Proposals to establish a decentralised structure permitting opportunities for community participation have been brought forward in Edinburgh where 30 local offices are envisaged. Decentralisation is seen as offering opportunities both for improved delivery of services and increased community participation.

CONCLUSIONS

Social service provision has distinctive features in Scotland which are most obvious in the apparatus of government. Essentially, however, power resides in London and, though a degree of distinctiveness is permitted in policy outputs, by far the most important influence on social services for which the Scottish Office and Scottish local government have responsibility is decisions made there. A major reason for this, of course, is the issue of resources which will remain of paramount importance.

Major reforms in the structure of local government and an important reorganisation of the Scottish Office during the 1970s combined with electoral volatility to give the impression of Scottish government in flux. The 1980s may not have been marked by the same excited political atmosphere, but dissatisfaction with the apparatus of government in Scotland may yet lead to major reforms affecting it at both the central and local levels. The lack of accountability of the Scottish central government apparatus to a distinctively Scottish representative body, together with a Secretary of State for Scotland enjoying the support of only a small minority of Scottish MPs, may make the case for legislative devolution more attractive. The consequences for local authorities of creating a Scottish legislature would be considerable, and the abolition of the regional councils and the establishment of single-tier local government might be seen as desirable. The problems of achieving a co-ordinated and integrated approach in local government in the context of the two-tier structure also suggest that changes are possible. Nevertheless, though a case can be made for radical changes in the way Scotland is governed, this does not mean that they will occur.

References

1. *Report of the Royal Commission on Local Government in Scotland* (Wheatley Report), Cmnd. 4510, HMSO, 1969.
2. J. G. Kellas *The Scottish Political System*, Cambridge University Press, (3rd ed.) 1984.
3. *The Government's Expenditure Plans 1987-88 to 1989-90*, Cm.56, HMSO, 1987.
4. R. Rose, *Understanding the United Kingdom: The Territorial Dimension in Government*, Longman, 1982.
5. *Future Strategy for Higher Education in Scotland*, Cmnd.9676, HMSO, 1985.
6. *Civil Service Statistics 1986*, HM Treasury, 1986.
7. *Report of the Committee on Scottish Administration* (Gilmour Report), Cmd.5563, HMSO, 1937, para. 37.
8. *Report of the Departmental Committee on Scottish Licensing Law* (Clayson Report), Cmnd.5354, HMSO, 1973.
9. *Scotland Will Win with Labour*, Labour Party, 1974.
10. *House of Commons: Official Report*, Vol.47, Col.862 (2 November 1983).
11. Letter to the author from Lord Barnett, 8 February 1985.
12. Committee on Scottish Affairs, *Scottish Aspects of the 1982-85 Public Expenditure White Paper: Minutes of Evidence*, HC413/1982.
13. HC413/1982.
14. Committee on Scottish Affairs, *Scottish Aspects of the Government's Public Expenditure Plans, 1983-84 to 1985-86: Minutes of Evidence*, HC354/1983, Appendix 3.
15. I. Levitt, *Welfare and the Scottish Poor Law, 1880-1914*, unpublished PhD thesis, University of Edinburgh, 1983.

16. A. Grierson, 'One Hundred Years of Scottish Local Government', *Public Administration*, Vol.13, 1935, p.232.
17. Wheatley Report.
18. *Report of the Enquiry into Local Government in Scotland* (Stodart Report), Cmnd.8115, HMSO, 1981.
19. Wheatley Report, para.873.
20. *Report of the Committee on the Management of Local Government* (Maud Report), HMSO, 1967.
21. *New Scottish Local Authorities: Organisation and Management Structures* (Paterson Report), HMSO, 1973.
22. *New Local Authorities: Management and Structure* (Bains Report), HMSO, 1972.
23. D. Bochel and M. MacLaren, 'Local Health Councils: The Consumers' Voice' in H.M. Drucker and N.L. Drucker (eds.), *The Scottish Government Yearbook 1979*, Paul Harris Publishing, 1978.
24. C. Martlew and G. Buchanan, *Councillors in Scotland*, Planning Exchange Occasional Paper No.28, 1986.
25. *Remuneration of Councillors* (Robinson Report), HMSO, 1977.
26. L.J. Sharpe, 'Theories and Values in Local Government', *Political Studies*, Vol.XVIII, No.2, 1970.
27. Martlew and Buchanan, *Councillors in Scotland*.

FURTHER READING

J.S. Gibson, *The Thistle and the Crown*, HMSO, 1985.

A semi-official, but readable, account of the development of the Scottish Office and its antecedents.

M. Keating and A. Midwinter, *The Government of Scotland*, Mainstream Publications, 1983.

A study of central and local government, their relationship and links with Whitehall.

J.G. Kellas, *The Scottish Political System*, Cambridge University Press, (3rd ed.) 1984.

Places Scottish political institutions within the context of Scottish society, distinctive party system and history.

G. Monies, *Local Government in Scotland*, Green, 1985.

A clear explanation of the organisation, structure and workings of local government in Scotland.

Public Expenditure: A Commentary on the Scottish Programme, Scottish Office, annual.

A useful review of Scottish Office expenditure, including that on education, health, personal social services and housing, with a brief discussion of developments in each field.

2
SOCIAL SECURITY

This chapter is concerned with the range of cash benefits which are available to individuals and families, either to provide an income during old age, sickness, unemployment or widowhood, or to meet particular needs related to family size, disablement and so on. Social security includes contributory national insurance benefits (such as retirement pensions), family credit, housing benefit and many other allowances and payments, as well as income support (formerly supplementary benefit). Social security is by far the most expensive social service in terms of public expenditure; indeed, it constitutes the largest of all programmes, accounting in the late 1980s for some 30 per cent of public expenditure, and about as much as the total of health and personal social services, education and housing put together.[1] Social security is unlike most social services in that it is not centred on the work of professional staff (such as doctors, social workers or teachers). Although large numbers of civil servants work in local benefit offices, only about four per cent of the cost of social security is accounted for by administration. From the point of view of Scotland social security is unusual in that it is the only major social service which is not the responsibility of the Scottish Office. It is run on a Britain-wide basis by the Department of Social Security (DSS) in London, and there is really nothing that is different about social security provisions north of the border.

A complication in looking at social security is that important elements in the system were reformed in April 1988 as a result of the 'Fowler' reviews. The government's objectives in changing the system will be examined and the new arrangements described. The chapter is concerned with the broad structure of benefits and underlying policy issues, and it will not deal with details of benefit entitlement which belong to the field of welfare rights. (Two welfare rights guides are listed in the further reading at the end of the chapter.)

The chapter has three main parts. First, the development of the benefits system is outlined because many of its present-day features reflect its growth over at least 80 years. In the recent past the Fowler reviews of the mid-1980s are discussed. Second, the current benefits system is described. Third, an attempt is made to assess the effectiveness of social security benefits and to examine some of the problems associated with them.

DEVELOPMENT OF SOCIAL SECURITY IN BRITAIN

Origins to the Second World War[2]

At the end of the nineteenth century the only source of cash income from public funds available to those in need was outdoor relief from the locally administered and financed poor law. The harsh terms on which poor relief was given meant that it was the last resort of a destitute minority of the population. The history of social security during the first half of the present century is to a large extent an account of how provision was made outside the poor law (and on a national rather than a local basis) on terms which were acceptable to the population as a whole.

There was also some provision through two voluntary channels: self-help and private charity. In the field of self-help there was an extensive network of friendly societies which provided benefits, particularly in times of sickness, in return for small weekly contributions. But the friendly societies were limited in their impact; they were largely confined to artisans – the skilled working class – because the unskilled could not afford contributions. Charities had grown in importance during the second half of the nineteenth century and their expenditure was very substantial by the standards of the time but they could only scratch the surface of need.

In the early 1900s there was a new awareness of the extent of poverty with the research of Charles Booth in London and Seebohm Rowntree in York.[3] They demonstrated that poverty was a more serious problem than had been generally assumed, and that its chief causes were factors such as old age and sickness rather than the personal failings of the poor. At the same time there was widespread dissatisfaction with the poor law and a feeling that it should be reformed. Although some believed that its administration ought to be tightened up and that the principle of less eligibility should be enforced, the more general view was that the poor law should be further liberalised and made less deterrent. A Royal Commission on the Poor Laws and Relief of Distress (distress meant unemployment) was set up in 1905 and reported in 1909.[4] But in the meantime the first social security scheme in Britain apart from the poor law was introduced by the Old Age Pensions Act, 1908. It was felt to be undesirable that large numbers of old people should be obliged to resort to poor relief and there had been a growing agitation for old age pensions. The Liberal government which came to office in 1905 agreed to introduce a scheme. Two of its features should be emphasised: first, pensions were financed from general taxation (rather than from local rates or special insurance contributions); and, second they were paid subject to a means test. Nevertheless, pensions were quite unlike the poor law; a standard national means test was used and almost everyone aged 70 with an income below a specified level had a right to a pension.

The introduction of health and unemployment insurance by the National Insurance Act, 1911 was the most important measure in the social security field until after the second world war. The approach of the 1911 act is significant because it marked the adoption in Britain of contributory social insurance – or national insurance – as a method of financing social security. Contributory insurance is the basis of many benefits today. Yet at the time, although there was controversy about how the poor law should be reformed, most interested people expected this and not contributory insurance to be the focus of government action. In the event, however, little was done about the poor law for many years.

The creation of entirely new contributory schemes was politically attractive for a number of reasons. First, insurance contributions from employers and employees were a convenient way of raising revenue which did not seem to be just another tax. Second, poor law reform was unattractive because of the enormous task of reconstructing local government administration and finance which it involved. Third, many advocates of poor law reform had a highly paternalistic approach and believed that relief should be 'conditional'; that anyone receiving assistance from the state should be required to behave in such a way that dependency would be ended as soon as possible. Contributory benefits, on the other hand, could be presented as a quasi-contractual return on contributions rather than a gift from the state demanding character reform. And the absence of a means test further emphasised the distinction between national insurance and the poor law. This approach of defining rights to benefit and of avoiding the personal investigation of claimants has been central to the national insurance system until the present time. The benefits under the 1911 act, as well as being financed from special insurance contributions (together with a contribution from the exchequer) and non-means-tested, provided only for the insured person with no allowances for dependants. Beyond these main features, however, the two schemes, for sickness and unemployment, differed in many ways.

Part I of the 1911 act dealt with national health insurance which was the larger (and more controversial) of the schemes. It covered all manual workers and lower paid white collar workers – the bulk of the labour force. National health insurance had two aspects: a cash sickness benefit and medical benefit. The latter was basically the free services of a general practitioner and free drugs (and became part of the national health service in 1948). Sickness benefit was payable for up to six months when it was replaced by a smaller disablement benefit. There was also a lump-sum maternity benefit.

Part II of the act covered unemployment insurance, the first state-run scheme of its kind in the world. It was small-scale and experimental, applying only to certain trades in which employment fluctuated, such as building and iron-founding. The scheme was administered through the recently established labour exchanges where the unemployed had to register in order to claim benefit. This was payable for a strictly limited period of one week's benefit for every five contributions with not more than 15 weeks' benefit in any 12 months. The scheme was primarily intended to tide over the normally employed workman for short periods. It did little for those suffering from casual and irregular employment who would soon run out of benefit even if they had paid enough contributions to qualify in the first place.

During less than a decade before the first world war, therefore, the beginnings of a system of social security benefits were established in Britain. But the years between the wars, dominated by economic crises and mass unemployment, saw only relatively modest improvements. In 1920 unemployment insurance was extended to practically the same categories of workers as were covered by health insurance. Shortly afterwards dependants' allowances were introduced as a cheaper way of making benefit more adequate at a time of inflation than increasing the rates for unemployed persons themselves. But the post-war boom soon collapsed, unemployment greatly increased and the insurance scheme entered a decade of chaos. It was politically unacceptable to force large numbers of the long-term unemployed on to poor relief, so that insurance was adapted to cater for them. The rules were relaxed until an unemployed person could draw benefit almost without limit, and as a consequence outgoings exceeded income from contributions. The exchequer had to make up the difference, but its payments were regarded as loans to the unemployment insurance fund so that a large debt was built up.

The problem of unemployment insurance came to a head in the political crisis of 1931 when economies in public expenditure were demanded to balance the budget. The new National government both cut benefits (their real value had increased owing to falling prices) and limited entitlement to six months so that, despite a high level of unemployment, the fund soon started repaying its debt. The long-term unemployed who ran out of insurance benefit could now obtain allowances only after a means test, and arrangements had to be made for carrying this out. Initially public assistance committees (which had assumed responsibility for poor relief when it was transferred from parishes to counties and large burghs in 1930) operated the means test on behalf of the government. But the divorce between providing and spending money was unsatisfactory, and in 1934 a new body, the Unemployment Assistance Board (UAB), was created to administer the allowances. This was an important innovation because for the first time responsibility for social assistance was given to a national body. The UAB, which set up a network of area offices, in 1948 became the National Assistance Board, the predecessor of the Supplementary Benefits Commission.

These events were significant for another reason because, though means testing had always been central to the poor law, only relatively small numbers of people had experienced it (and the personal means test for old age pensions was very different). The means test for the unemployed was on a 'household' basis, the needs of everyone living in the same house being aggregated. An unemployed son could therefore be ineligible for assistance and obliged to rely on his parents. Sometimes unemployed children moved into lodgings to get some income of their own.

The other innovations during the inter-war period affected pensions. There were a number of criticisms of the existing scheme. First, the pension age of 70 was seen as being too high; many found it difficult to carry on working until then. Second, the means test was disliked. Third, there was no provision for widows. The government decided to apply the principle of contributory insurance to pensions in order to finance improvements and it introduced the Widows', Orphans' and Old Age Contributory Pensions Act, 1925. For those who had been insured the pension age was reduced to 65 and the means test abolished, as well as widows' and orphans' pensions being introduced. The 1925 act did much to entrench the contributory approach to social security in Britain. Shortly after the outbreak of the second world war the Old Age and Widows' Pension Act, 1940 reduced the pension age for women from 65 to 60 (the origin of what may now seem a curious distinction between the sexes) and introduced supplementary pensions payable on a means-tested basis to pensioners and to widows of 60 and over. They were administered by the Assistance Board (previously the UAB), and removed substantial numbers from reliance on the poor law.

Thus by the second world war an extensive range of cash benefits had developed in Britain, mainly on the basis of contributory insurance. But they had severe limitations; for example, there were many separate schemes none covering precisely the same categories of people, they were administered by different organisations, and the level of some benefits was very low. As well as gaps in provision for the non-employed, the problem of inadequate wages in relation to family requirements was ignored completely.

The Beveridge Report

While the war was in progress the government started to consider reconstruction when peace came, and in 1941 an interdepartmental committee of civil servants under the chairmanship of Sir William Beveridge was appointed to undertake a 'survey of the existing national schemes of social insurance and allied services'.[5] Beveridge, who had long been concerned with social security, wanted far more radical reforms than had originally been envisaged and about which civil servants could not properly express views in public. They therefore became advisers and the report, published in November 1942, was signed by Beveridge alone. Though many changes have subsequently been made, social security benefits in Britain still owe much to the recommendations of the Beveridge report and, in order to evaluate their effectiveness, it is necessary to examine what he was seeking to achieve.

The theme which dominates the Beveridge report is the objective of guaranteeing to every citizen an income at subsistence level or, in other words, sufficient resources to keep people out of poverty (or what he called 'want'). In proposing rates of benefit Beveridge relied on pre-war poverty studies such as those of Rowntree, who acted as an adviser. Beveridge believed that the role of the state in social security should be limited to providing a subsistence income. He recognised that many people would wish to have a higher income when they were not working but believed that this should be obtained through voluntary insurance.

Beveridge identified two causes of poverty: the interruption or loss of earning power (for example during sickness, unemployment or old age), and the failure of wages to relate to the needs of families of different sizes. He believed that the abolition of poverty required a 'double redistribution of income'[6]: from those currently at work to those not at work, chiefly through social insurance; and from individuals and small families to larger ones through family (or, as he called them, children's) allowances.

The main part of the report was concerned with interruption or loss of earning power. Beveridge wholeheartedly approved of social insurance: he believed that people preferred benefits in return for contributions and without a means test. (There is no technical reason why non-contributory benefits should be means tested but in practice they usually are: family allowances (now child benefit) have been the major exception.) Social insurance should continue to be the main method of providing incomes for those not at work, and it would be necessary to improve the existing schemes in three directions: they should be extended to cover persons (chiefly white collar workers) and risks then excluded, and benefit rates should be raised to a subsistence level.

Social insurance was, however, to be only one of three methods of providing social security: the others were to be voluntary insurance and national assistance. The role of voluntary insurance in providing an income in excess of the subsistence level has already been mentioned but, as Beveridge's specific ideas have not had a great impact, this aspect of his proposals may be left aside. Social insurance on its own would not be capable of providing everyone with an income even at the subsistence level, and to supplement it (or to act as a 'safety net') there should be a non-contributory national assistance scheme of means-tested allowances for those in need. National assistance would cover all categories of need including those still met by cash payments from the poor law.

Assistance was envisaged as having only a very limited permanent role in meeting the few needs not covered by insurance benefits. (Beveridge proposed that increased retirement pensions should be phased in over 20 years so that in the interim assistance would cater for large numbers of old people. But higher pensions were paid immedately after the war.) There were in essence three kinds of need for which assistance would be required. First, there would be those who had not fulfilled the contribution conditions for insurance benefit, for example because they had not worked for a sufficient period. (The unemployed who run out of a benefit after a year are in a rather similar position, but this limitation was a divergence from the Beveridge report which did not propose a time limit on eligibility.) Second, there would be those in circumstances (or 'contingencies') which were thought not sufficiently widespread to warrant an insurance benefit: in practice lone parents (other than widows) have been the largest group in this position, but Beveridge did not foresee the rapid growth in their numbers. Third, there would be those who, although entitled to an insurance benefit, had exceptionally large needs. Insurance benefits were to be set at a level sufficient to provide a subsistence income for those with average needs, but they would be inadequate in cases such as a high rent or illness requiring a special diet. Only in this third category of need would assistance be paid in addition to insurance benefits.

Beveridge did not regard inadequate wages in relation to family needs as falling within his terms of reference, and instead he dealt with family allowances as one of three 'assumptions' which were essential to the success of his plan for social security (the others were a national health service and the maintenance of full employment). There had been a campaign for family allowances throughout the inter-war years, led by Eleanor Rathbone and the Family Endowment Society, which had made little progress.[7] As wages are unrelated to family needs, a combination of low income and dependent children can be a cause of poverty. But Beveridge was concerned with family allowances not only as a method of preventing poverty. He was also concerned about the potential overlap between the level of wages and benefits (especially during unemployment) from the point of view of work incentives. (This phenomenon is now known as the unemployment trap and is discussed below.) Without family allowances, paid whether the head of the household was working or not, either benefits for larger families would have to be set below the subsistence level (by paying very meagre amounts for children) or in some cases they would be higher than the wage which a claimant could earn.

Beveridge proposed family allowances, on a non-means-tested basis and financed by the exchequer, at an average of eight shillings a week (though they might in practice be varied according to age). Eight shillings was his estimate of the subsistence cost of keeping a child at the assumed post-war price level (taking into account benefits in kind such as subsidised school meals and milk to the value of a shilling). Family allowances were to be paid in respect of second and subsequent children so that separate child additions in the case of other benefits would not be required for them. Exclusion of the first child was justified on two grounds. First, Beveridge believed that 'very few men's wages are insufficient to cover at least two adults and one child'.[8] Second, he said that it was desirable that the cost of maintaining children should be shared between the family and the state. In reality Beveridge was also constrained by the level of expenditure to which the Treasury was willing to agree.[9] Exclusion of the first child approximately halved the cost of any given level of allowance, as about half of all dependent children are first or only children. On the assumption that wages were adequate for a one-child family, a subsistence level allowance would prevent additional children pushing a family into poverty, but the alternative of a smaller one payable in respect of every child could not do this.

The bulk of the recommendations of the Beveridge report were accepted by the government and implemented in a number of uncontroversial acts of parliament. The Family Allowances Act, 1945 was introduced by the Coalition government before the end of the war, while the rest were passed by the post-war Labour government: the National Insurance Act, 1946 which reformed contributory benefits; the National Insurance (Industrial Injuries) Act, 1946 which replaced workmen's compensation; and the National Assistance Act, 1948 which abolished the poor law and set up the National Assistance Board. Family allowances were first paid in 1946 while the other measures came into force in 1948. Nevertheless, there were divergences from the recommendations of the Beveridge report, chiefly affecting the rates of benefit, which were crucial. These changes undermined the whole approach of the Beveridge plan and greatly diminished the effectiveness of the post-war social security system in eliminating poverty.

In the case of benefits for those not at work (national insurance and national assistance) the divergences altered the proposed relationship between the levels of the two types of payment. It will be recalled that national insurance benefits were intended to provide a subsistence income in all normal cases. Those receiving insurance benefits would only require to have them supplemented by assistance where genuinely exceptional needs existed. Thus non-means-tested social insurance would generally be adequate to prevent poverty. But because many more people are entitled to insurance benefits than to means-tested assistance, the costs of providing a given level of payment through assistance is much less. Therefore, in setting the initial payment levels (whose relativities have been more or less maintained since 1948), the government decided to reduce the real value of insurance benefits below the levels proposed by Beveridge. This was done by fudging the adjustment for inflation of the amounts of benefit in the report which were at 1938 prices. National assistance rates could have been similarly reduced in real terms which, while being hard on those in need, would have maintained the intended relationship between the two benefits. In the event, however, the government set national assistance at a level approximating to the real value of Beveridge's subsistence scale. As a consequence a comparatively large minority of those entitled to national insurance benefits, including most of those without a separate source of income such as an occupational pension, have been entitled to have them supplemented by assistance.

What happened can be clarified by focusing on the treatment of rent. Beveridge recommended that a notional amount (he suggested ten shillings a week) should be included in insurance benefits which would generally be enough to meet rent, so that only those with housing costs in excess of this figure would, leaving aside any other exceptional needs, require assistance. In practice, however, because insurance benefit rates were (after taking account of inflation) lower than Beveridge proposed, no part of them was attributed to rent. Insurance benefits were similar to the rates of national assistance, but the latter paid housing costs in addition. Therefore housing costs were, until the introduction of housing benefit, an important cause of entitlement to assistance amongst insurance beneficiaries.

The much greater reliance on assistance than Beveridge intended – stemming partly from the limitation of entitlement to unemployment benefit and the growth in the numbers of single parents, but most importantly from the distortion of relative payment levels outlined above – had important consequences. Apart from an excessive reliance on what was in Beveridge's eyes a less desirable form of social security, the problems have centred on the incomplete take-up of means-tested benefits. In so far as the Beveridge plan envisaged a role for assistance there would, in any event, have been some problem of low take-up but it has in practice been very much exacerbated. It is the major reason why, in the case of those not at work, the post-war system of benefits has failed in its overriding objective of preventing poverty.

These disadvantages must, however, be balanced against the provision of higher benefits for a given expenditure through the concentration of resources on those with demonstrated financial need. Unless expenditure on social security could have been substantially increased, slightly more generous insurance benefits would have meant markedly lower rates of assistance. It is not clear that on balance this would have been to the advantage of the poorest households. After all, only a minority of eligible people fail to claim means-tested benefits. A smaller role for means testing would probably have meant, in effect, a lower poverty line (defined in terms of benefit levels) but one which many fewer people would have fallen below.

There was also a divergence from Beveridge's recommendations in the level at which family allowances were set. On grounds of cost the government set allowances at only five shillings a week (with unfulfilled promises of increased services in kind such as free school meals for all children) so that when they began to be paid after the war they fell far below the subsistence needs of a child. Not only were allowances initially inadequate to guarantee that family size would not be a cause of poverty but the reluctance of successive governments to uprate them to take account of inflation meant that they became increasingly ineffective. One measure of their inadequacy (and even of child benefit today) is to compare them with the much higher level of child additions under national assistance (supplementary benefit or income support) which may be taken to represent the government's view of the minimum costs of maintaining children.

The Beveridge report represented a major step forward in social security provisions and some of its proposals were radical, such as the extension of benefits to the whole population and the limitation of the role of means testing. But in others, like the emphasis on subsistence level benefits financed by regressive flat-rate contributions, it was conservative. The way in which the recommendations were implemented, however, has meant that the new benefits have been far from completely successful in achieving Beveridge's primary aim of abolishing poverty. Beveridge himself recognised this in the 1950s and became disillusioned with the treatment given to his plan.

THE FOWLER REVIEWS

In the 40 years after the second world war there were changes in and additions to the system of social security benefits. For example, national assistance was replaced by supplementary benefit in 1966 (not a great deal more than a change of name which was intended to create a better image); family income supplement was introduced in 1971, as were various benefits for the disabled in the next few years and the state earnings-related pension scheme in 1978; and in the late 1970s child benefit was phased in to replace family allowances (and child tax allowances). Nevertheless, the broad structure of the post-Beveridge system remained intact. Indeed, it still does because, although many means-tested benefits have been reorganised following the Fowler reviews, most non-means-tested benefits (with the exception of earnings-related pensions) were not affected. The reviews of certain benefits initiated by the then Secretary of State for the Social Services, Norman Fowler, which reported in 1985 were important, as were the actual changes resulting from them, but the exercise was much more restricted in scope than that carried out by Beveridge.

Four review teams were set up in 1984, concerned with provision for retirement, children and young people, supplementary benefit and housing benefit. The reviews were an exercise in 'open government', in that evidence was invited from interested organisations and individuals. Three of the four review teams included both government ministers and outsiders such as industrialists. Only the report of the housing benefit review team, which did not include any ministers, was published. In 1985 a consultative green paper, containing the government's provisional proposals for change, and various background papers were published.[10]

The background to the Fowler reviews was a combination of high and rising costs and the perceived shortcomings of the benefits system: administrative problems, particularly of supplementary benefit despite previous changes in 1980; low take-up of means-tested benefits and the consequent failure to provide an officially-defined adequate income to those in need (in other words to prevent poverty); and the poverty and unemployment traps (which are discussed below). The initiation of four separate reviews rather than a single inquiry more or less precluded proposals which might have altered the overall structure of the system and confined them to changes affecting individual benefits. At the end of 1985 a white paper[11] was published with the government's firm proposals (embodying some significant changes from the green paper) and they were enacted in the Social Security Act, 1986, most coming into force in April 1988. It is convenient to look at the changes under the headings of pensions, income support, the social fund, family credit and housing benefit.

Pensions: Every employed person who is not a member of an approved occupational pension scheme has, since 1978, been obliged to contribute (through a higher rate of national insurance contribution) to the state earnings-related pensions scheme (SERPS). Although the flat-rate state retirement pension is by far the most expensive social security benefit, the government did not propose any change to it (nor to most other national insurance benefits). But one of the main proposals in the green paper was for the phasing out of SERPS, everyone eventually having to join either an occupational pension scheme or to purchase a 'personal' pension from an insurance company. The justification for this change was that the future public expenditure costs of SERPS would be insupportable; but in fact the savings would be many years in the future and the Treasury was doubtful about them anyway. Furthermore, the resource cost to the employed population would not be altered unless the incomes of the elderly were reduced. The proposal to abolish SERPS was criticised by almost all those who responded to the green paper (including insurance companies). It is often the lower-paid who are in SERPS, those who work for smaller employers and those with less continuity of employment, the very people for whom occupational pensions are most difficult to organise. In the white paper the government retreated; the proposal to abolish SERPS was dropped but instead changes were to be made in the way pension entitlement is calculated. These changes are expected approximately to halve the long-term cost of SERPS and will inevitably also make it less effective.

Income Support: Supplementary benefit has been replaced by a combination of income support and the social fund (discussed below). To understand the basic problem with which the introduction of income support is intended to deal, it is necessary to recall the role assigned to its predecessor, national assistance, in the Beveridge plan. Assistance was intended to act as the safety net of the social security system, dealing with the exceptional needs of relatively small numbers on an individual basis, and was thus very labour intensive to administer. In principle a large number of additional payments were available under national assistance (supplementary benefit) – heating allowances, clothing and furniture grants and so on – and since the early 1970s these had generated a great many appeals to tribunals with the encouragement of the growing welfare rights movement. Assistance would no doubt have functioned reasonably well had it only had to cope with a restricted clientele as Beveridge intended, but over the years it came to have millions of claimants. In the early 1980s the strain on the supplementary benefit system was exacerbated by the greatly increased number of unemployed people. A move to reduce the role of discretionary decisions by officers by legally defining entitlements to additional payments (such as clothing grants) did little, on balance, to improve matters. The government decided in essence, therefore, to split the functions of supplementary benefit. Accepting the inevitability of a continuing large-scale role for means-tested assistance (there was no going back to the Beveridge ideal of most needs being met by national insurance benefits), the supplementary benefit 'scale rates', plus some new 'premiums' payable to broad categories of claimants, would become income support. The hope was that this would be a relatively streamlined system, in due course being operated from computerised offices. A variety of lump-sum grants remained, which would be radically altered and hived off to the social fund.

The weekly supplementary benefit scales were generally straightforward to administer and rarely a matter of dispute. They are continued, with some modifications, as income support (for example the distinction between higher 'long-term' and lower 'short-term' rates has been abolished, as has that between householders and non-householders). Under supplementary benefit, claimants might receive extra weekly amounts to meet 'additional requirements', for example a heating allowance. In the interests of simplification these have been abolished and 'premiums' introduced in their place which are paid to easily identifiable categories: families with children, pensioners, lone parents and the disabled. (The one major group not entitled to a premium are the unemployed, unless they have children.) In effect, different claimant groups receive different rates of income support depending on the government's view of their needs (and perhaps deserts). There is clearly an element of rough justice with gainers and losers: notable among the latter are claimants who received large amounts for additional requirements. To take an extreme case, a severely disabled and incontinent person might have been getting quite large amounts to cover heating, laundry and dietary costs and (leaving aside certain safeguarding provisions for existing claimants) is substantially worse off under income support. It may be felt that the absence of any provision for regular weekly allowances (the social fund only makes one-off payments) to meet genuinely exceptional needs is a shortcoming in the new arrangements.

The Social Fund: Lump-sum grants under supplementary benefit ('single payments') have been replaced by the social fund, which is formally separate from income support (though in practice operated from the same local DSS offices). The significance of this separation is that while appeals can be made concerning income support to independent tribunals (in much the same way as supplementary benefit appeals) the social fund is discretionary and without any independent appeals machinery. Dissatisfied claimants can, of course, 'appeal', but this is a matter of having their cases reviewed by the DSS itself. DSS staff will have to work within detailed guidelines, though it may be difficult to argue that a particular claimant has a definite right to receive a specific payment. The fund is cash limited and has an annual budget which may not be exceeded (rather than expenditure being determined by claimants' entitlements).

The social fund has two main roles: to provide interest-free loans, normally only to people receiving income support, and to encourage community care by making grants to enable individuals to live in the community rather than in institutions. The justification for loans is that the purposes for which they will be made – to buy clothing or bedding for example – are in principle covered by income support. (Supplementary benefit single payments often involved meeting needs which in theory had already been provided for by the scale rates.) The implication is that someone asking for a loan has failed to budget properly, and in serious cases people will receive financial advice from specially trained staff. Loans will normally be recovered by deduction from future income support payments, generally at the rate of 15 per cent of weekly benefit with a limit of 25 per cent. Non-repayable grants are made to enable those leaving hospitals or other institutions to re-establish themselves in the community by, for example, paying for furniture, and to allow people to move to more suitable accommodation and so avoid the need for institutional care. Grants may also be given to meet crises such as sudden illness. Finally, the non-means-tested maternity and death grants have been abolished (on the grounds that they were inadequate but it would be too expensive to increase them substantially). People with low incomes now have a right to claim a grant from the social fund to meet maternity or funeral expenses under defined circumstances.

Family Credit: Something should be said first about family income supplement (FIS) which family credit replaces in a modified form. FIS was a means-tested allowance payable to parents of dependent children. It was complementary to supplementary benefit; whereas supplementary benefit was not normally payable to persons in full-time work, FIS could only be claimed where at least one parent was in full-time work. Therefore a family with a low income might be entitled to either FIS or supplementary benefit but was never eligible for both (the same is true of family credit and income support). Compared with family allowances and child benefit, FIS covered only small numbers of recipients and had only a modest cost to the exchequer. The government justified the introduction of FIS in 1970, instead of increasing family allowances, on grounds of cost. FIS certainly concentrated resources on those in greatest need and provided the poorest with a scale of help inconceivable with a non-means-tested scheme. It suffered, however, like most means-tested benefits from low take-up.

FIS did not attempt to take into account the varying needs of households beyond level of income and number of children. It was normally assessed purely on the basis of a postal application form. 'Prescribed amounts', which varied with the number of children, were laid down and FIS made up half the difference between these and actual incomes if lower. The choice of a 50 per cent 'taper' was a compromise between conflicting objectives: to make up as much of the shortfall in income as possible, but to minimise the 'poverty trap' effect caused by additional earnings reducing benefit. Also to minimise the poverty trap (and for administrative convenience), once awarded, FIS was normally payable for a year at the same rate even if income changed.

Most of these features of FIS are carried over into family credit. One of the main changes which was proposed was that family credit would be paid through the wage packet rather than at the post office, so that in two-parent families it would be received by the father rather than the mother. The argument was that this would make clearer the financial advantages of taking a low-paid job compared with unemployment. But after a good deal of controversy the proposal was abandoned and family credit is, like FIS, directly payable to the mother. Family credit will normally be payable unchanged for six months rather than a year in the case of FIS. The family credit scheme covers a wider range of income than FIS so approximately doubling the number of eligible families.

In introducing family credit the government was concerned about the poverty and unemployment traps (see below). By making family credit more generous than FIS the total resources of low wage families with children will be increased (provided the benefit is claimed), thus reducing the unemployment trap and improving work incentives. Furthermore, only income after tax and national insurance contributions will be taken in account (rather than gross income). The use of a net income means test for family credit (and for housing benefit) means that the poverty trap is also diminished. Loss of free school meals as income rose could cause a drop in overall resources but this cannot occur under the new arrangements as they are not available to those receiving family credit. But although reductions in spending power of more than 100 per cent of a wage increase are no longer possible, there is likely to be a greater number of households facing withdrawal rates in the 80-90 per cent range.

In the absence of large sums of money for substantial increases in child benefit, policies to deal with the poverty and unemployment traps are necessarily a compromise. The more households that claim family credit, the more the unemployment trap will be eased; but at the same time greater numbers will be drawn into the poverty trap (though the move to net income means tests avoids the highest withdrawal rates).

Housing Benefit: There are several forms of assistance with housing costs (which are discussed in chapter 5) but here the concern is with means-tested payments of relevance mainly to tenants. A national scheme of rent rebates was introduced in 1972, together with a parallel scheme of rent allowances for private tenants (the only important difference being that the latter receive a cash payment rather than a reduced rent). Rate rebates, which are available to owner occupiers as well as tenants, had been introduced in 1966 following evidence of hardship suffered by lower income households. In 1974 the means test for rate rebates was put on a similar basis to that for rent rebates and allowances, and in the case of tenants the two benefits are normally dealt with together. The one category of person who was not eligible to apply for a rent or rate rebate or rent allowance was someone in receipt of supplementary benefit which itself met housing costs.

In 1983 rent rebates and allowances and rate rebates, as well as housing payments for those receiving supplementary benefit, were subsumed under a new housing benefit scheme. The change was, however, chiefly of significance to supplementary benefit claimants, because the rebate and allowance schemes continued much as before as part of housing benefit. In 1983 a limited number of claimants were floated off supplementary benefit (because their entitlement had been less than their rent and rates) and they could claim housing benefit separately. The majority, who continued to be entitled to supplementary benefit, were automatically awarded housing benefit to cover the whole of their housing costs. At central government level responsibility for housing rebates was transferred in 1983 from the Scottish Development Department to the Department of Health and Social Security (DHSS), thus recognising them as primarily income support measures.

Apart from the fact that the changes did nothing to rationalise the basis on which tenants and owner occupiers receive assistance with housing costs, at least two criticisms have been levelled at housing benefit. First, there was a continuing problem of low take-up. In the case of council tenants take-up of rent and rate rebates was comparable to that for supplementary benefit, but it was much lower in the case of private tenants. Second, housing benefit caused enormous administrative problems for local housing departments, particularly in liaising with the DHSS in the case of supplementary benefit claimants.

A number of structural changes were made to housing benefit in 1988, three of which affect the means test. First, like that for family credit, the means test will be on a net income (after tax and national insurance contributions) basis and it has been aligned with that for income support. Those in receipt of income support (as was previously the case with supplementary benefit) have their rent and rates (or community charge) met (subject to having to pay 20 per cent of rates or community charge). But those not getting income support (whether at work or living on other benefits) whose income is at or below the income support level will be in the same position; previously they were likely to have received only a proportion of their housing costs. Thus a person who is working for a low wage will not be in a worse position as far as assistance with rent and rates is concerned than someone on income support (though this may not be true of owner occupiers where the low wage earner is still likely to be at a disadvantage). As in the case of family credit, therefore, the changes seek to alleviate both the poverty and unemployment traps. A technical change which will simplify the calculation of housing benefit is the adoption of a single benefit withdrawal rate as income rises.

Second, whereas only actual income from savings was formerly taken into account in assessing eligibility for housing benefit, there is now a capital cut-off level as with income support. The capital limit excludes substantial numbers of pensioners from eligibility and, after considerable political controversy, it was raised from £6,000 to £8,000 with retrospective effect from April 1988.

A third change (which represents a continuation of a policy which has been pursued since the early 1980s) is a reduction in the income levels up to which eligibility for housing benefit reaches. Eligibility for housing rebates used to extend to substantially higher income levels than for most means-tested benefits. Now eligibility will disappear more quickly above the income support level, and this change is likely to be the main saving in public expenditure which results in the short term from the Fowler reviews (though the changes to SERPS will eventually produce larger economies). Taking all the changes resulting from the Fowler reviews together, there will be both losers and gainers. The government estimated that the effect of changes coming into force in April 1988 would be to leave some 3.7 million claimants worse off than they would have been under the existing system, while about 3.2 million would gain and 1.7 million would be unaffected.

THE BENEFITS SYSTEM

A good deal has already been said about a number of benefits in the context of the Fowler reviews, and in this section the main emphasis is on those which were not substantially affected by the 1988 changes, particularly national insurance benefits and child benefit. Benefits which are designed to provide the main or only income during loss or interruption of earnings, sometimes referred to as income maintenance benefits, fall into three categories: national insurance (contributory) benefits; income support; and a number of non-contributory, non-means-tested benefits such as the severe disablement allowance. Then there are benefits which are designed to meet particular needs rather than to provide a basic income, such as child benefit, family credit, housing benefit and various benefits for the disabled. (There is also a separate industrial injuries scheme which provides more generous benefits for those injured at work or suffering from industrial diseases.) Benefits can be grouped into three broad categories. These are national insurance, non-contributory and means-tested benefits which are listed in Figures 2.1, 2.2 and 2.3 respectively.

National Insurance (Contributory) Benefits

Contributory benefits have changed little, except for uprating, since they were introduced in 1948. They are financed from the national insurance fund into which are paid contributions by employees and employers plus a modest amount from the exchequer. They are payable without a means test to people suffering specified contingencies who have fulfilled the relevant contribution conditions (which vary between benefits). With the exception of unemployment benefit they are payable for as long as need lasts. A statutory sick pay scheme was introduced in 1983 under which employers became responsible for making at least a minimum allowance (which they can off-set against liability for national insurance contributions) in place of sickness

FIGURE 2.1 National Insurance (Contributory) Benefits

Unemployment benefit	Payable for up to a year.
Sickness benefit	Payable for up to 28 weeks, only to those not entitled to statutory sick pay from an employer.
Invalidity benefit	Invalidity pension, replacing statutory sick pay (or sickness benefit) and payable for as long as incapacity for work continues.
	Invalidity allowance, varying with age at which incapacity began, provided this was more than five years before retirement age, payable as long as incapacity continues.
	Earnings-related addition to invalidity pension based on earnings from 1978.
Maternity allowance	Payable for eight weeks if the mother has allowance worked and paid full contributions, but only where she is not entitled to statutory maternity pay from an employer.
Retirement pension	Basic pension paid on retirement at or after age 60 for women, 65 for men (plus addition if over 80 and increments for deferred retirement).
	Graduated pension based on earnings-related contributions paid between 1961 and 1975.
	Earnings-related pension (SERPS) based on earnings from 1978 (if not contracted out into an occupational scheme or personal pension).
Widows' benefits	Widowed mother's allowance payable for as long as the widow has a dependent son or daughter under 19 who is at school.
	Widow's pension payable if the widow is over 45 either on husband's death or when widowed mother's allowance ceases; but at a reduced rate if she is under 55 when husband dies or widowed mother's allowance ceases.
	Earnings-related addition to widowed mother's allowance or widow's pension based on husband's earnings from 1978.

benefit for the first eight weeks of incapacity. Statutory sick pay was extended in 1986 to 28 weeks, when it is replaced by invalidity benefit, so that sickness benefit is now generally only payable to the self-employed. Similarly, a statutory maternity pay scheme was introduced in 1987, replacing the maternity allowance for many working mothers. Since 1973 there has been a distinction between 'short-term' benefits (for sickness, unemployment and maternity) and 'long-term' benefits (for invalidity, widowhood and retirement) which are paid at a higher rate. Flat rate contributions (to which a graduated element had been added in 1961) were replaced by a wholly earnings-related system in 1975. This takes the form of a percentage of earnings paid by both employers and employees (subject to an upper limit in the case of the latter) with reduced rates for the low paid.

There is very little discretion in the administration of contributory benefits. When someone suffers a contingency for which a benefit exists, provided that the appropriate contributions have been paid, he or she is entitled to benefit regardless of other resources (such as savings or an occupational pension). Whether in a particular case someone is entitled to a benefit may occasionally be a complex question, but this is decided on the basis of legal entitlement and not whether the person is in financial need. If the conditions are not fulfilled, no matter how great the need may be, no benefit is payable. Nor do contributory benefits take account of individual variations in circumstances except of course family size.

The Beveridge plan did not include earnings-related benefits but in the 1950s there was a growth of occupational pensions and there were demands that higher incomes in retirement should be extended to the rest of the workforce through a state scheme. A very limited 'graduated' pension scheme was introduced in 1961 for those not entitled to an occupational pension (though another motive was that additional earnings-related contributions were a source of extra revenue for the national insurance fund). This scheme was widely seen as inadequate but it continued until 1975. There was a good deal of controversy – particularly about the proper role of state and occupational pensions – and two abortive attempts at reform which came to nothing owing to changes of government in 1970 and 1974. (Between 1966 and 1982, when they were abolished as an economy measure, there were also earnings-related supplements during the first six months of sickness, unemployment and widowhood.)

Legislation was passed in 1975 abolishing the graduated pension scheme and replacing it with the state earnings-related pension scheme (SERPS) which came into force in 1978. Every employee has to contribute towards an additional earnings-related pension; about half the workforce are 'contracted-out' of SERPS because they are members of an approved occupational scheme or, from 1988, they are purchasing a 'personal' pension. As time goes on a growing proportion of the elderly will enjoy increasingly more adequate incomes as people retire with a SERPS, occupational or personal pension, which will have important implications for the number of old people living in poverty.

Non-Contributory Benefits

These benefits are non-contributory and non-means-tested. The most important is child benefit whose predecessor (family allowances) dates from 1945. Otherwise, benefits of this kind were not envisaged in the Beveridge report and they are of comparatively recent origin, all being introduced in the 1970s. The non-contributory old person's pension was introduced in 1970 and is payable to anyone aged over 80 who is not entitled to a contributory pension. Its main purpose was to deal with the temporary problem of white collar workers who were not insured before 1948 and were not able to pay contributions for ten years thereafter in order to qualify for a contributory pension. The non-contributory invalidity pension (NCIP), the housewives' non-contributory invalidity pension (HNCIP) and the invalid care allowance (ICA) followed in 1975.

FIGURE 2.2 Non-Contributory (Non-Means-Tested) Benefits

Child benefit	Payable for each child under 16 (or under 19 if still at school) whether the parents are in work or not. An extra one-parent benefit is paid for the first child in a one-parent family. Child benefit is paid to whoever has responsibility for the child (not necessarily the parents).
Severe Disablement Allowance	Payable to people of working age who are severely disabled, incapable of work and do not qualify for contributory invalidity benefit. At lower rate than contributory benefit.
Attendance Allowance	Payable to severely disabled people needing continuous attention or supervision (at a lower rate if only during the day or night).
Invalid care Allowance	Payable to a person of working age caring for a severely disabled person who is getting attendance allowance.
Mobility Allowance	Allowance for physically disabled persons aged five or over and under 65 who are unable or virtually unable to walk. On reaching 65 those already getting the allowance can continue to receive it until they are 75.
Non-Contributory Retirement Pension	Payable at lower rate than the basic retirement pension, to those over 80 who would not otherwise get this amount of pension.
Guardian's Allowance	Payable to a person providing a home for a child whose parents are both dead (or sometimes on the death of only one parent where, for example, the parents are divorced).

The NCIP and HNCIP were designed to provide a non-means-tested income for those who, because of disablement, had not been employed and did not qualify for a contributory benefit. The difference between the NCIP and the HNCIP was that married women were subject to the additional condition that they must be 'incapable of performing normal household duties'. The rationale for this rule, which aroused much opposition, was that married women could normally expect to be maintained by their husbands. Following a ruling of the European Court, which held that the HNCIP discriminated against women, both were replaced in 1984 by the severe disablement allowance. So that the removal of the household duties test would not increase expenditure, a new rule that recipients had to be at least 80 per cent disabled (on the criteria used for industrial injuries benefits) was introduced. The ICA is payable to someone looking after a disabled person who is entitled to the attendance allowance, and is designed to help, for example, an unmarried daughter who stays at home to care for elderly parents. All these benefits have a serious limitation: their rate is only about 60 per cent of contributory benefits. For people with a private income they are a useful addition, but in the majority of cases they are simply offset against entitlement to income support so that the same payment is received under two heads rather than one. Thus many of those who are eligible do not bother to claim the benefits, and most of those who do so lose an equivalent amount of income support, so that their net cost to the exchequer is small.

Two non-contributory benefits are designed to provide an additional income to meet the special needs of the disabled. The attendance allowance was introduced in 1970 for severely disabled people in need of frequent attention or continual supervision during either the day or night (when the lower rate is payable) or both (when the higher rate is payable). It is not taken into account in calculating other means-tested benefits. Mobility allowance was phased in from 1976 and can be claimed by people between five and 65 who are unable to walk or virtually unable to do so.

Child Benefit: There are two schemes, child benefit and family credit (which has already been described), that provide an addition to wages which is related to number of children. Child benefit, which is the successor to family allowances, is also paid when earnings are interrupted but this is not the case with family credit.

Before the introduction of child benefit there were, apart from FIS, two main systems of income support for families with children: family allowances and child tax allowances. Family allowances were replaced by child benefit in 1977 and tax allowances were phased out over the following three years. Family allowances had continued in their original form with only occasional upratings. The reason for their neglect was that they were perceived by politicians as unpopular and unnecessary in an affluent society. The work on poverty by Brian Abel-Smith and Peter Townsend published in the mid-1960s challenged the view that family allowances were no longer required, and the Child Poverty Action Group was formed to campaign for their improvement. Substantial increases were implemented in 1968 which approximately halved the number of working families living below the poverty line. But in order to limit the cost to the exchequer the increases were effectively restricted to those who paid little or no income tax through the use of 'clawback', which made off-setting reductions in child tax allowances.

The chief justification for introducing child benefit was that the poorest families gained little or nothing from tax allowances while the highest paid gained most. The value of child benefit is the same for any family of a given size so that those affected least by the abolition of tax allowances had the largest net gain. There was controversy when Frank Field, then director of the Child Poverty Action Group, published confidential cabinet papers he had been given which suggested that the government might not go ahead with child benefit. It believed that at a time when incomes policy was severely restricting wage increases the reduction in (usually men's) take-home pay caused by the end of child tax allowances would be unpopular, but the embarrassment resulting from the leaks seems to have been instrumental in persuading the government to phase in child benefit.[12]

Apart from the distributional effects benefiting lower income families, there are two main difference between family allowances and child benefit. First, child benefit is not itself taxable (after the abolition of child tax allowances, adding it to husbands' incomes for tax purposes as was done with family allowances would mean that the more children they had the lower would be their take-home pay). Second, it is payable in respect of all children including first or only children. An additional one-parent benefit is payable for the first child of lone parents. Child benefit is not means tested and it is paid regardless of whether the parents are working or are in receipt of any other benefit. But it is taken into account in assessing means-tested benefits. Anyone under the age of 16 automatically qualifies for child benefit as do those under 19 who are in full-time school (or other non-advanced) education. It is normally payable to the mother.

Means-Tested Benefits

Income Support: This replaced supplementary benefit (frequently though incorrectly called 'social security') in 1988 as the British version of what in international terminology is referred to as social assistance. Supplementary benefit itself replaced national assistance in 1966; the name was altered when there were some modest administrative changes. Between 1966 and 1980 the

FIGURE 2.3 Means-Tested Benefits

Income Support	Weekly payments with 'premiums' for certain categories of claimants. Payable only to those not in full-time work (24 hours a week or more).
The Social Fund	Loans to meet needs which income support is intended to cover and grants to facilitate community care. Payable only to those receiving income support. Also means-tested grants to meet maternity needs and funeral expenses.
Family Credit	Payable to families with children where either the husband or wife is in full-time work (24 hours a week or more).
Housing Benefit	Rate rebates payable to tenants and owner occupiers. Rent rebates payable to local authority, new town and SSHA tenants. Rent allowances payable to private tenants. (Full rent and 80 per cent of rates/community charge of those receiving income support are met.)
Ancillary Benefits	Free dental treatment Free prescriptions Free welfare foods Free school meals Available to those receiving income support through the 'passport'. Free dental treatment and prescriptions are similarly available to those receiving family credit or after a separate means test.

scheme was under the control of the Supplementary Benefits Commission (the successor to the National Assistance Board), the chief function of which was to guide the exercise of, and to take responsibility for, discretion in individual cases. From 1980, when discretion in the administration of supplementary benefit was much reduced, the scheme was under the direct control of the DHSS, as is income support.

The functions of income support are essentially the same as those already outlined for national assistance: to meet the needs of those who are not entitled to a contributory benefit and to provide an addition to such a benefit when it is inadequate. The largest category of recipients, which grew rapidly in the early 1980s, are the unemployed most of whom have exhausted their entitlement to unemployment benefit. The second largest category are the elderly, practically all of whom receive income support to top up retirement pensions (though about four-fifths of pensioners do not have them supplemented). Income support, in contrast to national insurance benefits, is means tested but is not of course subject to contribution conditions. Nor is income support limited to specific contingencies like national insurance benefits (though claimants must have a legitimate reason for not working); in practice the main difference is that it is available to all lone parents and is not confined to widowed mothers. In principle anyone who is not in full-time work or education and whose resources are less than his or her needs can obtain income support. Only one claim can be made in respect of married (and cohabiting) couples and their dependent children, who are counted as a single unit.

The Social Fund: The functions of the social fund have already been outlined. It replaces single payments, a small part (in terms of expenditure only about five per cent of total costs) of the supplementary benefit scheme. The fund is perhaps the most innovatory aspect of the Fowler reforms, and the use of repayable loans and the absence of a formal appeals machinery have been widely criticised.

Remission of NHS and Other Charges: The use of charges in the social services was much reduced in the post-war reforms, but there has been a tendency for them to grow again. In particular, in 1948 virtually all national health service provisions were entirely free but charges were soon introduced for prescriptions, dental treatment and so on. At the same time, in order to safeguard lower income groups, exemptions from charges for those receiving national assistance were introduced, as well as for others with incomes at about the same level on a means-tested basis. With the introduction of FIS these exemptions were extended and the 'passport' procedure was introduced. Under the passport anyone who is receiving either income support or (for some benefits) family credit can obtain exemption from various charges on the basis of a simple application without a separate means test. Others can obtain some of the exemptions with a separate application and means test. While take-up of exemptions through the passport is reasonably good by the standards of other means-tested benefits, in the case of separate applications it is low. Since 1979 the government has followed a policy of increasing charges in the social services, although eligibility for exemptions from them has tended to be narrowed (for example in the case of school meals).

The main NHS charges from which remission can be obtained are those for prescriptions and dental treatment. (About half of prescriptions are in any case free to categories such as children under 16, pensioners and expectant mothers.) In the case of charges for dental treatment those with incomes somewhat higher than the income support level can obtain partial exemption. Until 1980 there was a national income scale for free school meals under which eligibility extended well above the supplementary benefit level. As an economy measure this was abolished (and local authorities were allowed discretion over what to charge for meals). From 1988 they have only have power to provide free meals for children whose parents are receiving income support.

SOCIAL SECURITY STATISTICS

Looking at expenditure on social security by broad groups of beneficiaries, the elderly account for about half the cost of all benefits (retirement pensions for about two-fifths). The unemployed, the sick and disabled, and families primarily dependent on wages are the other major categories, each accounting for between a sixth and a seventh of total expenditure. Over half of expenditure on supplementary benefit in recent years has been on the unemployed, about two-thirds of whom are entirely dependent (leaving aside any child benefit) on it. The relatively modest numbers receiving unemployment benefit reflect the fact that many of the unemployed have exhausted their entitlement to it. Despite the relatively large number of the elderly amongst supplementary benefit recipients, only about a seventh of expenditure has been on them because most also have retirement pensions. Fewer than a fifth of the long-term sick and disabled receive any supplementary benefit (income support), mainly because invalidity benefit is relatively generous. The position of the elderly is similar although in their case earnings-related pensions and savings are also increasingly important.

Table 2.1 provides an indication of the relative costs of different benefits and of the number of beneficiaries. It can be seen that the most expensive individual benefits are retirement pensions, housing benefit, child benefit and supplementary benefit. Non-means-tested benefits account for nearly three-quarters of expenditure, and over half of the total is on contributory benefits which are financed from the national insurance fund. Most of the fund's income comes from employers' and employees' contributions, each providing about 45 per cent of the total. The supplement from general taxation has been reduced to about nine per cent. About one-sixth of expenditure is on non-contributory non-means-tested benefits, of which some two-thirds is accounted for by child benefit. The non-contributory benefits for the disabled, such as the attendance allowance, are relatively cheap. Finally, rather more than a quarter of total expenditure is on means-tested benefits, mainly supplementary benefit (income support) and housing benefit.

TABLE 2.1: Proportion of Expenditure on and Number of Recipients of Different Benefits, 1986-87

	Expenditure[1]	Beneficiaries[2] (000s)
	%	
Non-means-tested benefits	73	
Retirement pensions (including SERPS)	42	9,620
Non-contributory retirement pension	1	35
Widows' benefits	2	385
Unemployment benefit	4	825
Sickness benefit	*	80
Invalidity benefit	6	965
Severe disablement allowance	1	245
Invalid care allowance	*	75
Attendance allowance	2	630
Mobility allowance	1	485
Maternity allowance	*	40[3]
Child benefit	11	6,820[4]
Industrial injuries benefits	1	200
War pensions	1	275
Means-tested benefits	27	
Supplementary benefit	19	4,930
Housing benefit	8	7,135
Family income supplement	*	205[5]

Notes: 1. Proportion of expenditure (excluding administration costs).
2. Estimated average number of beneficiaries, 1987/88.
3. Estimate after full introduction of statutory maternity allowance 25,000.
4. Twelve million children.
5. Families; estimate for family credit 400,000 families.
* Less than 0.5 per cent.

Source: *The Government's Expenditure Plans 1987-88 to 1989-90*, Cm. 56, HMSO, 1987.

In relation to the overall cost of social security, administration is a fairly minor item; as was pointed out above, it accounts for only about four per cent of the DSS budget. But there are considerable variations between benefits: in the case of the child benefit and retirement pensions administrative costs are only some two per cent of benefit expenditure but with supplementary benefit nearly twelve per cent. (Income support may be cheaper to run, though the social fund is likely to be expensive from this point of view.) Nevertheless, it would be vastly more expensive to provide the same level of payment without a means test. And a simple means test, as in the case of FIS (or family credit) need not cost much to operate; the administrative costs of FIS were only slightly above the average for all benefits. Whatever the arguments against means testing, administrative cost is not a very powerful one.

EFFECTIVENESS OF THE BENEFITS SYSTEM

The final section of the chapter is concerned with evaluating the effectiveness of social security benefits in Britain. Evaluation requires the selection of appropriate criteria, and the main one used here is the objective, which was central to the Beveridge report, of preventing poverty. The extent to which benefits during loss or interruption of earnings maintain normal income levels will also be examined.

Defining Poverty

Ever since 1948, given the objective of the Beveridge report, the national assistance (later supplementary benefit) scale rates can be seen as implicitly representing a poverty line. Income support is likely to fill a similar role in the future. This was at first rarely made explicit but from the 1960s it was widely accepted – by political parties, civil servants, pressure groups, academics and so on – that the supplementary benefit level was a very useful definition of poverty in Britain. Indeed, it was often referred to as the 'official' poverty line, and how this came about is worth outlining.

The systematic investigation of poverty was pioneered by Seebohm Rowntree who undertook his first study of York at the turn of the century. His approach to defining poverty, which was followed by many others up to the second world war, was to assemble scientific and medical evidence about the quantities of food and other 'necessaries' required to maintain a tolerable minimum standard of living (described in his first study as 'merely physical efficiency'). Poverty defined in this way is often called 'absolute' poverty, not because it presents a meagre standard of living (though it tends to do so) but because, in principle, it should be valid for all time (except for advances in scientific knowledge such as the discovery of vitamins). Poverty lines of this sort depend for their legitimacy – and a poverty line which does not enjoy widespread acceptance has little practical value for policy-makers – on the scientific knowledge of those responsible for their definition.

But in the 1960s the absolute approach to the definition of poverty came under attack. The essence of the criticism was that a poverty line is basically a social and political rather than a scientific entity. Notions of poverty are generally related to standards of living prevalent in a society, and vary over time and from place to place. An absolute approach, which claims to be based on objective scientific knowledge, cannot accommodate this reality except by fudging (which, for instance, Rowntree did in his second and third studies of York in 1936 and 1950, arbitrarily raising his poverty line). A distinction between 'necessities' and 'luxuries', on which an absolute definition must rely, may work well in poorer societies where the bulk of most people's expenditure is devoted to basic food, shelter and clothing, but it is difficult to apply in more affluent ones. One only has to list some common consumer durables – vacuum cleaner, refrigerator, freezer, radio, television, telephone – to see that what is a luxury is a matter of judgement, and changing judgement, rather than scientific fact.

Criticism of the absolute approach was crystallised by Brian Abel-Smith and Peter Townsend in *The Poor and the Poorest*, published in 1965.[13] Abel-Smith and Townsend did important empirical work on the measurement of poverty, and their method of using the Family Expenditure Survey (FES) has since been adopted in regular analyses of low incomes made by the DHSS. They are often credited with having 're-discovered' poverty and in a sense this is so in that they revealed a more widespread problem than had been thought to exist. But it may be truer to say that they redefined poverty. They rejected an absolute approach in favour of a 'relative' definition. (The poverty line is relative to general standards of living at a particular time and place, and is a national standard; it should not be confused with Runciman's concept of relative deprivation which is concerned with an individual's perception of his own circumstances.[14]) Relative poverty is centred on the notion of participation in the normal life of society; people are poor if their resources are so low as to exclude them from the ordinary activities of their relatives, friends and workmates. Thus, while an absolute poverty line, adjusted only for changing prices, is of interest in focusing attention on changes in the number of people living below a particular standard of living, a definition of poverty which reflects the current circumstances of a society is of more general usefulness.

A difficulty for Abel-Smith and Townsend was that no way had been devised of directly quantifying a measure of relative poverty (and indeed even after Townsend's subsequent work this problem has not been satisfactorily solved). They therefore decided to adopt the national assistance (as it then was) standard as a poverty line (though this had already been done less explicitly by others). The justification was not that they personally believed that the national assistance scales were necessarily right, but that they had legitimacy: 'Whatever may be said about the adequacy of the National Assistance Board level of living as a just or publicly approved measure of "poverty", it has at least the advantage of being in a sense the "official" operational definition of the minimum level of living at any particular time.'[15] But the national assistance, supplementary benefit or income support level does not only have the advantage of legitimacy as a measure of poverty; it also leads to an evaluation of the benefits system. The Beveridge plan was designed to guarantee a minimum income, so that if significant numbers of people in fact have incomes which fall below that level there must have been shortcomings in the proposals themselves or in their implementation. Some of these shortcomings have already been mentioned but, before the effectiveness of the current benefits system is examined, evidence on the extent of poverty will be briefly reviewed.

The Extent of Poverty

Evidence on the extent and incidence of poverty in Britain can only be dealt with in outline, but a number of studies of the topic are available.[16] It should be made clear first of all that there are technical and conceptual difficulties in using the supplementary benefit (or income support) standard, so that estimates are highly sensitive to the assumptions made. Two examples may be mentioned. First, there is the treatment of those actually receiving supplementary benefit who in principle should never be in poverty; their incomes should by definition be at the poverty line, and estimates based on FES data made by the DHSS assume that this is the case. Independent estimates, however, show that a significant number of those in poverty are in receipt of supplementary benefit, owing either to miscalculation of entitlement or recent changes in circumstances. This is a major cause of discrepancies between official figures and non-official ones which tend to be substantially higher. Second, FES data use the concept of 'normal income' which ignores periods of sickness and unemployment of less than 13 weeks, so reducing the apparent number with incomes below the poverty line. Furthermore, difficulties are inherent in the use of data from a sample survey. FES is a continuous survey of a cross-section of households in Britain carried out by the Office of Population Censuses and Surveys. Its primary purpose is to collect information about expenditure patterns so that the correct weighting can be given to different items in constructing the retail price index. The number of low-income households covered by FES is relatively small so that all statistics on numbers in poverty are subject to sampling error which may be substantial in the case of smaller groups such as one-parent families. For the same reason it is not possible to obtain detailed information about differences between Scotland and the rest of Britain from the FES.

Some statistics on the extent and incidence of poverty in Britain derived from the 1985 FES are contained in Table 2.2. This is a minimum estimate of numbers below the supplementary benefit level, and independent researchers using different assumptions have argued for substantially higher figures. The statistics can be looked at from two points of view: the relative importance of different causes of poverty and the 'risk' of poverty experienced by people in different circumstances.

It will be seen that there are significant differences in the relative importance of various causes depending on whether families or individuals are counted. The reason for this is that some categories, for example old people, tend to live in one or two-person households, and therefore bulk larger amongst the count of families than of individuals. The opposite is true of families with children. In 1985 those who were not working for whatever reason and were primarily dependent on benefits accounted for 85 per cent of families and 77 per cent of individuals in poverty. By far the largest category were the elderly who constituted nearly half of poor families and two-fifths of poor individuals. In recent years the numbers of elderly in poverty have not changed very much (on average older people have been getting better off but there are more of them) although they have been falling as a proportion of the (increased) number of the poor. Between 1979 and 1985 the total in poverty increased by about one-seventh (partly as a result of the higher real value of supplementary benefit scales). Despite the growth of unemployment it is a

TABLE 2.2:

Poverty in Britain, 1985

Families and persons[1] with 'normal incomes'[2] below supplementary benefit level

	Families (000s)	Proportion of poor families	'Risk' of poverty[3]	Persons (000s)	Proportions of poor persons	'Risk' of poverty[3]
		%	%		%	%
Total	1,600	100	6	2,420	100	4
Total OVER pension age	770	48	12	960	40	11
Married couples	200	13	8	390	16	8
Single persons	570	36	13	570	24	13
Total UNDER pension age	830	52	4	1,460	60	3
By family type:						
Married couples with children	160	10	3	630	26	3
Single persons with children	30	2	3	80	3	3
Married couple – no children	100	6	2	200	8	2
Single persons – no children	550	34	5	550	23	5
Of which large families (3 or more children)	50	3	4	250	10	4
By employment status:						
Normally in full-time work (or self-employed)	240	15	2	560	23	2
Sick or disabled for more than 3 months	50	3	6	60	2	4
Unemployed for more than 3 months	320	20	14	510	21	12
Others	230	14	7	340	14	6

Notes: 1. Estimates of persons living in private households derived from the 1985 Family Expenditure Survey, rounded to nearest 10,000.

2. Income from work where the head of household has been sick or unemployed for less than three months.

3. Proportion of families or persons with specific characteristics with incomes below the supplementary benefit level.

Source: *Low Income Families: 1985*, Department of Health and Social Security, 1988.

much smaller cause of poverty than old age, accounting for probably about one-quarter of the total if the figures in the table are increased somewhat to include those unemployed for less than three months. Nevertheless, between 1979 and 1985 the number of unemployed in poverty increased by some 220 per cent (families) and 240 per cent (individuals). A combination of low wages and number of children where the head of household was in full-time work accounted in 1985 for some 15 per cent of poor families and 23 per cent of individuals (though many more had incomes only slightly above the supplementary benefit level). Furthermore, the number in poverty would be much greater without second incomes provided by working wives.

Turning to the risk of poverty amongst families and individuals in different circumstances, it can be seen that two groups, the elderly (especially single people) and the unemployed, have the highest proportion with income below the supplementary benefit level. There is a very low risk of poverty where the head of household is in full-time work although, as there are many people in this position, they constitute a significant proportion of those with low incomes.

Statistics of poverty in Scotland are not regularly published, and in any case they could only be very approximate owing to the limitations of the FES sample. Such evidence as there is suggests that the extent of poverty in Scotland as a whole is not substantially different from the average for Britain (or at any rate that it is only slightly higher). Factors such as the proportion of the elderly in the population, the level of earnings and the unemployment rate confirm that this is likely to be the case. Variations within Scotland (as between different parts of England) are, however, very substantial. Although the FES cannot provide information at this level, it is well known that the Glasgow area and central Clydeside generally have above average levels of poverty.

In examining why the benefit system fails to prevent poverty as the Beveridge report intended, it is necessary to look separately at the non-working and the working poor.

The Non-Working Poor

The reasons for the ineffectiveness of social security benefits in preventing poverty amongst those not at work – the elderly, the unemployed, one-parent families and so on – were touched on in discussion of the implementation of Beveridge's proposals. They are in essence the extensive reliance on means-tested national assistance (supplementary benefit and income support) and the consequent problem of low take-up. The causes of this problem are examined below. There is no doubt that non-take-up of supplementary benefit – by about a quarter of those who were eligible to claim it – has been the chief cause of poverty, or at any rate why social security benefits failed to eradicate it, within the non-working population. There is no reason to expect that take-up of income support will be substantially higher.

When the new benefits system was being introduced after the second world war, politicians and civil servants were aware of the divergence from the Beveridge plan but they did not foresee the problem of low take-up. The intense dislike of means testing as it had been applied to the unemployed in the 1930s was believed to be a thing of the past; it was thought that all the objectionable features had been ended by the Determination of Needs Act, 1941 which introduced a personal (rather than a household) assessment of needs.[17] When, however, the assumptions of the post-war planners proved unduly optimistic and the extent of low take-up became apparent, it never seemed possible or a sufficient priority to spend the (admittedly large) resources required to return to the Beveridge plan of providing the national minimum primarily through non-means-tested benefits.

The Working Poor

Both the pre-war advocates of family allowances and Beveridge recognised that, as wages take no account of the cost of bringing up children, some households where the head is in full-time work would be in poverty. The persistence of this problem reflects the inadequacy of family allowances and child tax allowances and, more recently, child benefit, as well as the low take-up of FIS. Taking first the non-means-tested benefits, it is interesting to look at the value of the family allowances plus child tax allowances and of child benefit which replaced them. Owing to the irregularity with which family allowances were uprated, the real level of support fluctuated from year to year though a trend is apparent. The value of child benefit in the mid-1980s was not very different (after allowing for inflation) from that of family allowances and tax allowances combined immediately after the second world war. But a more significant criterion of the effectiveness of benefits for children is their proportional contribution to family budgets; as living standards rise so does the cost of rearing children. Over the 40 years from the mid-1940s the value of these benefits and tax allowances as a proportion of average earnings has been very roughly halved. This reflects a tendency over many years for the tax and benefits system increasingly to favour single people and childless couples at the expense of families with children.

The main problem with family income supplement has been low take-up. When FIS was introduced there was an extensive publicity campaign involving newspaper and television advertisements. Estimates of the number of eligible families, and therefore of the take-up of FIS, have been subject to large sampling errors owing to the limitations of FES data on incomes. Although a more up-to-date estimate is being prepared, the latest available figures relate to the early 1980s and suggest that take-up was only about 50 per cent.[18] About twice as many households are expected to be entitled to family credit than have been eligible for FIS, and this should diminish proverty among the families of low wage earners. Family credit would of course be even more effective if take-up could be raised substantially above that for FIS, but this is likely to be difficult to achieve.

Problems of Means-testing

The advantage of means-tested benefits (and other social services) in concentrating public expenditure on those in greatest need is obvious enough, but against this have to be set a number of important drawbacks. Argument about selectivity and universalism is one of the major debates in social policy and it cannot be discussed fully here. But three problems, low take-up, the 'poverty trap' and the 'unemployment trap', which are of particular importance to the social security system are briefly examined.

Low Take-up: It has been seen that low take-up is a major reason why social security benefits fail to raise the incomes of a substantial number of people to the poverty line. There has been some research into the reasons for low take-up and a number of causal factors can be outlined. First, there is the stigma of claiming means-tested benefits – in a society which places a high value upon economic success, some people regard it as shameful to declare their inability to manage without outside help. To say that means-tested benefits are a right of people in defined circumstances, while true (perhaps with the exception of the social fund), is not a complete answer because an entitlement which is conditional on need is widely seen as being qualitatively different from an absolute one. The association of means testing with the poor law is often used as an explanation but as time goes on this becomes increasingly implausible, and there is little doubt that stigma is not merely an historical hangover. Second, there is lack of knowledge about means-tested benefits. As they tend to be received by relatively small numbers of people there may be ignorance about the existence of some benefits (though this clearly has not applied, for example, to supplementary benefit). There may be a more general shortage of information about eligibility levels; there appears to be a widespread tendency to underestimate the amount of income someone may have from other sources and still make a successful claim. Third, there are problems involved in the actual claiming process such as filling in detailed forms and getting verification of earnings. Where problems arose with supplementary benefit, such as over irregular maintenance payments to lone mothers, claimants may have had to spend hours waiting in unattractive local DHSS offices. Income support is unlikely to be very different. It is not possible to weigh up the precise importance of the various factors behind low take-up, though research does suggest that even when people are informed about their eligibility they often still do not make a claim. Thus improved information about means-tested benefits would only be a partial solution.

Whatever the causes of low take-up, it is a substantial and intractable problem. In the case of supplementary benefit (and some other major schemes such as housing benefit) take-up rates of around 75 per cent have been achieved. Take-up of some other benefits, such as FIS, has been much lower. Overall rates for particular benefits hide the fact, however, that there is a relationship between the level of entitlement and take-up. Taking supplementary benefit as an example, while only a minority of those eligible for small sums in addition to a national insurance benefit may have claimed, those who would otherwise have been virtually destitute almost always overcame any feelings of stigma, lack of information or problems in claiming. In a sense, therefore, low take-up is less serious than it might at first appear, though even the loss of a modest amount of money is significant to people with incomes below the poverty line. There is no doubt that the simplification of claiming procedures and advertising campaigns could increase take-up to some extent, but experience suggests that it is virtually impossible to eliminate the problem. Low take-up is an inherent disadvantage of means-testing, though perhaps less so than the poverty trap.

The Poverty Trap: The term is widely used but not always properly understood. It has a specific meaning and refers to those, chiefly families with children, who are working for relatively low wages. If they get an increase in pay this is offset by income tax, national insurance contributions and the loss of means-tested benefits, notably family credit and housing benefit. Before 1988 a family could conceivably be worse off in terms of total resources following a pay increase, though more usually they were at least slightly better off. As was explained above, with the introduction of net income means tests for family credit and housing benefit, no family can lose more than 100 per cent of an earnings increase. But, leaving aside loss of family credit which is paid at the same rate for six months, a combination of income tax, national insurance contributions and withdrawal of housing benefit on rent and rates (community charge) will result in overall losses of about 90 per cent. Over a wide range of earnings the total income of a family with children (assuming means-tested benefits have been claimed in the first place) will rise only slowly. The term 'poverty plateau' which has also been used is apt.

The poverty trap became severe during the early 1970s owing to a combination of factors: the income tax threshold had dropped very low, national insurance contributions had been put on an earnings-related basis, and new means-tested benefits were introduced (especially FIS and the national rent rebate scheme). The poverty trap is the inevitable result of the extensive use of means-tested benefits (and of low tax thresholds) and it presents a dilemma for policy-makers. A large proportion of the shortfall below a target income level can be made up by means-tested benefits when the poverty trap will be severe (if 100 per cent of the shortfall is made up the whole of a pay increase up to the target income is offset). Alternatively, a relatively small proportion of income shortfall can be made up but then final income is likely to be substantially below the target level. The way out (though a costly one) is of course non-means-tested benefits (or at least means-tested ones which are withdrawn only slowly as income rises). The poverty trap can be seen as undesirable both from the point of view of incentives to move to a better paid job or to work longer hours (very like the arguments about the effects of tax rates paid by higher income groups), and from that of feelings of fairness.

The Unemployment Trap: This problem, which affects those who are out of work as well as those working for low wages, should be distinguished from the poverty trap. Where someone has children and only a modest earning potential, a job may bring little or no increase in income compared with unemployment. Since the mid-1970s and especially since 1979 the government has been concerned by the effects of the unemployment trap on work incentives, and its remedy has been to hold down the rate of benefits available to the unemployed (for example denying them the long-term rate of supplementary benefit). The Fowler reforms in 1988 further reduced the unemployment trap by aligning the means test for housing benefit with that for income support, as explained above. Some have argued, for example the Child Poverty Action Group, for increasing child benefit which raises incomes in work but not during unemployment (because it is offset against other benefits).

Benefits and Earnings

Finally, attention is turned to the effectiveness of income maintenance benefits in replacing previous income from employment. Although the proportion of previous income replaced obviously varies between households, a general indication can be obtained by comparing benefits with average earnings. At the same time, given the use of supplementary benefit entitlement as the 'official' definition of poverty, an indication is also provided of changes in the standard of living represented by the poverty line, both in terms of purchasing power and in relation to average incomes from employment.

As the levels of national insurance and supplementary benefits (excluding housing costs) remained close from 1948, the latter can be used for purposes of illustration. In 1973 a distinction was made between 'long-term' benefits (retirement pension, invalidity pension and widows' benefits as well as long-term supplementary benefit rates) and 'short-term' benefits (sickness benefit, unemployment benefit, maternity allowance and ordinary supplementary benefit rates). Until 1980 long-term benefits were uprated in line with earnings or inflation, whichever was higher, whereas short-term benefits were uprated in line with inflation. During the 1970s long-term benefits moved substantially ahead of short-term ones, and in the mid-1980s the value of the former was about a quarter higher than that of the latter. It was difficult to see that a difference in entitlement of several pounds a week was justified in terms of the greater needs of long-term claimants (excluding the unemployed). The distinction has, however, become less important: income support does not differentiate in this way (the premiums may be seen as a more subtle approach) while, with the introduction of statutory sick pay and maternity allowance, unemployment benefit is the only significant lower rate national insurance benefit.

Between 1948 and the early 1980s short-term benefits approximately doubled in real value while long-term benefits increased by about two and a half times. Since 1980 all benefits have in principle been uprated in line with prices, though in practice there has been some increase in their real value. Thus in absolute terms those on benefit, especially the elderly and others getting long-term rates, have enjoyed a very substantially increased standard of living since the second world war. But on a relative view of standards of living and poverty there must also be concern with how the value of benefits has changed compared with incomes in general. In relative terms (for example in comparison with average earnings) the increase in the value of benefits has been less dramatic.

Although the criteria used in uprating income maintenance benefits were not made explicit until the 1970s, it is clear that the policy from 1948 was to keep them broadly in line with average gross earnings. But, owing to increases in income tax and national insurance contributions, income maintenance benefits have risen in relation to net earnings. In the case of short-term benefits the change has been small but it has been more substantial with long-term ones. For a single householder national assistance and long-term supplementary benefit rates (excluding housing costs) rose from about a fifth of average net earnings in 1949 to about a third in the mid-1980s, and for a couple from less than a third to about half. In households containing dependent children replacement ratios are obviously higher. This is also the case even when child benefit is taken into account as an addition to income during employment because supplementary benefit (income support) allowances for children (except in the case of the very young) are larger than child benefit.

There has never been a formal commitment, however, to uprating non-income maintenance benefits although they generally have been regularly increased, at least since the 1970s. But child benefit has attracted controversy in this respect. Unlike family allowances it has been uprated annually, except on three occasions in the 1980s, the last in April 1988. There are suggestions that the government may freeze child benefit, or even means test it, as a way of reducing social security expenditure.

CONCLUSIONS

Whatever the shortcomings of the system of social security in Britain, income maintenance benefits are providing a substantially higher standard of living in absolute terms to those dependent on them than in 1948, though relative to incomes in general the improvement has been much less marked. Since the mid-1970s, however, short-term benefits have only been uprated in line with prices, and the Conservative government elected in 1979 is committed to doing no more than this in the case of all income maintenance benefits, thus only maintaining their value in absolute terms. But assuming that real (after inflation) earnings continue to increase, as they have done for most of the post-war period, unless corresponding increases are made to benefits both the living standards of recipients and the 'official' poverty line will fall in relative terms. To uprate benefits in line with prices when incomes are generally rising in real terms implicitly reflects an absolute rather than a relative notion of poverty. Measured poverty can be expected to diminish without any improvement in the incomes of the poor relative to those of the rest of society; all that needs to happen is that their incomes should rise in real terms, even if more slowly than the average.

The elderly are in a different position from most other groups of those not at work in that, as has been explained, people retiring in the future will be entitled to an additional earnings-related pension, either from their work, the state scheme (SERPS) or a personal pension. Thus, as more of the newly-retired will have contributed long enough to qualify for a substantial additional pension, despite the changes which have been made to SERPS, their incomes will rise well above the poverty line. Eventually, old people, the second largest group receiving supplementary benefit (income support), should have little need for this assistance. By the same token there should be much less poverty amongst the elderly. The chief problem with pensions is likely to be whether people of working age, who must bear the cost of providing for the elderly through reduced consumption in the expectation of themselves milar benefits, will be prepared to continue paying rising s.

velopment of social security in Britain has been marked by short nnovation and reform: the establishment of the system before the var, the Beveridge report and the changes which stemmed from it, and more recently the introduction of new benefits for the disabled, improved earnings-related pensions and child benefit in the 1970s. In the late 1980s the Fowler reviews have led to the most substantial changes to the benefit system since the Beveridge reforms. But means testing, except in the long term in the case of the elderly, is not being reduced and the best that can be expected is some improvement in take-up rates through advertising and simplification of claiming procedures. More complete take-up of means-tested benefits, if it could be achieved, would do much to diminish poverty.

If poverty is seen as an essentially relative condition, in the final analysis it can only be reduced through some redistribution of incomes in favour of the less well-off. The extent of redistribution required to close what has been called the 'poverty gap'[19] and to eliminate 'official' poverty – the central objective of the Beveridge Report over 40 years ago – would be comparatively modest. But the reforms of 1988 are unlikely to achieve it.

References

1. *The Government's Expenditure Plans 1987-88 to 1989-90*, Cm.56, HMSO, 1987.
2. On this topic see for example: B.B. Gilbert, *The Evolution of National Insurance in Britain*, Michael Joseph, 1966; B.B. Gilbert, *British Social Policy 1914-1939*, Batsford, 1970; and P. Thane, *Foundations of the Welfare State*, Longman, 1982.
3. C. Booth, *Life and Labour of the People in London*, Macmillan, 1903; and B.S. Rowntree, *Poverty: A Study of Town Life*, Macmillan, 1901.
4. *Report of the Royal Commission on the Poor Laws and Relief of Distress*, Cd. 4499, HMSO, 1909; and *Royal Commission on the Poor Laws and Relief of Distress: Report on Scotland*, Cd.4922, HMSO, 1909.
5. *Social Insurance and Allied Services: Report by Sir William Beveridge*, Cmd. 6404, HMSO, 1942.
6. *Social Insurance and Allied Services*, p.7.
7. J. Macnicol, *The Movement for Family Allowances*, Heinemann, 1980.
8. *Social Insurance and Allied Services*, p.155.
9. J. Harris, *William Beveridge: A Biography*, Oxford University Press, 1979.
10. *Reform of Social Security*, Volume 1 [Green Paper], Cmnd. 9517, Volume 2, *Programme for Change*, Cmnd. 9518 and Volume 3, *Background Papers*, Cmnd. 9519, HMSO, 1985; *Housing Benefit Review*, Cmnd.9520, HMSO, 1985.
11. *Reform of Social Security: Programme for Action*, Cmnd.9691, HMSO, 1985.
12. F. Field, *Poverty and Politics*, Heinemann, 1982.
13. B. Abel-Smith and P. Townsend, *The Poor and the Poorest*, Occasional Papers on Social Administration No. 17, Bell, 1965.
14. W.G. Runciman, *Relative Deprivation and Social Justice*, Routledge and Kegan Paul, 1966.
15. Abel Smith and Townsend, *The Poor and the Poorest*, p.17.
16. See for example: W. Beckerman and S. Clark, *Poverty and Social Security in Britain since 1961*, Oxford University Press, 1982; R. Berthoud and J.C. Cooper, *Poverty and Progress in Britain 1953-73*, Cambridge University Press, 1977; R. Layard, D. Piachaud and M. Stewart, *The Causes of Poverty*, Royal Commission on the Distribution of Income and Wealth: Background Paper No. 5, HMSO, 1978; P. Townsend, *Poverty in the United Kingdom*, Penguin Books, 1979; and Royal Commission on the Distribution of Income and Wealth, *Report No.6: Lower Incomes*, Cmnd. 7175, HMSO, 1977.

17. A. Deacon, 'An End to the Means Test? Social Security and the Attlee Government', *Journal of Social Policy*, Vol.11, Part 3, 1982.
18. *The Government's Expenditure Plans 1987-88 to 1989-90.*
19. Beckerman and Clark, *Poverty and Social Security in Britain since 1961.*

FURTHER READING

Social Security and Poverty

Reform of Social Security: Programme for Change, Cmnd.9518 and *Reform of Social Security: Background Papers*, Cmnd. 9519, HMSO, 1985.

These two papers from the DHSS were issued with the Fowler green paper and provide a substantial amount of useful information about the benefits system and its history.

P. Alcock, *Poverty and State Support*, Longman, 1987.

The most up-to-date general introduction to the field.

R. Berthoud and H.C. Brown, *Poverty and the Development of Anti-Poverty Policy in the United Kingdom*, Heinemann, 1981.

A wide-ranging review of the causes of poverty, with a chapter on the social security system, from the Policy Studies Institute.

G.C. Feighen, P.S. Lansley and A.D. Smith, *Poverty and Progress in Britain 1953-73*, Cambridge University Press, 1977.

A study of the problems of measuring poverty and of changes in its extent over time.

R. Layard, D. Piachaud and M. Stewart, *The Causes of Poverty*, Royal Commission on the Distribution of Income and Wealth: Background Paper No.5, HMSO, 1978.

An analysis of the factors causing low income based on data from the General Household Survey.

J. Mack and S. Lansley, *Poor Britain*, Allen and Unwin, 1985.

This book is based on a survey of low-income families carried out for a television series and also includes a useful general discussion of poverty.

P. Townsend, *Poverty in the United Kingdom*, Penguin Books, 1979.

As well as a discussion of the concept of poverty this major work includes the findings of a household survey.

Social Security Advisory Committee, *Annual Reports*, HMSO.

These reports, which have been published since 1981, contain useful discussion of current policy issues and statistics.

Welfare Rights

Child Poverty Action Group, *National Welfare Benefits Handbook* and *Rights Guide to Non-Means-Tested Social Security Benefits*, CPAG, annual.

These guides, which combine accuracy and clarity, deal with means-tested and non-means-tested benefits respectively, and are reissued when benefits are uprated.

3
HEALTH SERVICES

This chapter is mainly concerned with the national health service on which most people in Scotland, to an even greater extent than in the rest of the United Kingdom, rely. There will also be some discussion of the significant and growing contribution of the private sector. Services for the mentally ill and handicapped are, however, dealt with in chapter 4. In order to understand the present structure, functioning and problems of the NHS it is useful first to look briefly at the development of the state's involvement in the health field and at the establishment of the service after the second world war.

HISTORICAL BACKGROUND

A distinction can be drawn between public health – measures to deal with the environment and to control epidemic diseases – and the treatment and care of individuals. Public health became a concern of the state in the 1830s and 1840s, when population growth, industrialisation and urbanisation made problems of insanitary housing, and epidemics of cholera and typhoid, matters of acute concern to those with political power and influence. Various public health and housing acts were passed during the nineteenth century which gave both royal burghs and newly-established police burghs powers to undertake water supply and sewerage schemes, to make by-laws laying down minimum housing standards and to appoint medical officers of health and sanitary inspectors. In addition, by the late nineteenth century many areas had built isolation hospitals under their public health powers for infectious diseases such as smallpox and scarlet fever.

State and local authority involvement with individual health care in general was much slower to develop. This was partly because better-off people paid for their treatment and rarely used hospitals before the end of the nineteenth century. Free treatment was seen as being necessary only for the poor. The poor law authorities made some rudimentary provision, appointing district medical officers to treat out-door paupers, while poorhouses had sick wards in which basic care was provided. By the end of the century some of the largest towns had built separate poor law hospitals, many of which are still in use by the NHS. But the receipt of medical care from the poor law constituted parochial relief, which made the patient a pauper, and it was only used by a limited section of the population.

Tentative steps were taken before the first world war by the Liberal government of 1905-15 to expand state involvement in health care. The origin of the school health service – which was not finally absorbed into the NHS until 1974 – was the medical inspection of elementary school children in 1907. Medical treatment in school clinics followed within a few years. Much more important, however, was the introduction of national health insurance in 1911 (see chapter 2). Medical benefit provided free general practitioner care and drugs to most employed people (but not to their dependants) and the scheme did not cover hospital care. Nevertheless, it was of enormous importance in improving access to health care for the bulk of the population and the financial position of general practitioners. Then, during the first world war, as a result of concern about the high level of infant and maternal mortality, the maternity and child welfare service was established. This was generally operated by local authorities in conjunction with the school health service.

Another very important source of medical treatment for many people was the voluntary hospitals. Some of these dated from the eighteenth century or earlier and were established first in cities and large towns. By the end of the nineteenth century most towns had at least a cottage hospital. Voluntary hospitals relied on charitable contributions and the gratuitous services of doctors who sought honorary appointments for the prestige which they bestowed. During the inter-war years, however, hospitals came under financial pressure and increasingly relied on schemes whereby wage earners paid small weekly contributions in order to have the right to treatment and on direct charges to patients. In contrast to poor law and former poor law hospitals, which cared for a high proportion of the chronic sick, voluntary hospitals, with their greater prestige and better staffing, undertook much more surgery and innovative treatment.

By the second world war, therefore, a substantial amount of medical care was being provided at subsidised or zero cost to the patient: medical officers of health and public health isolation hospitals, tuberculosis sanatoria, poor law hospitals (some of which were taken over by public health authorities after 1930), the school health service, the maternity and child welfare service and national health insurance medical benefit – all of which were financed by taxes, rates or insurance contributions – as well as the voluntary hospitals. But provision was fragmented, both geographically and in terms of the groups covered. By and large the best provision was in big towns and cities with the most developed local authority services and voluntary hospitals, while national health insurance only covered employed persons. To take an extreme case, the medical care available to a non-working housewife in a rural area who could not afford private fees might be rudimentary. When the NHS was introduced in 1948 it was essentially an extension – to non-employed adults and higher-paid white collar workers as well as to under-provided areas – of free health care rather than an entirely new field of state activity.

Although there had been discussion in the 1920s and 1930s about the need for some sort of health service, the creation of the NHS essentially stemmed from the second world war. The war brought home the need for more comprehensive health services and as early as 1941 the Minister of Health announced the government's decision to create a national hospital service when peace came. In the following year the Beveridge Report[1], as one of its three 'assumptions' underlying the reform of social security, recommended the setting up of a comprehensive health service, and in the 1944 white paper, *A National Health Service*[2], the government's proposals were explained in detail. Attention is usually focused on the National Health Service Act, 1946 which created the service in England and Wales, but separate Scottish legislation, the National Health Service (Scotland) Act, 1947, was passed in the following year. In terms of broad structure and principles – a largely tax-financed service free at the point of use to the whole population – the legislation was similar, but there were a number of significant organisational differences.

The 1946 and 1947 acts, which both came into operation in 1948, contained a number of important principles and ideals which reflected both the shortcomings of the past and hopes for the future. The NHS was to be a comprehensive, universal service, available to all those who wished to use it, regardless of class, sex or locality. It would be free to the consumer at the point of use; it would be neither means tested like the poor law nor dependent on contributions like national health insurance; no-one would be denied its provisions. For the first time the state assumed overall responsibility for financing, planning and controlling the distribution of health services to bring them within reach of the whole population. Patients who had the desire and financial means to choose private treatment were, however, still free to do so, and doctors kept the right to practise privately alongside their health service responsibilities.

STRUCTURE AND DEVELOPMENT OF THE NHS 1948-1974

The organisation and administration of the NHS was based on a 'tripartite' structure in which there were three clearly differentiated elements: the hospital sector, managed by five regional hospital boards based in Aberdeen, Dundee, Edinburgh, Glasgow and Inverness; the general medical services, regulated by 25 local executive councils, providing dental, ophthalmic and pharmaceutical services as well as primary medical care from general practitioners; and the 55 counties, cities and large burghs which were responsible for the provision of auxillary and community services, such as maternity and child welfare services, district nurses and home helps. Ambulances, blood transfusion services and training needs were provided on a Scotland-wide basis.

During the early years of the NHS the primary task was to get the service established, and the main emphasis was on the development and expansion of staff and facilities. Expenditure on the service rapidly increased, and during the latter half of the 1960s and early 1970s grew at about three to four per cent a year. In 1962 a major ten-year hospital plan was announced for Scotland, and by 1966 it was already well under way with 11 new or modernised hospitals either ready or nearing completion. In 1966, however, future plans were modified as it had become apparent that hospital provision should be seen within the broader context of health care resources as a whole. More emphasis was placed on the need for local community-based services and plans were made for the development of 15 district general and specialist hospitals, as well as for a major programme of health centre building.

The disadvantages of the separate planning, management and financial structure of the tri-partite system had been widely recognised; it was clear that if the NHS were to be fully effective, hospital services would have to be better linked with primary medical services in the community and the variety of auxillary services then provided by local authorities. The efficient use of hospital beds, for example, depends on the availability of support from the personal social services for those who can be discharged but need care in the community. If services were to be provided in the right way at the right time, good communication and co-operative planning between the hospital, general practitioner and local authority were essential. All too often this was not happening and one study showed that 45 per cent of discharged hospital patients in two areas were not getting the practical assistance, information and advice that they needed.[3] It was clear that, unless these problems were addressed, litle could be done to improve the situation and provide a more integrated health care system.

Two major developments at this time provided an opportunity to make the necessary changes. First, in 1966 a Royal Commission on Local Government in Scotland was set up to consider the structure and function of local authorities. The recommendations of the Wheatley report[4] were implemented by the Local Government (Scotland) Act, 1973 and resulted in a radical restructuring of local authorities in 1975 (see chapter 1). Second, under the Social Work (Scotland) Act, 1968 the wide range of personal social services which had previously been run separately were brought together within the newly created social work departments (see chapter 6). Consideration of a new and better structure for the health service proceeded alongside these developments, with preliminary proposals being put forward in a green paper in 1967,[5] which was followed by a white paper in 1971[6] giving details of the new structure.

THE 1974 REORGANISATION

The new structure, created by the National Health Service (Scotland) Act, 1972, came into operation in 1974, at the same time as reorganisation took place in England and Wales. Both north and south of the border the main objectives of reorganisation were similar and were detailed in a green paper on the future structure.[7] They were to unify health services, to establish closer links with the local authority personal social services, to encourage public and professional participation in the running of the NHS and to ensure central financial control through clearly defined management structures. Whereas in England and Wales both regional and area health authorities were created, in Scotland there is no regional tier of administration. The agencies through which the NHS is administered are 15 area health boards which have a direct link to the Scottish Home and Health Department. Most of the boards were originally divided into districts for administrative purposes, but these have now been abolished. The Secretary of State became directly responsible for the provision of all health services with the elimination of local authorities from NHS administration. Staff providing primary care such as general practitioners, dentists and opticians usually continued to work as contractors rather than on a salaried basis.

Health Boards

Following the 1972 act the health boards took over most of the functions of the former regional hospital boards, executive councils and local health authorities. As the map (Figure 3.1) and Table 3.1 show, health boards vary greatly in the size of the geographical area they cover, the population for which they are responsible and the resources available to them. It is not, however, a simple matter of allocating resources to different areas to meet the health needs of the resident population. As medical technology advances and demands on the health service grow, an ever-increasing range of expensive specialist services and expertise is required that cannot be met by the smaller boards. Patients from throughout Scotland depend on hospitals in major centres such as Glasgow and Edinburgh for specialist consultation and treatment.

TABLE 3.1:

Health Board Resources, 1985-86

Health Board	Population	Revenue expenditure (£000s)	Capital expenditure (£000s)	Average equivalent full-time staff	Average available staffed beds
Ayrshire & Arran	375,212	99,937	4,384	6,065	2,999
Borders	101,705	27,943	10,005	1,749	933
Argyll & Clyde	446,637	129,571	11,795	8,286	4,387
Fife	344,019	90,634	4,968	6,207	3,204
Greater Glasgow	968,801	439,391	23,200	30,751	12,804
Highland	198,617	66,538	8,000	4,288	2,145
Lanarkshire	568,077	152,552	7,007	9,833	5,313
Grampian	500,566	155,406	7,887	10,775	5,556
Orkney	19,351	5,252	269	302	131
Lothian	745,229	274,019	19,651	18,757	8,162
Tayside	394,322	158,054	5,799	11,364	5,140
Forth Valley	272,426	83,295	12,665	5,756	3,412
Western Isles	31,545	9,587	798	519	199
Dumfries & Galloway	146,562	46,628	2,399	3,216	1,508
Shetland	23,440	6,356	566	326	160
TOTAL	5,136,509	1,745,163	119,357	118,194	56,053

Source: *Scottish Health Service Costs 1985/86*, SHHD, 1985; and Scottish Health Service Common Services Agency, *Scottish Health Statistics 1985*, ISD Publications, 1986.

FIGURE 3.1 Health Board Areas

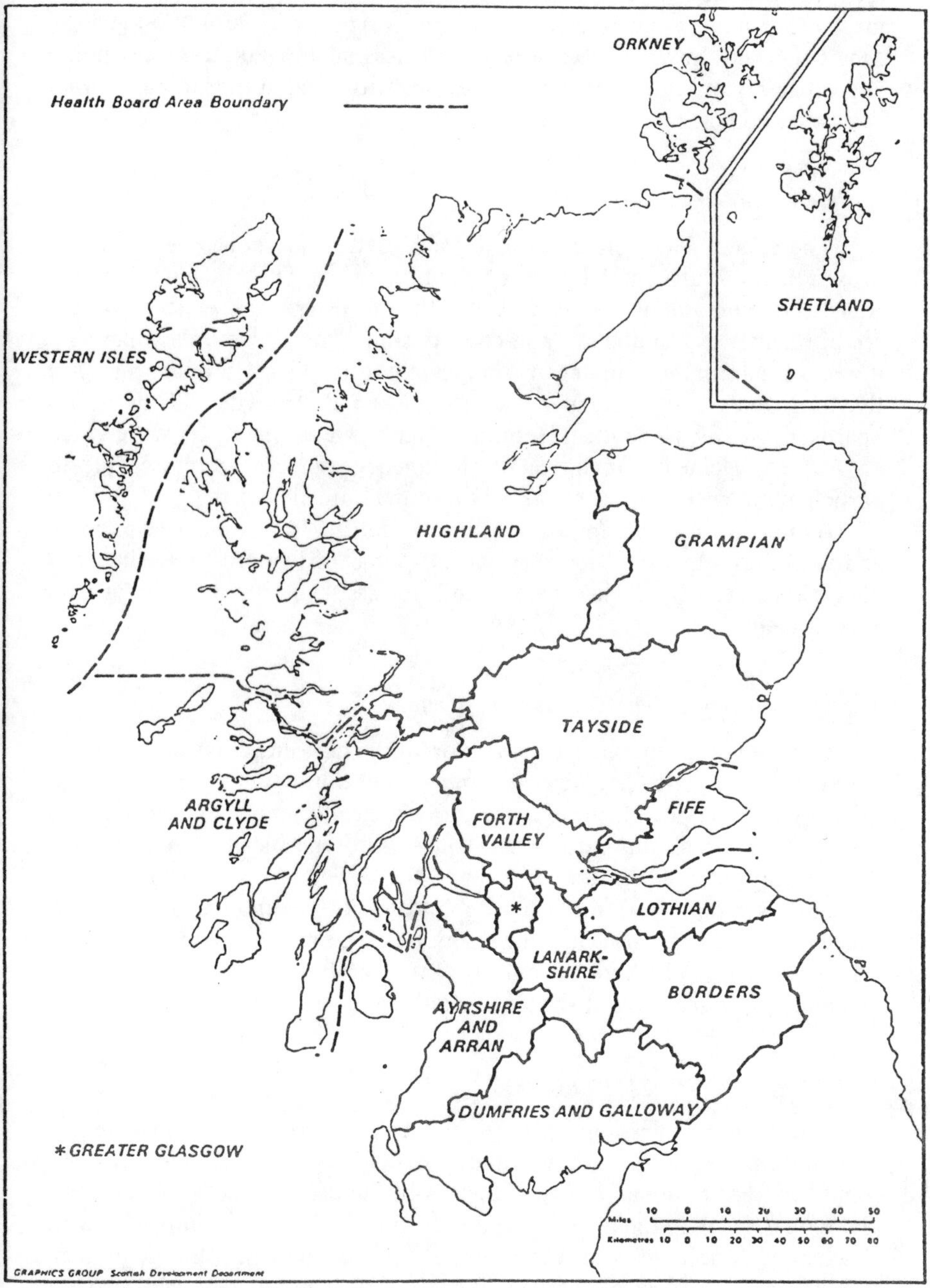

Membership of the boards varies according to the size of the population in the area, and members are appointed by the Secretary of State on the basis of their managerial ability rather than as representatives of particular interest groups. Membership is drawn from a variety of professional, voluntary, trade union and other organisations, after consultations with local authorities and other interested bodies.

The Common Services Agency

The agency has a number of divisions which are concerned with the provision of resources and services on a national scale. These include the blood transfusion and ambulance services, health education, legal services, and the recruitment and training of non-clinical staff. The agency also plays an important part in the planning and implementation of large capital projects, a function which is of particular value to the smaller boards. All the health boards, as well as the Scottish Home and Health Department, are represented on the management committee of the agency and are therefore able to participate in decisions about the way resources are allocated.

As part of the reorganisation of the NHS in 1974 a number of national and local consultative and advisory bodies were set up to represent the interests of various groups in the service and to assist in its monitoring and development.

The Scottish Health Services Planning Council

In broad terms the statutory function of the planning council is to advise the Secretary of State on matters relating to the health service in Scotland and to 'keep under review the development of the health service in Scotland as a whole and in the various parts of Scotland.'[8] More specifically, this entails the identification of needs in the service and the development of plans to meet those needs within the framework of political priorities and budgetary limits. There is a member from each of the health boards, each university in Scotland which has a medical school, six officers of the Secretary of State appointed by him and a representative of the local health councils.

Professional Advisory Committees

The major professional groups in the health service are involved in consultation at both national and local levels through the advisory committees. At national level the function of each committee is to advise the planning council on the planning and provision of the particular service with which it is concerned – medical, dental, pharmaceutical, nursing, optical, scientific or para-medical. The planning council is required to consult with national committees on relevant issues and may ask them to carry out detailed investigations into areas of health service provision. At local level the committees carry out a similar function in relation to the area health boards, advising on local needs and the provision of patient care. It can be seen from the structure of the consultative committees that professionals have a good deal of influence in both the planning and management of the health service. They are well represented at all levels and, although it can be argued that the medical profession still has the strongest voice, other professional groups can contribute to the decision making processes. The introduction of general managers into the NHS (see below) may, however, tend to diminish the influence of professionals to some extent.

Local Health Councils

There are 44 local health councils throughout Scotland which were established to represent the interests of the public and to give consumers an opportunity to express their views on health service provision. There are, for example, five local health councils in the Greater Glasgow area whereas some smaller board areas have only one. Like health boards they are composed of representatives of interested bodies such as local authorities, voluntary organisations and trade unions. Although regulations under the National Health Service (Scotland) Act, 1978 may make provision for a wide range of consumer participation, in practice the influence of the health councils has been limited.

The Health Service Commissioner

The commissioner, or health service ombudsman, acts as an independent investigator of individual complaints from patients or their representatives. He is empowered to deal with administrative complaints or failures to provide services but not clinical decisions about diagnosis and treatment. The complaint must be made in writing and usually within 12 months of its first coming to the attention of the aggrieved person. Before proceeding with an investigation the commissioner must satisfy himself that the subject of the complaint – usually a health board – has been given a reasonable opportunity to resolve the matter.

There is, in general, a lack of public awareness of the commissioner and his function. Health boards have shown little desire to publish their own complaints ratings, and no easily recognised body is available to help people prepare and present complaints. In addition, there is no separate commissioner based in Scotland. At a time when demands and costs are continuing to rise rapidly without a parallel increase in resources, it is not surprising that complaints are made about both the quantity and quality of health care. It is clearly important, therefore, that patients are provided with information and support to enable them to make their complaints as effectively as possible.

THE MANAGEMENT STRUCTURE SINCE 1984

Despite the 1974 reorganisation the NHS continued to be plagued by a variety of problems both in the organisation and provision of services.

Deteriorating industrial relations reflected unrest among both professional and ancillary staff. Costs increased and there was a general feeling that the NHS was failing to meet the demands being made on it. The Royal Commission on the National Health Service which reported in 1979[9] highlighted the inequitable distribution of resources between and within health boards and pointed to the resulting inequalities in service provision. However, as the royal commission pointed out, there was little hope of substantial additional resources for the NHS over and above what was already planned. Savings might, however, be achieved by greater efficiency and through the prevention of illness by means of a systematic programme of health education.

These factors, together with the imposition by government of cash limits on health board expenditure, heightened the growing need for a thorough examination of the management of the NHS. To this end a management inquiry was set up by the government in 1983 'to give advice on the effective use and management of manpower and related resources in the NHS'. The inquiry, which published its findings in the Griffiths report later in the same year, commented on the lack of a clearly defined general management structure at all levels of the NHS, defining this as 'responsibility drawn together in one person, at different levels of the organistion, for planning, implementation and control of performance'.[10] Without the leadership which would be provided by one person, with overall responsibility for the management of services in an area, it would not be possible to develop and implement new plans, bring about necessary change and control costs.

Although the inquiry did not cover Scotland, the Secretary of State informed interested bodies that he was in agreement with the principles of the report's recommendations and that he proposed a unit-based system of general management. Such a system would introduce into Scotland the management style favoured by the inquiry and bring decision making closer to the level at which services were delivered. Since 1984, therefore, each health board has been reorganised into a number of units, each comprising one or more hospitals managed by a team responsible for administration and finance, nursing services, works services and community medicine. Community services, such as health centres and clinics, are managed separately from hospitals by teams specifically responsible for them.

The first step in a phased programme for the implementation of the new structure, which is expected to take a number of years, was the appointment of general managers at health board level, responsible for the efficiency, economy and quality of service in their area. Second, there will be an examination of unit structures, and budgeting and information systems, as general managers are introduced at this level.

An important objective of these changes is to find ways in which clinicians can be increasingly involved in management. This was seen by Griffiths as critical to effective management, particularly at unit level, where doctors' decisions largely dictate the use of resources. He argued that it is necessary for them to accept the management responsibility which goes with clinical freedom and become actively involved in securing the most effective use of resources. At the time of writing many of the unit general managers are already in post and are beginning to implement the recommendations of the Griffiths report. The essential requirement laid down for these posts was the possession of general management skills and experience, and there is no doubt that such skills are vital in the difficult task that health board managers face.

Michael Beesley, a member of a district health authority in England, in examining recent developments in the implementation of the Griffiths report, notes that, unlike private sector organisations, the NHS has two distinct sources of management legitimacy. The first is financial and involves getting and managing the money from a central political market place, with its attendant values and priorities. The second is clinical, namely what provision and treatment doctors and other professionals think should be available to patients. Managing these two sources of legitimacy with their different and sometimes conflicting underlying values requires negotiation and consensus in establishing priorities, and making decisions about the allocation and distribution of available resources. Whether the appointment of general managers at a local level within a fundamentally unchanged structure will be sufficient to bring about an improvement in either the effectiveness or the efficiency of the service will not be apparent for some time and will largely depend on their ability to negotiate successfully between the two rival sources of legitimacy.[11]

HEALTH CARE NEEDS

When the NHS came into being in 1948 it was assumed that the new, universal and comprehensive service would gradually lead to a reduction in illness and disease, and that the maintenance of good health would result in a decreasing need and demand for medical treatment. In practice this did not happen and instead there has been a consistently rising demand for health care and related services. To understand why this should be so a number of factors have to be considered, such as changing patterns of illness, social and economic conditions, demographic changes and rising expectations of health care.

Changing Patterns of Illness

Certainly many diseases which were prevalent when the NHS was created have now disappeared or are only rarely encountered. This is particularly true of the major infectious and communicable diseases, such as tuberculosis and poliomyelitis, which have been virtually eradicated as a result of better living conditions and the development of vaccines. Unfortunately, however, as these diseases have declined others have taken their place so that today we are faced with different rather than fewer health problems. A look at the broad spectrum of disease in Britain today reveals three principal categories which are useful in considering the present position.[12]

The first group consists of those conditions and illnesses that can be seen as the result of the greatly increased proportion of elderly people in the community. More old people inevitably mean an increase in the disabilities and chronic degenerative diseases associated with old age. Quite apart from the life threatening and severely disabling illnesses such as strokes and heart disease, with advancing age defects of hearing and sight, loss of mobility and nutritional deficiency are also increasingly common. In addition, social isolation can lead to loneliness and depression. During the 1980s there has been a sharp increase in the oldest age groups of 75 and over (see chapter 10). This change will certainly increase the demand for both acute and long-term health care as well as making additional demands on residential and community social services.

The second group includes diseases which are associated with social behaviour and individual lifestyles. While low incomes led to malnutrition which was formerly a major cause of disease, affluence has brought its own problems. Eating more does not necessarily mean eating better and there has been much controversy in recent years about the role of diet in the causation of coronary heart disease and associated conditions. Smoking and alcohol abuse, misuse of drugs, changes in sexual behaviour, and the way we use our leisure time are other factors which have an important influence on health. Behaviour in these areas is to a very large extent a matter of individual choice but the consequences have important implictions, not only for the individual himself but in relation to the demands which are made on health care resources. The emergence of AIDS in recent years is perhaps the most striking example of the relationship between behaviour and health; in America where its spread is more advanced the estimated cost of treatment over the next few years is very substantial and we have yet to see the effects it will have on an already overburdened NHS.

Third, there are those illnesses which are associated with a changing social and physical environment. Although there have been improvements, such as the introduction of the Clean Air Act, 1956 which did a good deal to control air pollution in heavily populated areas, physical dangers in the environment have increased in other ways. Road traffic is constantly growing and road accidents are now the greatest single cause of death among children and young adults. On a wider scale the Chernobyl disaster in Russia in 1986 was a timely reminder of the hazards posed by radioactive pollution of the environment, while chemical pollution of various kinds has also become a matter of increasing concern. Both may have long-term effects on the health of children and young people.

Social and Economic Factors

Health hazards can also stem from social and economic factors such as poverty, poor housing and unemployment. The NHS, with its emphasis on treatment rather than prevention, has done little to address these problems which need to be tackled on a much broader front. It is also a matter of concern that the serious inequalities in health which have been well documented for many decades have persisted into the 1980s. The initial aims of the NHS to give everybody the opportunity of adequate and appropriate health care have not been reflected in any narrowing of the health gap between the Registrar General's occupational classes. Indeed, both the Black report[13] which drew on evidence from the early 1970s and a recent review commissioned by the Health Education Council[14] show that, although there have been improvements in the health of the population as a whole, the gap between different social groups has, if anything, widened in recent years. While there are a number of ways in which health inequalities may be explained, there is no doubt about the close relationship between health and social circumstances. Recent studies in Edinburgh, for example, indicate a clear link between housing tenure and health,[15] while an association between unemployment and health has also been established[16] as well as one between unemployment and attempted suicide.[17] It is important to remember that the social factors associated with poor health themselves interact and that many people will therefore be multiply deprived, living in poor housing on low incomes in areas with few amenities and lack of access to social, educational and other health promoting facilities. If people with poor social environments are more likely to have poor health, it is equally true that those with poor health are more likely to be downwardly mobile. They experience decreased chances of finding work in a society where employment is at a premium, with a consequent reduction of their income and standard of living. As was noted at a recent health symposium in Glasgow:

> those who are deprived because they are sick, disabled or mentally ill constitute a significant proportion of multiply deprived individuals, households, and residents of multiply deprived areas. It is also true that there is both social and geographical mobility in our society, and that those who move to 'better' positions or areas tend to be the healthiest and best educated.[18]

One may take the approach that poor health leads to poor social position, emphasise that deprived social circumstances are likely to result in poor health, or believe that the two explanations are inextricably intertwined. In any event one cannot avoid the conclusion that good health must be regarded as a matter for a wide range of central and local government policies as well as for the health service.

RESOURCE ALLOCATION IN THE NHS

As stated earlier it was the view of the government when the NHS was set up that, as better health care became available to everyone irrespective of his or her ability to pay, the amount of ill-health in the community would diminish and the proportion of national income devoted to the service would fall. We now know this has not been the case. Rather, as people become more conscious of health care, and as medical advances make it possible to treat and cure more illnesses, the demands for new treatments and the pressure to make them universally available are potentially unlimited. Consequently, the amount of money devoted to the health service has continued to increase with no sign of diminishing need for extra resources. As early as the 1950s expenditure on the

NHS had already become a matter of major concern and in 1953 the Guillebaud committee was set up 'To review the present and prospective cost of the National Health Service; to suggest means, whether by modifications in organisation or otherwise, of ensuring the most effective control and efficient use of such Exchequer funds as may be made available ...'[19] The committee found that in its first years the NHS had been absorbing a falling proportion of national income and that increased costs had been largely due to higher expenditure on salaries rather than any extravagant and inefficient use of resources; Guillebaud recommended no changes in organisation. Since the mid-1950s expenditure on the NHS has increased very substantially in real terms yet the question of funding has continued to be a problematic feature of the service. There have been calls for additional sources of finance to be found and for coherent rationing mechanisms to be developed, though it cannot be said that very much has yet been achieved. The main focus in recent years has been on the fairer allocation of resources between areas and on the achievement of greater efficiency, especially in hospitals.

In any consideration of funding three aspects need to be considered: sources of finance, level of funding and distribution of the financial resources available. By far the major part of funding for the NHS, nearly 90 per cent of the total, comes from general taxation with about ten per cent from national insurance contributions and between two and three per cent from direct charges for certain services such as prescriptions and dental treatment. The level of funding is ultimately a political decision but whatever the ideologies of various governments the amount of public money allocated to the service has never proved to be sufficient for the ever increasing demands upon it. In any event, arguments about the level of spending are fraught with difficulties. International comparisons, for example, show that, while Britain spends a relatively small proportion of national income on health care, there is no clear link between the level of spending and the health status of the population.[20] It may be that it is the way money is spent rather than the amount which is the most influential factor in determining the effectiveness of health care. It is widely accepted that the NHS provides good value for money compared with insurance based arrangements where cost control tends to be weaker. Furthermore, as we have seen, many of the factors which affect health status are outside the field of health care expenditure altogether.

The distribution of resources in the NHS is of fundamental importance if there is to be appropriate access to health care for those with differing needs. It was increasingly recognised during the 1960s and 1970s that, in spite of ever-increasing expenditure, there were large regional inequalities which stemmed largely from historical factors which had been reinforced by the methods used to allocate resources in the NHS since its inception. In the mid-1970s efforts were made to provide a formula that would redistribute resources on the basis of need, and the results were published in 1977 in *Scottish Health Authorities: Revenue Equalisation* (SHARE).[21]

The criteria of need which were identified as the main determinants of health expenditure were the size and structure of the population; patterns of illness and social factors which play a part in these; the cost of providing care which varies from area to area depending on factors such as population density; the cost of maintaining existing facilities; and the teaching responsibilities of universities.

For historical reasons Scotland enjoys higher spending per head on the NHS (over 120 per cent of the United Kingdom average) as on most public services (see chapter 1), but the task of allocating it between health board areas in response to the above-mentioned criteria is not straightforward. Even though the SHARE formula allows for adjustments to take account of, for example, population movements, these are not always possible to forecast accurately; there have been larger shifts in the last decade than the SHARE report anticipated. Other constraints include the level of public expenditure, and the ability of the local authority personal social services to accommodate a shift in the focus of care for certain groups, such as the elderly and handicapped, from hospitals to the community. Nevertheless, in spite of the difficulties in implementing SHARE, allocations in 1987-88 ranged from five per cent above the parity target to eight per cent below, compared with 15 per cent above and 34 per cent below in 1977-78 when the scheme was introduced.[22]

Although expenditure on the NHS in Scotland rose by about 27 per cent in real terms between 1979-80 and 1987-88[23] the service is widely perceived as being under increasing financial strain. Hospitals and community health services have in fact had a slightly slower rate of increase in resources than the NHS as a whole, while family practitioner services (which are not subject to cash limits) have fared substantially better. There are a number of reasons for the financial difficulties which are being experienced by hospitals. First, costs in the NHS have risen faster than in the economy as a whole, partly as a result of the continual introduction of new and expensive treatments. But a more important cause has been the relative price effect whereby NHS costs increase more rapidly than general inflation, mainly because a high proportion of expenditure is on wages and salaries which tend to rise in real terms. Second, the growth in the number of the very elderly, who make much more use of health care than the average, increases demands on the service. When these factors are taken into account it is doubtful whether the hospitals are even as well funded as they were ten years ago in relation to the demands which are being made upon them. It is often claimed that no matter how much is spent on the NHS increasing demands and higher expectations can never be fully met. While in principle this may be true, there can be no doubt that the slowing down in the rate at which resources have been increased each year since the mid-1970s has made funding problems very much more acute.

Priorities for the 1980s

In 1976, soon after the reorganisation of the NHS, a report, *The Health Service in Scotland: The Way Ahead*,[24] was published by the Scottish Home and Health Department setting out guidelines for the development of the service and reviewing health care priorities for the period up to 1980. As the report made clear, the adverse economic situation facing the United Kingdom at that time meant that there would be severe restrictions on public expenditure and that the NHS would not be immune from these. Some expansion would be maintained but this would be at a lower level than previously. In the report six main principles were identified which were intended to inform the general approach to future planning. The first was the need to work within available budgets. Second, attention was given to the importance of the development of health services within areas of multiple deprivation. The next two principles focused on the changing emphasis between hospitals and the community, with recommendations that there should be a lessening of the growth rate in the acute hospital sector but continued improvements in both hospital and community health services for the elderly, the mentally ill and handicapped and the physically handicapped. Finally, encouragement was to be given to the growth of preventive measures and the development of a responsible attitude to health on the part of the individual and the community.

In summary, then, the report clearly set out the preferred strategies for dealing with health problems, emphasising the importance of the social environment and the need for preventive measures, particularly in the areas of multiple deprivation in central Scotland. Its recommendations also reflected an awareness of increased demands on the NHS as a result of the growing proportion of old people in the community.

Following the 1976 report, it was expected that the Health Service Planning Council would work towards a long-term programme based on these priorities and provide comprehensive guidance to health boards. Their report, *Scottish Health Authorities: Priorities for the Eighties* (SHAPE),[25] was published in 1980 and was based on the work of the council's programme planning groups and recommendations from professional advisory bodies.

The programme put forward in SHAPE placed services in three categories according to their priority for expenditure during the 1980s. Category A consists of the development of preventive services, services for the multiply deprived, care of the elderly, mentally ill, mentally and physically handicapped, and community nursing services. Programmes in this category would be given first priority. Category B services, which consist of maternity services and primary medical, dental and ophthalmic services, would also be allowed to grow but at a slower rate. Category C services were to remain almost static in real terms or actually decline. These include child health, acute hospital services and the general pharmaceutical service.

Included in the report were recommendations for capital expenditure which would be required as a consequence of the priorities. In general the proposals for category A services would only involve substantial capital outlay for the development of residential and hospital accommodation for the elderly, young chronic sick and for day centres. Only minimal capital expenditure was envisaged for services in category B. In category C any expansion in child health would take the form of extra out-patient and day-care facilities, paid for by the closure of in-patient paediatric units which were too small to meet the needs of children adequately. Tables 3.2 and 3.3 show some indicators of the

TABLE 3.2:

Hospital Beds and Patient Discharges by SHAPE Categories, 1980 and 1985

SHAPE category	Average available staffed beds			Discharges		
	1980	1985	% change	1980	1985	% change
A Care of the elderly	9764	10690	+9.5	21203	28432	+34.1
A Elderly with mental disability	2742	3765	+37.3	2632	4166	+76.4
A Mental illness	17040	16307	−4.3	27242	28543	+4.8
A Mental handicap	6617	6016	−9.1	2013	3240	+61.0
A Physical handicap	470	536	+14.0	973	1846	+89.7
B Maternity	2689	2563	−4.7	105759	105490	−0.3
B Maternity and neonatal	3315	3142	−5.2	125961	120511	−4.3
C Child health	1257	1173	−6.7	50308	53846	+7.0
C General and acute	19745	18470	−6.5	546546	549192	+8.7
TOTAL	58208	56334	−3.2	774246	830610	+7.3

Note: Figures refer to years ending 30th September.

Source: *Scottish Health Statistics 1985*, ISD Publications, 1986.

TABLE 3.3: Community and Family Practitioner Services by SHAPE Categories, 1980 and 1985

SHAPE category	1980	1985	% change
Community Services			
A Community nursing			
Community nurses WTE[1]	4907	5237	+6.7
Home visits (000s)[2]	6823	7208	+5.6
B Community dentistry			
Dentists WTE[1]	285	289	+1.3
Courses of treatment (000s)	260	284[4]	+9.2
Family Practitioner Services			
B General medical services			
Doctors	3256	3575	+9.8
Consultations (000s)	23392	23907[4]	+2.2
B General dental services			
Dentists	1280	1407	+9.9
Courses of treatment (000s)	2549	2857	+12.1
B General ophthalmic services			
Opticians[3]	583	776	+33.1
Sight tests (000s)	727	918	+26.3
C General pharmaceutical services			
Chemists shops[4]	1107	1134	+2.4
Prescriptions dispensed (000s)	35607	37821	+6.2

Notes: 1 Whole-time equivalents.
2 Home visits by district nurses, health visits and midwives.
3 Ophthalmic opticians and ophthalmic medical practitioners.
4 Data relate to 1984.

Source: *Scottish Health Statistics 1985*, ISD Publications, 1986.

resources devoted to the SHAPE programmes between 1980 and 1985, as well as outputs in terms of courses of treatment and so on. The SHAPE priority category is indicated for each programme.

THE PRIVATE SECTOR

The private sector has a role in the provision of health care in two essentially different ways: through the privatisation of NHS cleaning, catering and laundry services, and through medical insurance and private hospitals. Both of these have been encouraged by the Conservative government since 1979 and they will be discussed in turn.

Privatisation within the NHS

The government takes the view that ancillary services in NHS hospitals, which have traditionally been provided by health service employees, tend to be run inefficiently and that substantial 'efficiency savings' can be achieved if they are put out to competitive tender. The Scottish Home and Health Department has brought pressure to bear on health boards to privatise these services and this is increasingly being done. South of the border in-house tenders have often been successful and in these cases services have continued to be provided by NHS employees.

It appears to be the case that substantial savings have been achieved through privatisation; a recent study concluded that in six contracts which were put out to tender savings of between one-third and two-thirds were achieved.[26] Nevertheless, there is a great deal of controversy about privatisation. First, there have been allegations that in some instances standards of service have deteriorated: wards are not being properly cleaned nor sheets adequately washed. Second, even if standards have not deteriorated, it is not clear how far the savings have resulted from greater efficiency or simply from lower wage rates, sick pay or holiday entitlements. The last consideration raises a general issue in the social services: the conflict which may arise between the public sector as a 'good' employer and the economies that can be obtained by exploiting a generally plentiful supply of unskilled labour and holding down pay levels.

Two other examples of forms of privatisation within the NHS are increased charges and the disposal of physical assets. Although the health service is mainly financed from taxation, and GP and hospital care is free, charges for prescriptions and dental treatment have been sharply increased since 1979, while the ophthalmic service has been largely privatised. As far as physical assets are concerned, health boards have been encouraged to sell off surplus land and buildings and, indeed, have often been eager to do so as a way of obtaining resources to finance new developments. In 1986, for example, they were urged to dispose of residential accommodation which has traditionally been provided for nurses and junior doctors. Although it can be argued that some of the £130 million represented by the value of housing accommodation could be more appropriately used in direct patient care, low-paid or ı staff may suffer hardship and recruitment become more difficult.

Private Health Care

Individuals have always had the right to obtain health care privately, either through insurance or by direct payment. In addition, the 1947 act enabled accommodation for private patients to be made available in NHS hospitals. These 'pay-beds' subsequently became the subject of increasing controversy and in the mid-1970s the Labour government established the Health Services Board (since abolished) to preside over their gradual phasing out and to control the development of private hospitals. Some commentators believe the threat to NHS pay beds was of considerable benefit to the private sector as it encouraged the development of separate independent hospitals.

With the advent of a Conservative government in 1979 there was a reversal of the previous policies and an increasing emphasis on the role of the private sector in health care. The argument from the political right is that good health care is best achieved by a combination of public and private provision, and that people should be encouraged to take financial responsibility for medical treatment to a much larger extent than at present. The government accepts that the state should provide a health service for those who want to use it or do not have access to private care, but they also argue that anyone who wishes to do so should be encouraged to make alternative arrangements. Because health care costs are unpredictable, people who make substantial use of the private sector usually subscribe to an insurance scheme to cover specialists' fees and hospital or nursing home charges.

More use is being made of private sector health care, though in most cases only for a limited range of hospital treatment, and the number of people in Britain covered by medical insurance has doubled over the last decade to about ten per cent of the population. Many firms now take out group subscriptions with organisations such as BUPA on behalf of their employees, and trade unions are increasingly doing so for their members. Private facilities to meet the growing demand have also increased: there are more private hospitals and nursing homes, and a greater number of private beds.[27] At the same time the number of beds available in NHS hospitals has fallen (although the number of patients treated has increased) and waiting lists have lengthened. Between 1980 and 1985, for example, the number of people awaiting in-patient treatment in Scotland increased from 13.1 to 15.1 per 1,000 population.

While there may be argument about the reasons for the increase in health insurance, it is clear that many of the operations carried out within the private sector are for non-urgent, but nevertheless irritating and often painful, conditions. Within the NHS the waiting time for such operations is frequently lengthy and the only alternative, in order to get surgery more quickly or at a convenient time, is to arrange for private treatment.

Unless there is a substantial reduction in the length of NHS waiting lists this trend is likely to continue. In addition, facilities offered in private hospitals and clinics may also be seen as better and more congenial than those in the health service. Reports of ward closures resulting from a severe shortage of nurses as large numbers leave the profession, and of dangerously early discharges of patients caused by pressure on hospital facilities, have undoubtedly combined to undermine confidence in the present state of the NHS.

In considering the role of the private sector in health care, however, it is important to remember that it is, at present, only a very small part of the total available provision, and this is particularly so in Scotland. Nevertheless, it can be argued that its presence, however small, can lead to the development of a two-tier system which favours those who can afford to pay and draws trained staff from the NHS. An example of these arguments has recently been seen in relation to a planned private hospital in Clydebank, which will cater mainly for foreign patients. The scheme is backed by an American company, Health Care International, and will apparently provide 4,000 permanent jobs in an area of extremely high unemployment. Opponents of the scheme argue, however, that it will lead to a depletion of NHS medical and nursing staff in the Greater Glasgow area. In addition, there have been fears that the demand for blood transfusion products, which a high technology hospital requires, could affect their availability to the health service.

CONCLUSIONS

It is frequently said that the NHS is in crisis: that it is under funded, overstretched and increasingly unable to meet the growing demands upon it. In some ways, as we have seen earlier in the chapter, it has become the victim of its own success, no longer able to meet the needs and expectations it has to a large extent created.

More people are being treated by the NHS every year with more operations being performed and hospital discharges recorded. The question must be asked, however, how far this increased throughput is a reflection of a more efficient and effective NHS or how far it is a response to an overloaded system, with patients being discharged too early without appropriate community support.

There seems little likelihood in the near future of more than a modest real growth in the resources available to the NHS. Expenditure on the service has continued to increase in real terms but in recent years it has scarcely kept pace with rising needs and costs. In this context the setting of priorities, and the allocation and distribution of resources, have assumed a position of primary importance.

References

1. *Social Insurance and Allied Services: Report by Sir William Beveridge*, Cmd.6404, HMSO, 1942.
2. *A National Health Service*, Cmd.6502, HMSO, 1944.
3. R.G.S. Brown, *The Changing National Health Service*, Routledge and Kegan Paul (2nd ed.), 1978.

4. *Report of the Royal Commission on Local Government in Scotland* (Wheatley Report), Cmnd.4140, HMSO, 1969.
5. *Royal Commission on Local Government in Scotland: Minutes of Written Evidence, Vol.7*, HMSO, 1967; and Scottish Home and Health Department, *Administrative Reorganisation of the Scottish Health Services*, HMSO, 1968.
6. *Reorganisation of the Scottish Health Services*, Cmnd.4734, HMSO, 1971.
7. *The Future Structure of the National Health Service*, HMSO, 1970.
8. National Health Service (Scotland) Act, 1978.
9. *Report of the Royal Commission on the National Health Service*, Cmnd.7615, HMSO, 1979.
10. *Report of the NHS Management Inquiry* (Griffiths Report), DHSS, 1983, p.11.
11. M. Beesley, 'Management and the Health Service', *Social Policy and Administration*, Vol.19, No.2, 1985.
12. *Prevention and Health: Everybody's Business*, HMSO, 1980.
13. *Inequalities in Health: Report of a Research Working Party Chaired by Sir Douglas Black*, DHSS, 1980.
14. *The Health Divide: Inequalities in Health in the 1980s*, Health Education Council, 1987.
15. S.M. Hunt et al, *Housing and Health in a Deprived Area of Edinburgh* and D.P. Strachan, *The Home Environment and Respiratory Morbidity in Children*, unpublished papers presented at a conference of the Legal Research Group, Warwick University and the Institution of Environmental Health Officers, 1986.
16. A. Maclure and G.T. Stewart, 'Admission of Children to Hospital in Glasgow: Relation to Unemployment and Other Deprivation Variables', *Lancet*, 1984, Vol. 2.
17. S. Platt and N. Kreitman, 'Unemployment and Parasuicide in Edinburgh, 1968-1982', *British Medical Journal*, Vol.289, 1984.
18. S. McIntyre, 'Sociological Perspectives on Health Promotions in Multiply Deprived Areas' in J.K. Davies (ed.), *Health Promotion in Areas of Multiple Deprivation*, Scottish Health Education Group, 1986.
19. *Report of the Enquiry into the Cost of the NHS* (Guillebaud Report), Cmd.9663, 1956.
20. J. Allsop, *Health Policy and the National Health Service*, Longman, 1984.
21. Scottish Home and Health Department, *Scottish Health Authorities: Revenue Equalisation* (SHARE), HMSO, 1977.
22. *Public Expenditure to 1990-91: A Commentary on the Scottish Programme*, Scottish Office, 1988.
23. *Public Expenditure to 1990-91.*
24. Scottish Home and Health Department, *The Health Service in Scotland: The Way Ahead*, HMSO, 1976.
25. Scottish Home and Health Department, *Scottish Health Authorities: Priorities for the Eighties* (SHAPE), HMSO, 1980.
26. R. G. Milne, 'Competitive Tendering in the NHS,' *Public Administration*, Vol.65, No. 2, 1987.
27. *Regional Trends 22*, HMSO, 1987.

FURTHER READING

J. Allsop, *Health Policy and the National Health Service*, Longman, 1984.

This book discusses policies related to the distribution of health services, the funding and management of the NHS, and the policy problems that have faced governments, particularly since the 1970s.

J.K. Davies (ed.), *Health Promotion in Areas of Multiple Deprivation*, Scottish Health Education Group, 1986.

A report of a symposium held in Glasgow, which examines the challenge of multiple deprivation and offers some suggestions for future action.

D.N. Hamilton, *The Healers: A History of Medicine in Scotland*, Canongate Press, 1981.

The most authoritative source on the history of specifically Scottish aspects of health services.

Scottish Home and Health Department, *Scottish Health Authorities: Priorities for the Eighties*, HMSO, 1980.

The SHAPE programme outlines proposals for the development of the NHS in Scotland and sets out priorities for expenditure.

Inequalities in Health, Penguin, 1988

This book combines a reprint of the 1980 report of the DHSS working group on inequalities in health (the Black Report), edited by P. Townsend and N. Davidson, and of *The Health Divide* by M. Whitehead, the report of a review commissioned by the Health Education Council, which discusses studies on inequalities in health since Black.

4
MENTAL HEALTH SERVICES

This chapter is concerned with an important aspect of the health services, the care of the mentally ill and handicapped. With the slow shift of emphasis from institutional to community care for these groups, the contributions of the personal social services and of voluntary organisations has become increasingly important, and that contribution will also be examined. Finally, the chapter will deal with services for those with alcohol-related problems which in some respects raise similar issues to the treatment of mental illness.

SERVICES FOR THE MENTALLY ILL

In Scotland, as in England and Wales, a central feature of the debate about the care of the mentally ill has been uncertainty as to the future role of specialist mental hospitals. Although the average size of these institutions was smaller than south of the border, and although they have in general been less remote from the populations that they served, they embodied an essentially similar tradition and set of assumptions about the nature of mental illness.

Most mental hospitals came into existence in the latter part of the nineteenth or early in the twentieth century as 'lunatic asylums' – institutions for the custodial care of the incurably insane. Their medical staffs were with a few notable exceptions not of the highest quality, and their attendants untrained with functions a good deal closer to those of prison warders than of hospital nurses. Some asylums no doubt offered greater comfort than others and some greater kindness; but the range of variation must necessarily have been limited, as the knowledge and skills necessary for the effective treatment of mental illness did not exist. Contemporary attitudes were both reflected in and influenced by the legal framework within which mental illness was managed.[1]

Both the role and the image of the mental hospital began to alter in the 1930s, though at first only slowly, as a result of the discovery of physical methods of treating some mental illnesses. Then, in the post-war period, administrative, clinical and attitudinal changes interacted so as to bring about quite rapidly a re-drawing of the whole pattern of psychiatric care. With the inauguration of the NHS, psychiatric hospitals were removed from the control of local authorities, vested in the Secretary of State, and administered together with general hospitals through a common system of regional hospital boards. This may have helped a little to remove some of the stigma attaching to these institutions, but it was of less importance than the impact of the rapid advances in the 1950s in the development of drug treatments for psychiatric disturbances. These gave added impetus to the greater liberalism that was becoming apparent in public attitudes towards mental illness and the mentally ill, and to a more enlightened and better informed approach on the part of general medical practitioners. As a result of such changes, the hospitals came to emphasise more and more a therapeutic rather than a merely custodial role. Admission rates rose, there was increasing emphasis on voluntary admissions rather than the use of compulsory powers, and the average length of stay in hospital dropped sharply. Some, though not all, psychiatric hospitals began to develop an active interest in social and industrial rehabilitation to balance the generally predominant emphasis on drug treatment. There was also a steady growth of out-patient services, though little in the way of other community provisions developed on either side of the border.[2]

MENTAL HEALTH LEGISLATION

There has been a long history of legislation relating to mental illness and to mental handicap, which in part has had the aim of protecting vulnerable members of society who might be subject, although this is much less common today, to compulsory measures of care. Since the enactment of the reforming Mental Health (Scotland) Act, 1960 services for both the mentally ill and handicapped have been covered by the same legislation. The 1960 act was modified by the Mental Health (Scotland) Act, 1983 and the legislation was subsequently consolidated in the Mental Health (Scotland) Act, 1984. The act is concerned with mental disorder as a whole, which is defined as including 'mental illness or mental handicap however caused or manifested'. This section of the chapter deals with the provisions relating to the mentally ill. The 1960 act had the same general purpose as an English act passed in the previous year: to ensure that legal formalities did not stand in the way of the most effective utilisation of recently-developed medical knowledge. It was designed to keep to a minimum the use of compulsory powers for the admission of patients to, and their detention in, psychiatric wards and hospitals. So far as possible, patients should be free to enter and leave such establishments with no more formality than is associated with the use of general medical and surgical facilities; and indeed these conditions now apply to more than 90 per cent of psychiatric patients. There are, however some patients who, for their own health or safety or for the protection of others, need hospital treatment but are unable or unwilling to seek it voluntarily. When in such cases compulsory measures are required, the Scottish act incorporates a legal safeguard for which the corresponding English legislation makes no provision; the approval of a sheriff is normally required to an application for compulsory admission. The application (as in England) must be made by a mental health officer or the patient's nearest relative and supported by recommendations from two doctors, one of whom should generally be the patient's family doctor and the other a psychiatrist. The welfare of psychiatric patients who are unable to look after their own interests is the concern of the Mental Welfare Commission for Scotland. This has independent powers to discharge any psychiatric patient if it considers that detention is no longer necessary, to advise and assist any patient whether voluntary or compulsory, and to investigate complaints of improper detention, ill-treatment or inadequate care.

But, whereas in England and Wales the Mental Health Act, 1959 was followed by a ministerial decision to reduce drastically the scale of in-patient provision with the closure of many mental hospitals and a major shift of emphasis to psychiatric units in general hospitals, the official view taken in Scotland was much more cautious and non-committal. In the event, the run-down of in-patient provision in England has proved to be a good deal less fast than was originally forecast, and the build-up of community services slow and patchy. In Scotland, however, the move from a hospital-oriented to a community-oriented system of care has been even slower.

While the 1983 amending legislation was intended to reinforce the trend towards care in the community, admission to hospital is sometimes necessary and occasionally this cannot be achieved voluntarily with the patient's consent. In these latter cases the act tightened up the procedures which have to be followed. Regional social work departments are now required to appoint mental health officers, who are social workers with additional special training. Where compulsory admission is being considered an officer has a duty 'to interview the patient and satisfy himself that detention in hospital is in all the circumstances the most appropriate way of providing the care and medical treatment the patient needs'.[3] The legislation also strengthened the membership and powers of the Mental Welfare Commission for Scotland, in large measure as a response to a growing concern about its weakness in the face of threats to the civil liberties of compulsorily detained patients. This concern had been reflected in decisions of the European Court of Human Rights. The membership of the commission was increased from seven to ten, of whom at least three must be women, and it was required to interview long-term detained patients at least once every two years and to publish an annual report. In addition, the act made more rigorous the conditions relating to the registration and control of private hospitals for the mentally ill.

TRENDS IN THE USE OF PSYCHIATRIC SERVICES

Between 1960 and 1985 the number of consultant posts in psychiatry in Scotland increased from fewer than 100 to over 200 while the total nursing staff rose from approximately 7,000 to 11,000. The number of patients admitted each year either to a mental hospital or to a psychiatric unit attached to a general hospital rose steadily until the early 1970s; since then it has remained fairly constant at around 27,000, corresponding to a frequency of about five per 1,000 of the Scottish population. The majority of these are patients who have been admitted on a previous occasion. The resident population has fallen from around 19,000 in the late 1960s and early 1970s to some 14,000 in 1985,[4] equivalent to about one in every 330 of the population. This may be compared with the position in England and Wales where the corresponding proportion is half that in Scotland.[5] Clearly, the degree of dependence on hospital in-patient provision has remained markedly higher north than south of the border.

There has also been a considerable expansion of psychiatric out-patient provisions in hospital clinics. Between 1965 and 1985 the number of new out-patients went up from about 18,700 to 34,000: an increase of 80 per cent. This was very much greater than the overall growth of 45 per cent in out-patients went up from about 18,700 to 34,000, an increase of 80 per cent. with the data on hospital admissions and discharges, it is evident that the out-patient services have been bringing psychiatric assessment and treatment to a wider range of the emotionally disturbed rather than providing an alternative service for those who would otherwise have been admitted to a psychiatric ward.

These figures remind us that hospital treatment statistics cannot provide an accurate estimate of the frequency of psychiatric illness in the community. We know from general population surveys that although there are some persons who seek no professional help with the treatment of symptoms as serious as those with which psychiatrists are regularly confronted, the majority do in fact consult their general practitioners. In most instances the latter are the only treatment agency involved. The extensive availability of psychotropic drugs, which can in many cases alleviate the symptoms of mental illness, has made this possible. Nevertheless, it may be argued that a higher proportion of patients might benefit from more specialised investigation, and the proportion actually receiving it, although still very much a minority, seems in fact to have been on the increase.

Future Trends

However desirable the objectives of the 1983 legislative changes, in reducing the risk of avoidable compulsion and in giving better protection to patients' civil liberties, in themselves they will do little or nothing to achieve a better balance of hospital and community services for the mentally ill or to improve the quantity and quality of supportive services available to them and their families. The problems of comprehensive care arise from the fact that although modern drug treatment can indeed bring about impressive improvements in the condition of a high proportion of patients in a short space of time, the underlying condition is frequently not eradicated but remains and is liable to cause further breakdown, perhaps within months of discharge from hospital. We have noted already the high proportion of re-admissions to hospital among psychiatric patients. There is a good deal of research evidence to show that social and personal crises can in many cases serve both to precipitate and to reactivate psychiatric disturbance; at the same time, both vulnerability to stress and the capacity to resist it are shaped in part by personal relationships and earlier life experience.[6] In short, it can be argued that an excessive concentration on a view of mental illness that is narrowly conceived in conventional medical terms has led to an under-estimate of the part played by social and psychological factors, and that this in its turn has been responsible for a badly balanced approach to the planning of services for treatment and prevention.

This imbalance in our understanding and interpretation of psychiatric disturbance, which has only recently begun to be corrected, is matched by a disproportion in the distribution of resources between hospital-based and community-based services. This has not developed as a result of a calculated if erroneous national plan. In fact, there is not and never has been a national policy for the care of the mentally ill. Hospital and personal social services for the mentally ill have each been left to develop within the respective frameworks of the NHS and the local authority system, with no planned integration between them nationally, regionally or (with some isolated exceptions) locally. Within these services, separately administered and separately financed, the extent and standard of provision for the mentally ill and their families have depended on the relative degrees of priority they have been able to achieve in the struggle for resources. In common with other branches of medicine dealing with long-term and recurrent conditions, psychiatry could not easily compete with the claims of high cost, high technology medicine during the years of expanding NHS resources. This is not to say that the available provisions were reduced – as we have seen both medical and nursing staffs expanded during the 1960s and 1970s – only that their rate of growth was relatively modest. While many advances could undoubtedly have been achieved had there been further shifts in resource allocation in favour of psychiatric hospitals, at least an established service of long standing has been maintained and often enhanced.

The problem as far as local authority services are concerned has been that, unlike the NHS, there was no established base on which to build. In the rapid expansion of local authority social work services after the Social Work (Scotland) Act, 1968 (see chapter 6), priority was given to statutory responsibilities, to the management of social crises, and to work in the child care field. There was virtually no tradition of community provision for the mentally ill, and it would have required extraordinary dedication and persistence for staff and finance to be channelled to meet the needs of this client group. Given the established view of mental illness as essentially a medical problem, it was easy for those with competing priorities to argue that local government could not afford to meet what were seen as NHS responsibilities. It is not altogether surprising therefore that in the 1980s there were in the whole of Scotland fewer than 200 persons living in hostels or group homes provided by local authorities, with another 40 in similar accomodation run by voluntary bodies. Only one centre for the mentally ill was open in 1985 with a mere 35 places.[7]

The idea that people with mental illnesses (or handicaps) should, as far as possible, be cared for in the community is not new. It was the intention at the time of the 1960 act that resources should be made available for the development of community services to enable the large number of such individuals who do not require long-term hospitalisation to be cared for at home. There has in fact been a steady decrease in the hospital population but without a commensurate development in community services to support patients discharged from hospital. Although there has been greater progress south of the border, the Audit Commission's report in 1986, *Making a Reality of Community Care*[8] was severely critical of the slow and uneven development of such services, not only for the mentally ill and mentally handicapped but also for the elderly and physically disabled. While additional resources would undoubtedly help, the Audit Commission was of the opinion that the expenditure already devoted by the NHS, by the local authority personal social services and by the DHSS to social security benefits taken together would, if effectively co-ordinated and managed, be sufficient to provide adequate community services. The report of a similar review, under the chairmanship of Sir Roy Griffiths, of community care in Scotland is not available at time of writing.

Meanwhile, although the resident population of Scottish mental hospitals is larger than it needs to be, its rapid reduction would not be acceptable given the present inadequate state of community care services. They are so under-developed that it would be difficult to justify either a large-scale emphasis on rehabilitation and discharge programmes for long-stay patients or a significant move to direct new cases away from in-patient care. There is a striking lack of integrated thinking, directed at the design of comprehensive caring services, as well as the more obvious lack of integrated action to provide such services. The small amount of finance now specifically available to support social work developments that would reduce the burden on health services has so far made little impact.

The designation and training of mental health officers should however, lead to the creation of a body of community-based social workers with a major interest in the field. This in turn may perhaps lead to some pressure within local authorities to respond more effectively – in some areas to respond at all – to the needs of this neglected client group. Welcome though such a trend would be, it would need powerful support and reinforcement, not least from central government, if Scottish services for the mentally ill are to move decisively forward.

SERVICES FOR THE MENTALLY HANDICAPPED

There are some parallels between the way in which ideas about the care and management of mentally handicapped people have evolved and the development of services for the mentally ill. Central to professional thinking about both these client groups has been a shift away from the traditional emphasis on large custodial institutions. There are, however, important differences between mental illness and mental handicap, in spite of the fact that they are covered by the same legislation as far as compulsory hospital admission is concerned.

When we speak of mental handicap we are concerned first and foremost with intellectual retardation. Mental deficiency, mental defect and mental subnormality are all terms that have been used in the past (in legislation as well as in professional writing) to refer to the same broad range of problems. The 1984 act now refers to mental impairment which is defined as 'a state of arrested or incomplete development of mind which includes ... impairment of intelligence and social functioning'. The causes of mental handicap are still imperfectly understood; or, to be more precise, a wide variety of conditions may give rise to or be associated with mental handicap. Research has thrown light on the causes of some of these conditions, but by no means all. In general, we are dealing with conditions that are present from birth, whether resulting from damage to the foetus, from birth injury, from the operation of rare recessive genes or from the interaction of genetic processes that give rise to the 'tail-end' of the normal distribution of intelligence. In exceptional cases infection or brain injury after birth may also be responsible for mental handicap. Whatever the causal background, however, the problem is not one of illness which can be relieved or cured by treatment in the medical sense.[9] The practical question is how best to maximise whatever potential the mentally handicapped person may have and to ensure that he or she is enabled to live the fullest and most satisfying life possible.

This has not always been the objective of social policy. Special institutions for mental defectives, as they were then known, were initially an outgrowth of the poor law. The Mental Deficiency Act, 1913, which extended the scope of compulsory certification, was intended in part to protect society from the mental defective, who was assumed to contribute disproportionately to the sum total of pauperism, vice and crime, and in part to protect the defective from ill-treatment and exploitation at the hands of the unscrupulous. By extending provision for certification to the large class of high grade defectives, it encouraged the growth of large and overcrowded asylums. By setting up social inefficiency as the criterion by which mental defectives became 'subject to be dealt with', the act gave almost unlimited currency to an essentially custodial conception of care. It is only in the past three decades that we have seen the emergence of a decisive shift away from traditional approaches to the mentally handicapped. This change to some extent reflects more tolerant and understanding public attitudes, but it has been powerfully reinforced by the findings of research, undertaken by educational and clinical psychologists, which has shown how changes in the pattern of care and training can produce significant improvements in competence. It will be some time, however, before service provision is sufficiently reoriented to take full account of modern knowledge.

Research and its Implications

What we have learned from research is that mentally handicapped children tend to make better progress in both intellectual and social development if they are brought up by their parents rather than in institutions, and that if residential care is unavoidable the emphasis should be on small, family-like homes rather than institutions on the traditional scale. There is evidence that small residential establishments can be planned to meet the needs of identifiable communities, and can be more readily integrated into them than those which draw their inmates from a large area and are geographically remote.[10]

Few would go so far as to argue for the abolition of all residential care for the mentally handicapped. The most severe cases generally have serious physical disabilities and need constant attention; the resulting burden is one that many parents feel they are unable to accept, and there are no compelling reasons why their wishes should not be respected. Even in the case of those who are 'seriously' rather than 'profoundly' handicapped – for example most children suffering from Down's syndrome – parental attitudes may include large elements of shame, guilt and anxiety; while it is right that such parents should receive careful advice and sensitive help in reaching a decision, their right to opt for residential care should not be denied. What is important is that this choice should offer the prospect not merely of good physical care – though even that has been shown to be lacking in some institutions (including a number in Scotland) where major scandals have erupted – but also of education and training. One very significant development in recent years has been a greatly increased interest in more effective methods of training mentally handicapped children. Among the well-founded practical approaches that have emerged are procedures by which professionals train parents, who in turn can then train their own children.[11]

Some handicapped children may of course be capable of attending school, and the majority of the least severely handicapped go to ordinary schools. In the case of children with 'pronounced, specific or complex' educational needs (which may be the result of physical or mental disabilities) it is the duty of the local education authority to assess their educational needs and to record its decisions as to how they should be met. Parents have the right to be involved in such assessments and to appeal against any plans for their children's education with which they are in disagreement. In principle, whenever possible, even children with quite substantial mental handicaps should be integrated into ordinary schools. Some, however, are sent to special schools run either by the local authority or by a voluntary organisation. The numbers attending special schools have been declining steadily with the move towards integrated education. For some very severely handicapped children part-time tuition by a visiting teacher is provided in their own homes or in hospital.

Although a great deal of the discussion and research into mental handicap has focused on problems of childhood, it is vital not to lose sight of the dramatic changes that have taken place in the life expectancy of the mentally handicapped. Because modern medicine can cope with the infectious and other diseases which used to kill large numbers of mentally handicapped children, the majority now survive to middle age and beyond. Expectations about the level of functioning of the mentally handicapped adult have also changed, and there is a good deal of experience to show that under suitable conditions a high proportion can be trained to carry out a variety of industrial tasks. Some of the less severely handicapped are helped by the employment services to find training and then sheltered employment in Remploy factories or in workshops run by local authorities or voluntary organisations. Those with more severe handicaps may be given places in adult training centres which provide occupational and recreational facilities as well as valuable social contacts. However, in a period of high unemployment marginal groups such as the mentally handicapped and the mentally ill are likely to be doubly disadvantaged in finding employment. But even under better economic circumstances one would still expect to find a continuing need for some kind of support in a high proportion of cases; and very frequently the death or increasing infirmity of an elderly parent precipitates a crisis in the life of a mentally handicapped person. Admission to institutional care for the first time in middle age is common, and in the opinion of many observers should be unnecessary. Hostels offering a high degree of independence and some forms of group tenancy arranged by housing associations have attractive posibilities as community-based alternatives.

Recent Trends in Scotland

If the type and quality of service provision in Britain have so far fallen short of the standards that modern knowledge has shown to be appropriate to the needs of the mentally handicapped and their families, the discrepancy in Scotland between the actual and the ideal has been and remains particularly striking. The Scottish Society for the Mentally Handicapped, like its English equivalent, has performed a valuable task in bringing together the families of the mentally handicapped to exert pressure for reform on central and local government, and has also moved into direct service provision. Excellent work is also done by smaller, specialised bodies such as the Down's Children Association, which bring parents together for mutual aid and support, and help to diffuse relevant knowledge. In spite of these forces for change, however, the general pattern of services has been slow to alter. Dependence on hospital provision remains high, and the build-up of community services has been slow. Although both the staffing position and the characteristic pattern of usage of the hospitals have improved, many of them are both larger in scale and more remote from the populations they serve than is desirable.

Since the early 1970s, hospital nursing staffs, including trained as well as student and auxiliary nurses, have increased by about 50 per cent. There has been no growth in the number of medical consultants, but more clinical psychologists are now involved in this area of hospital work. Over the past two decades the number of hospital in-patients has fallen from about 7,400 to 6,700, in spite of an admission rate which has risen from about 1,000 to 2,000 per year.[12] This apparent contradiction points, of course, to a reduced average length of stay. The number of discharges has doubled in a decade, and the average length of time spent in hospital by those discharged has been halved. The increased admission rate conceals two opposite trends: the number of first admissions has tended to fall while the number of re-admissions has risen steeply. More patients than in the past, it would seem, now alternate between hospital care and life in the community; what quality of life they and their families experience and what factors are associated with re-admissions are questions that research has not so far addressed.

For some of these hospital patients foster care under the guardianship of a social work department might be a practical alternative if the immediate family cannot cope and completely independent living in the community is beyond their capacity. An application can be made by the mental health officer to the sheriff court for a guardianship order, provided he or she considers that it is in the interest of the patient's welfare. If the application is granted the officer and the social work department have the responsibility of appointing a guardian, who may be a family member, social worker or appropriate volunteer, and of carrying out any requirements of the order as to place of residence, education, training, occupation and attendance for medical treatment. Together with the required three-monthly visits to the person concerned, this obviously puts very heavy responsibilities on the staff of social work departments and on their facilities such as hostels and adult training centres. It is therefore not surprising that, in spite of the renewed interest in guardianship generated by the 1983 legislation, the numbers of persons, including a few mentally ill patients, for whom orders have been sought is small (72 at end 1985) and is in decline.

A major problem is the failure of the local authority sector to allocate adequate resources to work with the mentally handicapped or to plan provisions in partnership with the NHS. The failure has, however, been less extreme than in the case of mental illness; where mental handicap is concerned there is a longer tradition of involvement and perhaps also a sense that the dimensions of the problem are more clearly understood. There was a genuine spurt in developments in the early 1970s, but with a slow-down since about 1976 under the impact of financial restraints. An official committee, reporting in 1979 on services for the mentally handicapped in Scotland, referred to a shortfall of about 2,000 places in local authority or voluntary residential homes and of nearly 3,000 places in adult training centres. The same report identified needs, as yet very imperfectly met, for social work assistance for families, in terms of practical help, emotional support and short-term respite care. The report's conclusion, that 'the steps so far taken by all statutory agencies in Scotland to achieve this desirable end (that is an increasing emphasis on care in the community) have been inadequate and almost without exception have had little effect on the transfer of patients from hospital to community care'[13] cannot easily be brushed aside. Economic constraints have been and remain a major obstacle. While these must be overcome before there can be significant progress, it will be at least equally important to create the means by which disparate services can rise above the barriers which at present inhibit joint planning, joint financing and joint implementation of provisions. These barriers are in part administrative and institutional but are also embedded in attitudes and values.

ALCOHOL-RELATED PROBLEMS

We turn now to problems associated with the use, or abuse, of alcohol. In many respects their treatment raises similar issues to mental illness, and each year some 4,000 people are admitted to psychiatric hospitals or psychiatric units in general hospitals in Scotland for the treatment of alcoholism, amounting to about one-seventh of all admissions.[14] These admissions represent of course only a fraction of all the people whose lives are adversely affected by alcohol abuse, but it is virtually impossible to say what is the total size of the group. 'Alcoholism', 'alcohol-related problems' and 'problem drinking' are all imprecise terms. They would not provide a basis for accurate measurement even if we were in a position to survey complete populations and could rely upon receiving reliable information in answer to the questions. A certain amount is in fact known about levels of expenditure on alcohol. These have been rising many times faster than expenditure on food or other items of consumption and expenditure on wine and spirits faster than on beer. At the same time the price of alcohol has been falling in relation to both incomes and the prices of other goods, which may account for much of the increased consumption. The data are not, however, precise, because it is clear that there is a significant tendency, for example in the Family Expenditure Survey, for spending on alcohol (and on tobacco) to be under-estimated. But even more important is the fact that, although we have reasonable working assumptions about what constitutes a 'safe' level of drinking, it would not take us very far to define as an alcoholic everyone who exceeded that level.

Although the vast majority of people in our society consume alcoholic drinks from time to time, only a small proportion develop alcohol dependency. By alcohol dependency we mean a state in which there is a sense of compulsion to drink; a feeling that alcohol is a necessity for which the person craves. The withdrawal of alcohol leads to painful physical and mental symptoms, which can be dissipated only by a return to alcohol, and – perhaps for a considerable period of time though not indefinitely – the body becomes able to tolerate increasing levels of alcohol without obvious social or physical breakdown. Commonly the development of alcohol dependency is spread over a number of years. It is principally with the problems of those with alcohol dependency that the NHS and personal social services have become increasingly concerned since the 1960s. Welcome though this attention is, we should remember that the period which leads up to a full-scale alcohol dependency, during which drinking becomes increasingly heavy and compulsive, can produce very serious personal and social problems, but also that it offers time for helpful intervention.[15]

The harmful consequences of excessive drinking and alcohol dependency are hard to estimate with any degree of precision, for they are wide-ranging in nature and their human costs are borne not only by the drinkers themselves but also by members of their immediate families and by the wider society. Perhaps most obvious and easily identified are the consequences in terms of ill-health and reduced life expectancy. Follow-up studies of patients admitted to psychiatric wards with a diagnosis of alcoholism indicate high comparative mortality rates, not only for cirrhosis of the liver, which is universally agreed to be alcohol-related, but also for violence, suicide, accidents and cancers. Peptic ulcer is disproportionately common among heavy drinkers, and some forms of damage to the brain and nervous system are particularly associated with prolonged excessive alcohol consumption.

This section of the chapter began with a reference to those alcoholics who are admitted to psychiatric hospitals or psychiatric units in general hospitals. Although severe mental disturbance is far from rare, many more excessive drinkers experience deterioration of personality which, although it may not receive psychiatric help, is nevertheless of a degree sufficient to cause profound disturbance in their family, employment and wider social relationships. How seriously and how rapidly the personal and social life of the excessive drinker disintegrates depends upon the interaction of many factors in his or her environment. Without attempting to quantify all such effects, it can be said that alcohol dependency contributes massively to marital tension, unhappiness and breakdown; to violence towards women and children; to extreme pressure on family budgets and a consequent build-up of unmanageable debts; and to incompetence at work, absence from work and loss of employment. Alcohol is a contributory factor in a very large proportion of social problems, not least in the industrial areas of Scotland. In a class of its own is the effect of excessive consumption of alcohol on road traffic accidents; various studies suggest that between one-third and one-half of serious accidents are associated with high levels of blood alcohol, and 20 per cent of all road deaths are caused by drunken drivers.[16]

Causation and Treatment

Because of the difficulty of measuring accurately the frequency of heavy drinking or of alcohol dependency, international comparisons are hazardous. All the indicators available, however, suggest that alcohol-related problems are significantly more common in Scotland than in England. If we consider such varied measures as the number of deaths from cirrhosis of the liver, the number of hospital admissions associated with alcoholism and the number of convictions for drunkenness, we are likely to conclude that Scotland is about twice as heavily afflicted with alcohol dependency; and this would suggest that Scotland should be included among the more seriously affected European countries. Why this should be the case is not immediately obvious; the pattern of causes underlying alcoholic excess is complex, and does not lead to a simple generalisation which neatly explains national differences.

In respect of all forms of behaviour that are damaging to the individual and are seen as harmful to society, there is a widespread public preference for straightforward, preferably single-factor, explanations. Alcoholism is no exception, and tends to be 'explained' in terms of moral weakness or personality disturbance or social pressures, according to the prejudices of the person who is giving expression to his opinions. In fact, a dispassionate examination of the large body of research evidence indicates that genetic factors, personality make-up and socio-cultural influences may all be implicated, and that the relative contribution of each of these can vary. As far as present-day Scotland is concerned, it is by no means a circular explanation to say that the prevalence of heavy drinking at least in part reflects a tradition of heavy drinking, even though it leaves open the question of how the tradition became established. Patterns of drinking tend to be self-perpetuating over the generations. The young person growing up is presented, not with a 'tradition' in some abstract sense, but with a set of assumptions woven into the everyday behaviour of adult relatives and neighbours, including assumptions about the appropriateness and social acceptability of certain styles and levels of alcohol consumption. Research suggests that in many sub-cultures, including perhaps those that prevail in several sectors of Scottish society, heavy drinking is a means by which an image of hard masculinity is created and presented and, at a deeper level, a way in which the need for personal power can be satisfied in fantasy terms.[17]

This does not explain, however, the growth in female drinking which in Scotland, as in England and Wales, is a comparatively new and disturbing aspect of the alcohol problem. More tolerant attitudes to women's drinking, in some cases income of their own from employment, and easier access to alcohol through supermarkets may account at least in part for the phenomenon. It is perhaps also significant that in some cases the problem arises when children have left home and the mother has more time on her hands and a less well-defined role. Female alcoholics, whose drinking is often secretive, are more difficult to treat and their problems may have more traumatic effects on the family. Of even greater concern perhaps is the rapid increase in teenage and even child drinking which, as well as long-term effects on the number of heavy drinkers, contributes in the shorter-term to football hooliganism, vandalism, unwanted pregnancies and road accidents.

For a variety of reasons, a view of the person with severe drinking problems as someone in need of help and treatment rather than moral condemnation and exhortation has been slow to develop. It is of course arguable that there was little to be gained from promoting such a view until such time as useful, practical help could in fact be made available on acceptable terms to those who needed it. However, during the past two decades there has been an increasingly open recognition of the scale and severity of alcohol-related problems, and a marked increase in provision by the health services, social work departments and the voluntary sector, as well as a significant investment in health education directed at the prevention and early recognition of alcohol-related problems.

Although it has in recent years become unfashionable to speak of alcoholism as a 'disease' and of people with alcohol dependency as 'sick', it remains the case that a large part of the responsibility for meeting the needs of those alcoholics who seek help rests with the health services. We do not know with any certainty how far general practioners are involved in this work, but it seems unlikely that their contribution (other than as referral agents) is a substantial one. Most medical or medically-related treatment of alcoholics is the responsibility of psychiatrists. In addition to the in-patient admissions referred to earlier, psychiatrists run a number of out-patient clinics, including some that are not geographically linked with a hospital. While a minority of in-patients suffer from severe psychiatric disorders associated with brain damage caused by prolonged excessive drinking and may require traditional long-term hospital care, most of them and virtually all out-patients are less permanently damaged; their need is to gain control of their drinking habits and often to obtain help with a variety of associated personal problems. The treatments available are varied, and include group therapy and the use of drugs to aid withdrawal from alcohol. Clinical psychologists as well as psychiatrists are on the staff of most alcohol treatment units and have developed the use of behaviour modification techniques by which the patient learns new ways of dealing with his or her inner needs and tensions.[18]

There has been a marked growth of interest in recent years in 'detoxification' – a process involving a rapid, enforced withdrawal from alcohol with the use of drugs to counter the painful and dangerous symptoms associated with such withdrawal. These procedures require carefully controlled conditions and the use of well-trained nursing staff. So far, detoxification has tended to be associated with the management of deteriorated, often homeless alcoholics, who might otherwise find themselves occupying police and prison cells. Section 5 of the Criminal Procedure (Scotland) Act, 1980 empowers a police officer who arrests an offender and has reason to believe that he (or she) is drunk to take him to a 'designated place' for detoxification instead of making an arrest. The first such centre in Scotland has been established in Aberdeen.

Voluntary bodies also play an important part in helping those with drinking problems. Indeed, it could be said that Alcoholics Anonymous (AA) has had a unique pioneering role in offering the alcoholic access to help in a non-medical setting, as well as raising general public awareness of the significance of drinking problems and of the fact that these can often be treated. The activities of AA, which emphasise group support, have steadily expanded and it is now concerned also with the families of alcoholics. Another major development on the voluntary front has been the growth of local councils on alcoholism. In the early 1980s there were some 24 of these bodies in Scotland, offering both individual and group counselling to clients with alcohol-related problems of varying degrees of severity. More than 300 counsellors provided this service and worked with about 4,000 new clients each year. The counsellors, who are trained under a national scheme organised by the Scottish Council on Alcoholism, come from a wide variety of backgrounds including some who have themselves in the past been dependent on alcohol.[19]

Although alcohol enters directly or indirectly into a high proportion of all the problems dealt with by social workers, the latter have on the whole been reluctant to become involved in this difficult and sensitive area. Recently some social work departments have identified alcoholics as a group with which they should be actively involved.[20] Strathclyde region is running a number of advice and resettlement centres for alcoholics and is concerned to improve the competence of social workers in this aspect of practice.

The proliferation of services raises questions about a rational division of responsibility. Which clients find their way to which facilities seems to be very much a matter of chance. To make best use of the resources available, we need to have a clearer understanding of the ways in which people with alcohol dependency of varying degrees, and with associated personal problems of varying types and severity, are brought into contact with different treatment agencies. We also need to have firmer knowledge of the extent to which alternative approaches to treatment are more or less effective with different types of clients. Reported 'success' rates vary between 20 per cent and 60 per cent, but it is by no means certain that in comparing outcomes in different agencies we are really comparing like with like. That services should have developed in an unco-ordinated fashion is vastly preferable to their not developing at all. The next step forward, however, seems to call for a greater shared awareness of what each can accomplish most effectively, with an associated strengthening of mutual referral systems based on agreed criteria.

CONCLUSIONS

The care of the mentally disordered raises sensitive questions of civil liberties, in that occasionally measures of control may be needed both to ensure the safety of the individual against harm from himself or exploitation by others and to protect society against deviant behaviour. The legislation of the nineteenth and early twentieth centuries was largely concerned with issues of this kind and the answer was too often long-term institutionalisation. Increasing knowledge about the causes and treatment of mental illness and handicap have laid the foundations for new approaches which are reflected in the legislation of the last 30 years. The emphasis has shifted from institutionalisation and compulsory detention of the mentally disordered to their care in the community.

Hospital treatment, as far as possible on a voluntary basis, is seen as a last resort for those unable to cope with the strains and stresses of life in the wider society. Unfortunately, the ideal and actuality are far apart, more so in Scotland than south of the border. As a result an unnecessarily large number of people are occupying expensive hospital beds. There is, however, no general shortage of hospital facilities for the mentally ill and handicapped, although the quality of care may on occasion leave something to be desired, and they are financed by the exchequer out of national tax revenues. The hostels, day-care centres, and occupational and recreational facilities which are often necessary to make life in the community possible for the mentally disordered, on the other hand, have to be provided by local authorities or voluntary organisations with local authority support. Funds must come from tightly-stretched local resources. The mentally ill and mentally handicapped, and still more alcoholics, do not carry a great deal of political weight and are unlikely to enjoy a high priority for the allocation of extra resources. New attitudes on the part of society as a whole towards those who do not always conform to 'normal' patterns of behaviour are needed, as well as for more adequate facilities to be financed. They must also be accepted as full members of society and as neighbours if community care is to have the possibility of fulfilling its potential role in enhancing their quality of life.

References

1. K. Jones, *Mental Health and Social Policy 1845-1959*, Routledge and Kegan Paul, 1960.
2. G.F. Rehin and F.M. Martin, *Patterns of Performance in Community Care*, Oxford University Press, 1968.
3. Scottish Home and Health Deparment and Social Work Services Group, *Review of the Mental Health (Scotland) Act, 1960*, SHHD and SWSG, 1982.
4. Scottish Health Service Common Services Agency, *Scottish Health Statistics 1985*, HMSO, 1986.
5. Department of Health and Social Security, *Health and Personal Social Services Statistics for England, 1987 Edition*, HMSO, 1987.
6. G. Brown and T. Harris, *Social Origins of Depression*, Tavistock Publications, 1978; and G. Brown, J.L.T. Birley and J.K. Wing, 'Influence of Family Life on the Course of Schizophrenic Disorders', *British Journal of Psychiatry*, No. 121, 1972.
7. Social Work Services Group, *Statistical Bulletin*: *Residential Accommodation 1985* and *Home Care Services, Day Care Establishments and Day Services 1985*, Scottish Office, 1986.
8. Audit Commission, *Making a Reality of Community Care*, HMSO, 1986.
9. A.M. Clarke and A.D.B. Clarke (eds.), *Mental Deficiency: the Changing Outlook*, Methuen, (3rd edition) 1974.
10. J.K. Wing and R. Olsen (eds.), *Community Care for the Mentally Disabled*, Oxford University Press, 1979.
11. Wing and Olsen, *Community Care for the Mentally Disabled.*
12. *Scottish Health Statistics 1985.*
13. Scottish Home and Health Department and Scottish Education Department, *A Better Life for the Mentally Handicapped in Scotland*, HMSO, 1979.
14. *Scottish Health Statistics 1985.*
15. Royal College of Psychiatrists, *Alcohol and Alcoholism,* Tavistock Publications, 1979.
16. S. Hollerman and A. Burdrace, *The Costs of Alcohol Misuse*, Department of Health and Social Security, 1981.
17. D.C. McClelland, W.N. Davis, R. Kalin and E. Warner, *The Drinking Man*, Free Press, 1972.
18. Royal College of Psychiatrists, *Alcohol and Alcoholism.*
19. R.I.F. Brown and P.J. O'Donnell, *Barefoot Counsellors on Alcoholism: The Scottish Experiment*, unpublished paper presented at 26th International Institute on Prevention and Treatment of Alcoholism, 1980.
20. Strathclyde Social Work Committee, *Addiction: Collusion or Cover Up?* (Report of an Officer/Member Group), Strathclyde Regional Council, 1978.

FURTHER READING

A. Clare, *Psychiatry in Dissent*, Tavistock Publications, (2nd edition) 1980.

An admirable discussion of present-day psychiatry and its problems which is both scholarly and readable.

D. Goldberg and P. Huxley, *Mental Illness in the Community*, Tavistock Publications, 1980.

An account of the findings of research into the processes that bring people into contact with psychiatric services.

L. Hunt, *Alcohol Related Problems*, Heinemann, 1982.

A clearly presented review of alcohol problems and their management which is broadly based but with a fairly strong social work orientation.

F.M. Martin, *Between the Acts: Community Mental Health Services 1959-1983*, The Nuffield Provincial Hospital Trust, 1984.

An examination of factors which are associated with success or failure in the implementation of mental health policies.

J. Wing and R. Olsen (eds.), *Community Care for the Mentally Disabled*, Oxford University Press, 1979.

A series of essays reviewing modern ideas on provisions for those with long-term problems of mental illness and mental handicap.

5
HOUSING

There is debate about whether housing should be included among the social services, and it certainly has important differences from, for example, health care. Housing is far from being free at the point of use and it costs most people a substantial amount in rent or mortgage repayments. Direct public sector provision in the form of council housing caters for only a minority of households, and many houses are bought and sold in the market rather than being allocated administratively on the basis of need. Finally, professionally trained staff have a relatively small role in the housing field. Nevertheless, housing does possess characteristics which justify regarding it as a concern of social policy.

State intervention in housing markets has gone far beyond the provision of council housing. The majority of households, both tenants and owner occupiers, are subsidised by the taxpayer and do not have to meet directly the full cost of their accommodation. The rent acts may limit what a private landlord can charge. The building regulations lay down minimum standards for housebuilding, relating to such aspects as room size and possession of basic amenities. Local authorities can compulsorily improve or demolish unsatisfactory dwellings. Thus, although the state is not the dominant provider of housing, it extensively regulates and subsidises its provision. Furthermore, without claiming that anything which is essential for basic human well-being is necessarily the concern of social policy, the availability of adequate housing is important from the point of view, for example, of good health.

There has been public involvement in housing since the second half of the nineteenth century though for many years the concern did not extend beyond attempting to ensure that minimum standards were achieved. The city of Glasgow, for example, was a pioneer of slum clearance in Britain. In 1917 the Royal Commission on the Housing of the Industrial Population of Scotland reported.[1] The commission had been appointed before the outbreak of the first world war, but new problems arose during the war from the cessation of building and the movement of workers to munitions factories, with consequent increased pressure on housing in areas such as Clydeside. It was shown that working class housing in Scotland was deplorable, that standards were lower than south of the border, and that a substantial building programme was urgently required. Not only were houses often insanitary, badly built and falling into disrepair; many were far too small for the families which lived in them. Overcrowding was widespread and acute: nearly a quarter of the population was living at a density of more than three persons a room and approaching half at a density of more than two persons per room. (Today only a small proportion of the population lives at a density of more than one and a half persons per room.)

The commission believed that it would not be realistic to expect private landlords to build the new houses which were urgently required and recommended that local authorities should be given the responsibility of providing them. Exchequer subsidies would be needed to make up the difference between the costs of building the houses and income from rents. These were first provided in 1919 and over the years council housing has become, especially in Scotland, an important form of provision.

In Scotland there are 56 housing authorities – 53 district councils and three islands councils – which have a wide range of responsibilities. They are responsible for keeping the housing requirements of their areas under review and for ensuring that land is available to private builders. They also have to secure the improvement or demolition of sub-standard housing and to provide improvement grants, as well as themselves building and allocating council houses. This chapter will necessarily often generalise at the level of Scotland as a whole, but each authority has to deal with a unique set of circumstances relating to the condition of its housing stock, shortages or surpluses of accommodation, tenure mix and many other factors.

As well as council housing, public rented housing is also provided by the Scottish Special Housing Association (SSHA), other housing associations and the new towns. The SSHA, unlike housing associations in general which are relatively small-scale organisations financed by the Housing Corporation, is a central government agency. It was set up in 1937 to supplement local authority housebuilding throughout Scotland.[2] SSHA housing is much more like council housing than that provided by other housing associations. In 1986 the SSHA owned about 85,000 houses or some four per cent of the total stock.

There are five new towns in Scotland, each under the control of a development corporation. East Kilbride and Glenrothes were designated in 1947 and 1948 respectively, Cumbernauld in 1956, Livingston in 1962 and Irvine in 1966. The new towns owned some 47,000 houses in 1986 though they of course contain many more which have either been sold to tenants or built by private developers.

Housing policies in Scotland generally follow those south of the border at least in broad terms because they reflect the views and priorities of the government of the day. Nevertheless, there are some significant differences, especially relating to the public rented sector (which is relatively much larger than in England and Wales). These differences reflect the separate Scottish legal system and distinctive building methods (for example flats are much more common in Scotland). The Scottish Development Department (SDD) is responsible for housing in Scotland rather than the Department of the Environment, and to some extent it has followed its own policies. Nevertheless, as was pointed out in chapter 1, the extent of the Scottish Office's freedom of manoeuvre is severely limited, especially where issues of finance or political commitment are involved. Thus, for example, council tenants' right to buy and the policy of raising council rents in recent years have applied throughout Britain. There is even more uniformity of policy in the case of owner occupation where, for instance, there are few separate Scottish building societies and income tax relief on mortgage interest is dealt with by the Inland Revenue.

A final point which should be made by way of introduction is that, for the sake of simplicity and following ordinary usage, all types of dwellings will be referred to as houses, except where it is necessary to distinguish flats.

THE SCOTTISH HOUSING STOCK[3]

The physical adequacy of the housing stock has improved enormously over the last 70 years, both in terms of numbers of dwellings and their quality. The problems of severe general shortages and overcrowding, and of vast numbers of houses lacking basic amenities such as a bathroom, have been overcome, though this does not mean that other problems do not exist today. Nevertheless, problems such as homelessness and the shortcomings of some council estates, serious as they are for the people affected by them, are suffered by relatively small numbers. Whereas 20 or 30 years ago a substantial part of the population regarded themselves as inadequately housed, this is no longer the case.

The Size of the Housing Stock

Some data on the size of the population, number of households, their average size and the number of dwellings are given in Table 5.1. It can be seen that while there has only been a small increase in the size of the population

TABLE 5.1:

Population, Households and Dwellings in Scotland, 1921-86

	Population (000s)	Average Household size	Households (000s)	Dwellings (000s)	Dwellings: surplus (deficit)[1] (000s)
1921	4,883	4.4	1,099	1,058	(41)
1951	5,096	3.5	1,436	1,375	(61)
1961	5,179	3.3	1,570	1,627	57
1971	5,229	3.1	1,686	1,809	123
1981	5,180	2.8	1,854	1,987	133
1986	5,121	2.7	1,931	2,057	126

Note: 1. Crude surplus or deficit of dwellings compared with number of separate households.

Sources: *Scottish Housing: A Consultative Document*, Cmnd.6852; and Scottish Development Department, *Scottish Housing Statistics*.

TABLE 5.2:
Housing Completions in Scotland 1971-87

	Housing associations (except SSHA)	%	Other public sector[1]	%	Private sector[2]	%	Total
1971	244	(1)	28,925	(71)	11,614	(28)	40,783
1972	332	(1)	19,825	(62)	11,835	(37)	31,992
1973	413	(1)	17,405	(58)	12,215	(41)	30,033
1974	766	(3)	16,331	(58)	11,239	(40)	28,336
1975	1,152	(3)	22,800	(66)	10,371	(30)	34,323
1976	544	(1)	22,279	(61)	13,704	(38)	36,527
1977	546	(2)	14,642	(54)	12,152	(44)	27,320
1978	1,127	(4)	10,189	(40)	14,443	(56)	25,759
1979	544	(2)	8,063	(34)	15,175	(64)	23,782
1980	881	(4)	7,488	(36)	12,242	(59)	20,611
1981	1,928	(10)	7,066	(35)	11,021	(55)	20,015
1982	1,167	(7)	3,733	(23)	11,529	(70)	16,429
1983	1,271	(7)	3,492	(20)	13,178	(73)	17,941
1984	2,076	(11)	2,647	(14)	14,118	(75)	18,841
1985	1,099	(6)	2,828	(15)	14,449	(79)	18,376
1986	1,466	(8)	2,301	(12)	14,832	(80)	18,599
1987[3]	1,119	(6)	2,778	(16)	13,913	(78)	17,810

Notes: 1. Local authorities, new towns, SSHA and government departments.
2. Virtually all for owner occupation.
3. Provisional figures.

Source: Scottish Development Department, *Scottish Housing Statistics*; and Scottish Development Department, *Statistical Bulletin*.

since the 1920s, the number of households (defined as persons living alone or groups of people who take their meals together) and dwellings has almost doubled. As a result there is less sharing of houses by more than one household and far less overcrowding. The increase in the number of households within an almost stable population has been caused in particular by the growing number of elderly people and by families having fewer children, and it is reflected in a fall in average household size from over four to under three persons. There has been a crude surplus of dwellings over households in Scotland for about 30 years, though the surplus has been fairly stable for much of this time. But for a number of reasons this apparent surplus should be treated with caution: for example, some houses are always empty at any time because they have recently been completed or the previous occupants have just moved out. Local shortages can occur in areas of increasing population. Furthermore, vacant dwellings are often of relatively poor quality, for instance in unpopular council estates.

Overcrowding, which was once a very serious problem, has been greatly reduced, but with 14 per cent of households living at a density of more than one person per room at the time of the 1981 census, Scotland was still in a worse position than England and Wales with three per cent. As well as a shortage of large houses there are not enough small ones. There has been a rapid increase in one and two person households which now account for over half the total. Many of these households consist of elderly people and, while some are happy to continue to occupy larger accommodation, a substantial number would welcome a move to a more easily managed home. Local authorities have concentrated on building small units for the elderly including sheltered housing since the 1970s, while in recent years there has also been a rapid growth in purpose-built owner-occupied housing for them.

The rate of housing completions in Scotland has fallen to less than 20,000 a year (Table 5.2) and the figures for the crude surplus of dwellings mentioned above suggest that building is scarcely keeping up with demand. It can be seen that there has been a dramatic change in the relative importance of building by the public and private sectors. In 1978, for the first time since the 1920s, council houses did not constitute a majority of the output of new dwellings in Scotland. With the further sharp decline in public sector building, which in part has been a result of government policy, the owner-occupied sector has recently accounted for 75 to 80 per cent of completions. Within the public sector, building by housing associations has grown as that by local authorities has fallen.

The Quality of the Housing Stock

The quality as well as the quantitative adequacy of the Scottish housing stock has greatly improved. About three out of four houses have been built since 1918 and virtually all of these are satisfactory in the sense of possessing basic amenities such as an inside wc and a bathroom (though some are unsatisfactory in other respects, for example because of dampness). It is, however, among the one-in-four houses which were built before the first world war that the problem of lack of basic amenities is concentrated. Nevertheless, most houses of this age have been improved and provided with bathrooms if they did not originally possess them. A system of improvement grants has existed since 1949, and more recently procedures have been developed for the improvement of areas of older housing which are discussed below. Taking the availability of a fixed bath or shower as an example, in 1951 about half Scottish households did not enjoy this amenity, dropping to 13 per cent in 1971 and to less than three per cent in 1981 (which was lower than the figure for England and Wales).

Another, more severe, criterion of unsatisfactory housing is the statutory tolerable standard. Sub-tolerable (or BTS) houses are the worst of the stock and local authorities have a duty to deal with them either by improvement or clearance. The tolerable standard is broadly equivalent to unfitness for human habitation, which is still used in England and Wales, but it is explicitly linked to lack of internal amenities as well as the general condition of the building. Crucially, a house lacking an inside wc or a hot water supply (though not a bath) is BTS. The number of BTS houses has fallen steadily and in 1987 there were officially estimated to be some 55,000 or about three per cent of the stock.

Unlike its counterparts in England and Wales, the Scottish Development Department has not been willing to finance a sample house condition survey so that estimates of BTS houses are obtained from local authorities. When Glasgow district council undertook its own survey in 1985, it classified nearly 15 per cent of the city's stock as BTS, nearly four times as many as the figure previously reported to the SDD. Much of the increase was accounted for by council houses being classified as BTS, chiefly on the grounds of dampness.[4] Without arguing that Glasgow's experience could be generalised, it is plausible to expect that a house condition survey in Scotland might result in a substantially larger number of houses falling below the tolerable standard.

The distribution of BTS houses is both uneven and surprising. The lowest proportions are mainly found in predominantly suburban districts around Glasgow, with relatively modern and high-quality housing stocks: Bearsden and Milngavie, Eastwood, and Cumbernauld and Kilsyth all had less than one per cent in 1987. So did Clydebank, reflecting the extent to which it has been rebuilt since the second world war, and also rural Wigtown. On the other hand, the six areas with over ten per cent of their stock officially falling below the tolerable standard were in the Highlands and Islands: Argyll and Bute, the Orkney Islands and the Western Isles all with 14 per cent, Ross and Cromarty with 13 per cent, Skye and Lochalsh with 12 per cent and the Shetland Islands with 11 per cent. The problem of rural cottages which lack, say, an adequate water supply or sewerage system is very different from that of nineteenth century slum tenements in Glasgow but it is none the less real.

Another characteristic of Scottish housing is the importance of flats which constitute about two-fifths of the stock, twice the proportion south of the border. Flats often provide excellent homes and may be particularly suitable for some types of households, such as the elderly. Nevertheless, there is no doubt that a house with a garden is preferred by many people, while the large number of flats is a reason why Scottish dwellings are on average somewhat smaller than those elsewhere in Britain.

Housing Tenure

The distinction between the different tenures is of great importance in housing policy. They are characterised by varying terms of access and types of accommodation, and they tend to be used by different groups in the population. The main tenure categories are owner occupation, public sector renting and private sector renting. Most public sector renting consists of council houses, with relatively small contributions from the SSHA and new town development corporations. Housing associations other than the SSHA are sometimes included in the public and sometimes in the private rented sector. Table 5.3 shows the breakdown in tenure at the end of 1986, with comparative figures for England and Wales. The largest sector in Scotland is public renting, with just under half all dwellings, which is relatively much larger than south of the border. Owner occupation is less important than south of the border with rather more than two-fifths of the Scottish housing stock

TABLE 5.3:
Housing Tenure, 1986

	Number of dwellings (000s)	Owner occupied %	Public rented[1] %	Housing association rented[2] %	Private rented & other %
Scotland	2,068	43	49	2	6
England and Wales	20,104	66	24	3	8

Notes: 1. Includes dwellings owned by local authorities, new town development corporations and the Scottish Special Housing Association.
2. Excludes the SSHA.

Source: Department of the Environment, Scottish Development Department and Welsh Office, *Housing and Construction Statistics.*

compared with two-thirds in England and Wales. Housing associations and the private rented sector are small tenure categories throughout Britain.

These statistics are, however, only a snapshot relating to a particular time, and the importance of the different tenures is constantly changing. For some 60 years from the end of the first world war there were two important growing tenures – owner occupation and public sector renting (mainly council housing) – with private renting in decline. In 1919 about 90 per cent of the housing stock was privately rented, about ten per cent owner occupied and a negligible proportion rented from local authorities. The public rented sector ceased to grow as a proportion of the Scottish housing stock in 1978 because since then more new houses have been built for owner occupation than for renting. Since 1981 the size of the public sector has also been falling in absolute terms because sales have exceeded building; at the end of 1987 it had been reduced to about 46 per cent of the total. Very few privately rented houses have been built for many years while most existing ones have either been sold to owner occupiers or demolished. It is likely that owner occupation will continue to grow at the expense of public sector renting. Housing association renting is also likely to grow but can be expected to remain a relatively small tenure.

The relative size of the public rented and owner occupied sectors varies widely between areas in Scotland. At one extreme, Clydebank, Monklands and Motherwell had over three-quarters of their housing stock in the public sector in 1987, while Bearsden and Milngavie, and Eastwood had only 13 and ten per cent respectively.

There are major differences in the quality of housing both within and between the different sectors. Some council housing has serious problems such as dampness and poor environment although virtually all of it possesses basic amenities. The owner-occupied sector is generally the highest quality but it also includes older dwellings of poor standard. The small private rented sector is a mixture of old houses, often of a low standard, which date from when it was the dominant tenure and a wide variety of flats and bedsitter accommodation.

In terms of the income of households and their socio-economic status there are very important differences between who lives in the various tenures. The private rented sector once accommodated nearly the whole population, but it is now left with those lower income and often older households which have not moved on to other tenures, together with groups such as students that use it as a short-term solution to their housing needs. When owner occupation started to expand between the wars it first attracted mainly the middle classes but more recently it has also been gaining skilled and semi-skilled manual workers in large numbers. The role of the public sector is changing as private renting contracts and owner occupation grows, a process which is sometimes referred to as 'residualisation' of council housing. In broad terms, down to the 1960s it was predominantly families with children headed by skilled or semi-skilled manual workers which moved into council housing, but they are now increasingly opting for owner occupation. This is partly because of its financial advantages and partly because of the difficulty of getting access to good quality accommodation in the public sector. Most people setting up home for the first time who can afford to do so become owner occupiers while some middle aged council tenants have taken advantage of the right to buy since 1980. The lower income groups, on the other hand, which once mainly used the private rented sector have become council tenants on a large scale. These include unskilled manual workers, the unemployed and single parents as well as the elderly.

IMPROVEMENT AND REHABILITATION

In the 1950s, when the worst post-war housing shortages had been overcome, attention was increasingly turned to dealing with the poorest quality dwellings. These houses were unfit for human habitation or, to use the present term, sub-tolerable. For 20 years until the mid-1970s the main approach was slum clearance, and at this time large numbers of dwellings were demolished and most of their occupants rehoused in the public sector. Since then, however, relatively few dwellings have been demolished, and clearance has dropped to a very low level of less than 2,000 a year since 1984. One reason for this is the improvement in the quality of the housing stock so that less demolition has been necessary, but it is also a result of the development of area improvement policies which have been seen as preferable to clearance.

Improvement grants were introduced in 1949 but for a quarter of a century they were used on only a small scale. They were mainly taken up by owner occupiers rather than by private landlords, and little impact was made on the worst of the housing stock. A weakness was that no machinery existed to ensure that all sub-standard houses in an area were improved. Until the end of the 1960s most grants were used to install basic amenities, such as an inside wc or bath, in individual houses. Grants have normally met half the cost of improvement work up to a maximum approved expense limit.

A key event in the development of improvement policies was the publication in 1968 of *The Older Houses in Scotland: A Plan for Action.*[5] This white paper and the subsequent Housing (Scotland) Act, 1969 saw the development of policies for the improvement and rehabilitation of areas of sub-tolerable housing. (Whereas improvement refers mainly to the installation of basic amenities, rehabilitation tends to be used for the more radical modernisation of BTS dwellings.) Housing treatment areas which were introduced in 1969 were replaced by housing action areas (HAAs) in 1974. (It should be noted that HAAs in England and Wales are rather different.) The size of HAAs varies from a handful of houses to more than a hundred.

The change of emphasis from slum clearance to improvement and rehabilitation was the result of a number of factors. Perhaps the most important was the demonstration by economists that improvement was likely to be less expensive than demolition and rebuilding.[6] There was also a view that large-scale slum clearance often perpetuated some of the problems which it was intended to solve by spreading blight to other areas. Another consideration was widespread dissatisfaction among people who were being rehoused in new council housing when high flats and non-traditional building methods were in vogue. The desirability of preserving communities was also emphasised.

HAAs enable local authorities to deal with concentrations of houses which do not meet the tolerable standard or lack basic amenities. They can be either for demolition or improvement but most are for the latter purpose. A great deal of work is generally required to rehabilitate the houses, which owner occupiers who tend to have low incomes and may be elderly are often not in a position to undertake themselves. The higher grant rate in an HAA of 75 per cent, and up to 90 per cent in cases of financial hardship, does not always overcome the problem. Some houses are still privately rented but landlords frequently prefer to sell their property rather than to improve it. Rehabilitation of an area of poor quality housing over a period of years may be unacceptably slow as well as impractical in tenemental property. For all these reasons a public agency, either the district council or a housing association, has an essential role in HAAs. The local authority or housing association usually acquires most of the rented houses and many of the owner-occupied ones. Staff are required to liaise with residents to discover their particular needs and to assist those owner occupiers who prefer not to sell to arrange improvements. Local authorities and housing associations do not receive improvement grants but the work is subsidised in the same way as their other capital expenditure. In 1986 about one-third of houses improved in HAAs were dealt with by housing associations, one-third by owner occupiers, some one-fifth by private landlords and rather more than ten per cent by local authorities.

Glasgow, with its large stock of old tenemental housing, has taken the lead in the use of HAAs since the mid-1970s when area improvement superseded a large-scale clearance programme. In the late 1980s about two-fifths of houses being dealt with in HAAs were in Glasgow, and over half of these were the responsibility of some 27 housing associations. These community based associations, which directly involve the residents of relatively small areas, were pioneered in Glasgow.

As well as the installation of basic amenities, grants can cover a wide range of work such as electrical rewiring. Up to half of improvement grants may be spent on repairs, and since 1974 grants have also been available solely for repairs including the replacement of lead plumbing. The conversion of a large house into a number of smaller dwellings, or of a building used for other purposes into residential accommodation, may also be grant aided. In 1986, when about 25,000 grants were approved, over half were for repairs and most of the rest for improvements. The number of grants has, however, fluctuated widely over the years, with a peak of nearly 80,000 approvals in 1983. Between 1982 and 1984, primarily to increase employment in the building industry, the government temporarily increased the level of grant to 90 per cent. The level has since returned to 50 per cent (except in HAAs) but another important reason for the reduced number awarded has been central government restrictions on capital expenditure by local authorities. The government has proposed the introduction of a unified improvement and repairs grant which will be means-tested (eligibility will be aligned with that for income support). The tolerable standard may also be revised (inclusion of a bath or shower has often been suggested). But these changes are not included in the current housing bill and will be the subject of future legislation.

HOUSING SUBSIDIES

The housing costs of most people, whether owner occupiers or tenants, are subsidised by the taxpayer, though in entirely different ways depending on tenure. Housing subsidies are a complex topic but some points of particular relevance to Scotland can usefully be made about them. For the sake of simplicity discussion will focus on the two most important tenures of council housing and owner occupation.

The main purpose of housing subsidies is presumably to ensure that people are not prevented by low incomes from obtaining adequate accommodation. This may be thought important because, apart from the value of decent housing to individuals, it benefits the community as a whole, for example by improving the general standard of health. Indeed, the origins of state involvement in the housing field in the nineteenth and early twentieth centuries can be seen as an aspect of its concern with public health. But some subsidies clearly go far beyond an objective of ensuring reasonable housing regardless of income. Particularly as far as owner occupation is concerned, a great deal of the expenditure on subsidies goes to households where there is no question of inadequate housing or low income. It is difficult to see, however, that there is much justification for public expenditure on housing beyond ensuring socially acceptable standards, such as the avoidance of overcrowding and the availability of basic amenities. Desirable as bigger and better houses may be from the point of view of individuals, wider benefits from them are hard to identify. A more realistic explanation for the existence of some subsidies, especially income tax relief on mortgage interest for owner occupiers, may be that they have grown up over the years and it is politically almost impossible to end them.

Council Housing

An important distinction in housing subsidies, particularly those affecting council housing, is between general assistance and means-tested assistance. General assistance is a subsidy which reduces the general level of council rents and therefore benefits all tenants of a local authority regardless of their individual incomes. On the other hand, means-tested assistance, now represented by housing benefit, reduces the rent paid by particular households which have low incomes. Basically what has been happening since 1979 is that general assistance to council tenants has been much reduced, resulting in higher rents and a greater reliance on housing benefit.

Exchequer subsidies for council housing have existed since 1919 and until the 1970s they were paid mainly in the form of general assistance. A national rent rebate scheme was introduced in 1972 and was later incorporated into housing benefit. The present arrangements for general assistance were introduced by the Housing (Financial Provisions) (Scotland) Act, 1978 which replaced existing exchequer subsidies with housing support grant (HSG). The 1978 act did not fix any particular level of subsidy but provided a mechanism whereby this could be determined each year by the government.

Every housing authority has to maintain a housing revenue account (HRA) relating to its council houses. Capital repayments and interest on loans for building houses on average constitute about 60 per cent of HRA outgoings, repairs and maintenance 25 per cent, and supervision and management ten per cent. The three main sources of HRA income are rents (before housing benefit), HSG and rate fund contributions (RFCs) made by most local authorities from their own resources. Table 5.4 shows how the relative importance of these sources of income changed between 1979-80 and 1987-88. A baseline is provided by 1979-80 in that it was the last financial year which started before the Conservative government took office. For most of the 1970s rents provided rather less than half HRA income, and the present government

TABLE 5.4:

Sources of Housing Support Grant Income, 1979-80–1987-88

	79/80 %	81/82 %	83/84 %	85/86 %	86/87 %	87/88 %
Rents (before HB)	44	55	67	72	78	83
HSG	39	25	11	9	6	6
RFCs	14	16	18	14	11	6
(RFC guideline/limit from 85/86)	(na)	(11)	(16)	(13)	(10)	(6)
Other	3	4	4	5	5	5

Notes: na: not applicable.
HB: housing benefit.
RFC: rate fund contributions.

Source: Scottish Development Department, *Scottish Housing Statistics*.

has followed a policy of increasing this proportion until it is now over 80 per cent. At the same time the contributions from HSG and RFCs have been reduced. The government can be seen as having two main objectives: to reduce public expenditure (though about half of rent increases disappear into higher expenditure on housing benefit), and to reinforce the attractions of owner occupation and in particular council house purchase for moderate income tenants who are not eligible for housing benefit.

In broad terms, HSG is paid to meet the deficit (if any) between a local authority's HRA income from rents and RFCs (the 'local contribution') and expenditure. On the income side the SDD announces each year its view of what would constitute a reasonable average council rent, and it assumes that local authorities will charge this. It also specifies an assumed RFC (if any) for each local authority. (Since 1985-86 the SDD has also specified a maximum RFC which may be higher than the assumed contribution for HSG purposes.) On the expenditure side the SDD similarly specifies an amount for management and maintenance in respect of each house; to this is added actual loan charges at a specified rate of interest which represents the current cost of borrowing. If assumed expenditure exceeds the local contribution, HSG is payable to the local authority.

In 1987-88 only 25 of the 56 Scottish housing authorities were still in receipt of HSG. The level of HSG has been fairly stable recently but this reflects reductions in assumed RFCs; once these have been phased out HSG is likely to fall again. It seems probable that in a few years only a small number of authorities with very high costs, for example Skye and Lochalsh, the Shetland Islands and Western Isles, will still be eligible for HSG, provided that the government continues to require local authorities receiving HSG to make substantial rent increases.

Between 1979-80 and 1987-88 average council house rents rose from less than £5 a week to nearly £15, an increase of about two-thirds in real terms. Since the government has limited maximum RFCs, local authorities have little alternative but to increase rents by the assumed amount. Increases have sometimes been resisted at the margin but the main effect of this has been a squeeze on resources available for the repair and maintenance of the stock.

In 1987-88 all but a handful of local authorities in Scotland were still making RFCs and none was making a substantial HRA surplus. But in future local authorities which are making no RFC will have the option (as happens frequently south of the border) of either imposing only modest rent increases to cover rising costs or making larger ones and generating surpluses which can be used for the relief of rates (or the community charge) or to improve other services.

Housing benefit is both a housing subsidy and a social security benefit, and it is discussed from the latter point of view in chapter 2. The number of tenants receiving housing benefit (and its predecessors before 1983) has increased during the 1980s despite its being made less generous on a number of occasions. The increase has been the result partly of the rise in unemployment and partly of increased rents. About two-thirds of public sector tenants were receiving housing benefit before the changes in April 1988, rather more than half of whom were entitled to it because they were receiving supplementary benefit. Fewer public sector tenants will be eligible for housing benefit under the revised scheme implemented following the Fowler reviews. Nevertheless, the underlying trend may still be for the proportion of tenants who are eligible to increase as council housing is steadily residualised, but much depends on the level of both rents and unemployment. In due course, as owner occupation becomes increasingly widespread, the number of tenants who are not eligible for housing benefit and pay full rents might become very small.

Before leaving public sector housing finance it is useful to distinguish control over capital spending by local authorities from exchequer subsidies. Councils finance house building and major renovations with loans, and this spending is limited by capital allocations. These are in effect permission from central government for local authorities to spend money they have to borrow and repay. A local authority does not receive a payment from the exchequer (although capital spending may increase eligibility for HSG). Capital allocations are determined in the light of housing plans which local authorities have to submit every four years (every year in the case of Glasgow) to the SDD. Housing plans include an assessment of local housing needs, taking into account factors such as population trends and the condition of the housing stock. These needs may be met by new building or renovation, and by owner occupation or the public sector, depending on local circumstances. The housing plan system was introduced in 1977 but less emphasis has perhaps been placed on it by central goverment since 1979.

Owner Occupation

Whereas subsidies to public sector tenants are in the form of conventional public expenditure and appear in the annual public expenditure white paper, this is not the case with most of those received by owner occupiers. These are in the form of relief from paying taxes to which owner occupiers would otherwise be liable and are sometimes called 'tax expenditures'. Owner-occupied housing receives favourable treatment through the tax system in two main ways. As well as interest paid on the first £30,000 of mortgages for house purchase not being treated as taxable income, an owner's main or only dwelling is exempt from capital gains tax. Although tax expenditures are not always recognised as subsidies, it may be more realistic to see the main difference as one of method of payment rather than of principle. If someone has a lower income tax liability because he is repaying a mortgage this means that either tax rates in general have to be higher or the government has less money to spend. Furthermore, although eligibility for relief is still calculated through the income tax system, most owner occupiers now receive it through the mortgage interest relief at source (MIRAS) arrangements. A direct payment is made by the exchequer to the building society or other lender so that the borrower only pays interest net of relief. Oddly, MIRAS is not counted as public expenditure.

The larger a person's mortgage, or if his income is high enough for him to pay higher rate tax, the greater will be the benefit he receives from tax relief. A house buyer who has a £12,000 mortgage which bears an interest rate of ten per cent pays interest of £1,200 a year. If, like most people, he pays only the basic rate of income tax at 25 per cent, he in effect receives a subsidy of £300 a year. A better-off person may have a mortgage of £30,000 (or more) and a marginal tax rate of 40 per cent. On his eligible interest payments of £3,000 this person will receive a subsidy of £1,200 a year, four times as much as the other. A subsidy which operates in this way may be seen as somewhat inequitable. In 1987-88 income tax relief cost over £4 billion for the United Kingdom as a whole, although Scotland received substantially less than a proportionate share in relation to the size of the population. The lower benefit from tax relief in Scotland partly reflects less owner occupation and partly house prices that are below the national average which is inflated by those in London and the south-east of England. As well as the inequity of mortgage interest tax relief, its effectiveness in reducing the cost of owner occupation is probably not very great. This is because tax relief enables buyers to afford bigger mortgages and therefore to pay more for houses. But the supply of houses is inelastic and responds slowly to increased demand, and in any case only about ten per cent of purchasers buy new dwellings. Thus much of the benefit of tax relief disappears into higher prices.

CURRENT ISSUES AND PROBLEMS

In this final section of the chapter attention is turned to a number of issues in the housing field. Homelessness and unsatisfactory council housing may be seen as problems from all points of view, but the sale of council houses is better regarded as a somewhat controversial policy which can cause problems for some people but also brings gains to others.

Homelessness

Homelessness is the most acute form of housing need though in numerical terms it is a relatively small problem affecting, as far as official statistics are concerned, around one per cent of Scottish households a year. The extent to which the state makes provision for people who have nowhere to stay raises the question of how far housing can be seen as a basic right, similar to education or health care, that is available regardless of ability to pay. Very important changes were made in provisions for the homeless by the Housing (Homeless Persons) Act, 1977 and the problem will be examined in the context of that legislation. The act increased local authority responsibilities for the homeless and transferred them from social work to housing departments.

Under the 1977 act (since consolidated in the Housing (Scotland) Act, 1987), an applicant for assistance has to be actually homeless or threatened with homelessness. This means that the applicant, or anyone who normally lives with him (or her) as a member of his family, has no accommodation which he is entitled to occupy or has accommodation but is unable to use it (for example because of a risk of domestic violence). If a household is deemed to be in 'priority need' the local authority must secure at least temporary accommodation for it. Priority need means that the applicant or a member of his household has dependent children, is pregnant, is vulnerable because of old age or mental or physical disability, is the victim of fire, flood or other disaster, or has 'other' special reasons for being homeless. Most local authorities make little provision for homeless single people without children, who are generally not regarded as being in priority need, and they have to rely mainly on voluntary organisations.

Housing authorities can, however, declare an applicant in priority need to be 'intentionally homeless' if, in the words of the legislation, he 'deliberately does or fails to do anything in consequence of which he ceases to occupy accommodation which it would have been reasonable for him to occupy'. Local authorities are required to secure only temporary accommodation for those who are classified as intentionally homeless. This provision was intended to be used in exceptional circumstances to deal with cases of flagrant abuse though some local authorities have resorted to it with surprising frequency. In 1985-86, however, the overall proportion of applicants in Scotland regarded as intentionally homeless had fallen to some three per cent of the total, and it was no higher than about ten per cent in any area.

The number of applications to local authorities in Scotland rose to over 20,000 a year in 1985 and 1986, and in nearly 60 per cent of cases accommodation was secured for them. This was usually permanent accommodation which normally meant a council house though often one in a low demand area. Local authorities in Scotland do not find it necessary to make much use of bed and breakfast accommodation as often happens in the London area. Indeed, in the many local authorities where council housing in unpopular estates is available without a lengthy wait, the distinction between households which are officially classified as homeless and others in urgent need may in practice often not be very great. Accommodation for the homeless is not free though a council rent or other charges which may be met by housing benefit.

In recent years over three-quarters of applicants have been classified as being in priority need, by far the most important reason being that the household included dependent children. The majority of applicants were staying temporarily with parents, other relatives or friends. The most common reason for homelessness was that those with whom applicants were staying could no longer accommodate them, though the underlying reason was often a family dispute of some kind. In practice, homelessness is frequently a matter of someone being under great pressure to move rather than having nowhere at all to stay. Thus the increase in the number of homeless people since the 1977 act came into force is likely to be in part a reflection of a greater awareness of the service provided as well as of greater need. In so far as greater need exists, it can be seen more as a result of increased marital breakdown and similar problems than of general housing shortage in Scotland.

Council House Sales

An important aspect of housing policy in recent years has been the sale of council and other public sector houses to their tenants. The Tenants' Rights, Etc. (Scotland) Act, 1980 gave most public sector tenants of three (later reduced to two) years' standing the 'right to buy' at a substantial discount on market value. Few council houses had previously been sold in Scotland as most local authorities did not favour the policy. Table 5.5 shows the number of council and other public sector houses sold to sitting tenants between 1980 and 1986. Sales have been a very important source of increased owner occupation since 1980, and since 1981 they have approximately equalled or, in 1982, 1983, 1984 and 1987, substantially exceeded new building for sale. The rate of sales fell after a peak in 1983, but then reached a record level in 1987, in part as a result of increased discounts on flats. Applications to buy were also at a record level in 1987 and, although the rate of sales may diminish again, it is likely to remain substantial as more tenants feel able to purchase. The long-term constraint on sales is likely to be the availability of dwellings which are felt to be worth buying rather than a fixed pool of potential purchasers.

Discounts are generous at 32 per cent of market value after two years as a public sector tenant plus one per cent for each year up to 60 per cent. Since 1987 discounts on flats have been even higher, starting at 44 per cent and rising to 70 per cent after only 15 years. The average discount is around 50 per cent. Another incentive to buy has been the substantial increases in council house rents since 1980.

Between 1979 and 1987 more than 110,000 public sector houses were sold to sitting tenants, including nearly 80,000 council houses.[7] The latter constituted about nine per cent of the stock of council houses though there were major variations between areas. North East Fife sold over 20 per cent of its stock and eight other authorities more than 15 per cent. Some 28 districts sold over ten per cent of their stock and most were predominantly rural,

TABLE 5.5:

Council and Other Public Sector House Sales in Scotland, 1980-87

	Local authorities	New towns	SSHA	Total
1980	2,396	2,129	1,417	6,482
1981	7,336	1,845	1,989	11,170
1982	11,811	1,362	1,933	15,106
1983	13,006	2,390	2,919	18,315
1984	12,832	1,963	2,444	17,239
1985	11,594	1,573	2,463	15,630
1986	13,294[1]	1,653	2,073	14,261[1]
1987	13,328[1]	2,141	3,015	19,636[1]

Note: 1. Provisional total.

Source: Scottish Development Department, *Scottish Housing Statistics*; and Scottish Development Department, *Statistical Bulletin*.

though suburban Bearsden and Milngavie was a high seller. On the other hand, a dozen districts all in central Scotland sold less than five per cent of their stocks, while Clydesdale, Glasgow, Monklands and Motherwell all sold less than three per cent. On the whole it is in areas where council housing is most dominant, and where the greatest tenure adjustment is needed if the government's objective of widespread owner occupation is to be achieved, that there have been fewest sales. Another difference is that in rural areas, where there is a demand for holiday and retirement homes, former council houses may be resold at prices which put them outside the reach of local people.

The dwellings purchased have not been typical of the public sector stock. Relatively few flats and maisonettes have been sold while houses with gardens in more attractive estates are the most popular.[8] About 80 per cent of sales have been of houses, though by the second half of 1987 flats and maisonettes were constituting about half the total, reflecting the increased discounts on them.[9] The popularity of houses is not surprising, because as well as being seen as worth buying it tends to be longer established and better off tenants who live in them as a result of how allocation and transfer systems operate. Thus, while in rural areas characterised by modest public sector housing stocks and high rates of sales, shortages of council housing in relation to demand may develop, the effect in urban areas is more one of creaming off the good quality stock. There may continue to be more than enough council dwellings in relation to demand though an increasing shortage of houses with gardens in pleasant and sought-after areas.

A large public sector remains in Scotland, and the government is now concerned with its future management. A recent white paper[10] and legislation now before parliament which is discussed below may result in some estates being taken over by housing associations, housing trusts or private landlords. Another development has been for remaining tenants to be transferred from unpopular estates with high vacancy levels and for the houses to be sold to builders for refurbishment and resale to owner occupiers.

Unsatisfactory Council Housing

The public sector was intended to be a solution to housing problems by making available good quality accommodation to people who otherwise would not have been able to obtain it. In terms of the conventional indicator of housing quality, the possession of basic amenities, the public sector is of uniformly high quality. Yet in reality some council housing is unsatisfactory and may be difficult to let. Increasingly, as sub-tolerable houses lacking amenities are dealt with, attention is being turned to the public sector. A variety of factors may make housing relatively less attractive, such as building type, location, state of repair and environment. Other things being equal, houses are likely to be preferred to flats (particularly those in large blocks), central to peripheral areas and modern or modernised to older dwellings. Some council houses are unsatisfactory by any standards but others would be considered acceptable in one area but not in another. A great deal depends on the alternatives which are available.

Almost invariably unpopularity and difficulty in letting housing lead to a deprived and unstable population. Such estates tend to have a disproportionate number of larger families, high child densities and a concentration of 'difficult' tenants. These factors exacerbate and interact with the basic physical shortcomings of the housing itself: for example, blocks of flats do not provide a very satisfactory environment for children. A vicious circle of increasing unpopularity and population imbalance can be set up.

Attention is often drawn to grading of applicants according to their housekeeping standards or to alleged 'dumping' by local authorities, but the preferences of applicants themselves are probably more important. In most areas applicants for council housing are permitted to choose where they will live. As a result the best housing tends to be occupied by applicants who are in a position to wait a substantial time for a vacancy. Those who require a council house as quickly as possible, usually because their existing accommodation is either very unsatisfactory or in danger of being lost altogether, are constrained to accept an offer in an unpopular area for which there is no waiting list. Such people are also likely to be disadvantaged in other ways as well: for example, to be unemployed, single parents or simply to have low incomes.[11]

The shortcomings of less popular council estates and the concentration of disadvantaged people in them through the operation of the allocation process may make pre-existing problems worse. The availability of even the best housing solves only one problem of poverty. With the decline of the private rented sector the poorest have increasingly been moving to council housing. A combination of policies is required in fields such as social security and employment as well as housing.

Action can, however, be taken in the housing field to alleviate some of the problems. Housing which is in a poor state of repair can be rehabilitated. In some cases buildings can be modified to make them less unsatisfactory. Amenities such as shops and pubs can be provided in estates where they are absent. But some housing will always be more popular and some less popular. As well as action to alter physical conditions, therefore, allocation policies need to be changed if the concentration of disadvantaged people and the restriction of their housing opportunities are to be alleviated. Allocation procedures could give more emphasis to housing need as against waiting time in determining who obtains popular accommodation.

GOVERNMENT PROPOSALS

Important changes to housing policy in Scotland were included in the white paper published at the end of 1987[12] and many of these are incorporated in legislation that will be passed during 1988. The new policies mainly affect rented housing, in both the public and private sectors. Since 1979 the main emphasis of policy has been on the extension of owner occupation, particularly through the introduction of the right to buy, and this will continue. The government has, however, now turned its attention to the future of rented housing. In the public sector, where most council houses have not been, and are unlikely to be, purchased by individual tenants, the government believes that management can be improved and that some of the stock should be transferred from councils to new owners. In the private rented sector the government hopes that it will be possible to achieve some expansion after years of decline. A key development will be the establishment in 1989 of a new agency, Scottish Homes, which will bring together the Scottish Special Housing Association and the Housing Corporation in Scotland.

The white paper set out four objectives for housing policy: the continued spread of home ownership; the revitalisation of the private (or 'independent') rented sector; a changing role for local housing authorities with less emphasis on providing council housing and more on acting as enablers to facilitate the work of other agencies; and a more effective focusing of public finance with a greater contribution from private sector funding. It is really only the second, third and fourth objectives which are to any extent new, and the policy changes are directed towards achieving them.

Scottish Homes

The government's proposals for the establishment of Scottish Homes were the subject of a discussion document issued earlier in 1987.[13] It stated that there was no unified agency in the housing field with a promotional role, comparable with the Scottish Development Agency or the Highlands and Islands Development Board. Scottish Homes will assume responsibility from the Housing Corporation for supervising and financing housing associations, as well as being landlord of the large stock of houses which it will inherit from the SSHA. The new agency is likely to acquire other houses which are in need of modernisation from local authorities, something which is already being done by the SSHA. Scottish Homes will also have power to provide financial assistance to private sector housing projects, either through grants or loans. It is clear that the government sees Scottish Homes as playing a major role in the future of rented housing in Scotland, particularly in the field of urban regeneration.

Local Authorities

Local authorities are likely in the future to have a reduced role in the direct provision of rented housing, though they will remain substantial landlords, albeit on a diminishing scale. Councils are already building few houses and the government does not expect this to change. Their existing stock will be eroded through sales of individual houses under the right to buy and of estates under a new 'right to transfer' to a new landlord. Any landlord which is approved by Scottish Homes will be able to approach local authority tenants and invite them to transfer. Housing associations, co-operatives and private landlords are mentioned in the white paper. The written consent of individual tenants will be required. The trade-off for tenants may often be between the promise of early improvements to unsatisfactory housing and higher rents. The transfer of housing in peripheral estates to Scottish Homes for improvement may, however, be more significant.

The Private Rented Sector

The government takes the view that if controls over rent levels are removed, new investment can be attracted into private rented housing. At present most privately rented houses are within the system of regulated tenancies where 'fair' rents, which are generally substantially below free market levels, can be set by rent officers. Although existing regulated tenancies will continue until the tenant moves or dies, no new ones will be created. In future the standard form of tenure, except in council housing, will be assured tenancies, which will also extend to housing associations. Rents under assured tenancies will be 'freely negotiated' between landlord and tenant (though they may be less than a market rent if a landlord, for example a housing association, has access to subsidies). The tenant will have security of tenure, subject to a number of grounds for eviction, and when the period for which a rent has been agreed expires he can if necessary go to a rent assessment committee for arbitration over a new one. The 1988 budget extended the business expansion scheme (BES) to investments in housing to let on assured tenancies. This gives exemptions from income tax on initial investments and from capital gains tax. The BES may attract significant amounts of private finance into rented houses.

There is still likely to be the constraint, however, that very few people who can afford to become owner occupiers will be willing to rent for more than short periods. The financial attractions of owner occupation, in terms of falling real costs and the acquisition of a valuable asset, are simply too great. But people who cannot afford owner occupation are unlikely to be able to afford a rent which would give a worthwhile financial return to investors. The BES may do a little to bridge the gap, but the key factor will undoubtedly be the availability of housing benefit. If the government is prepared to inject much larger amounts of money into housing benefit, there might be a substantial expansion of the private rented sector although it is likely to remain relatively small compared with the other sectors. Rent officers will have to approve private sector rents as being reasonable for housing benefit purposes.

It is difficult to predict how the rented sector will evolve, but there is likely to be more varied provision within which council housing will become less important. The government now talks about an independent rented sector which will include both housing associations and private landlords. Most housing association developments will in future receive substantially lower levels of exchequer subsidy through housing association grant, so that rents will be much higher than they are now. A range of rented housing may develop, from council housing and that provided by Scottish Homes with relatively modest rents, through housing associations, co-operatives and housing trusts with higher rents, to commercial landlords charging market rents. Thus there will be a much less clear-cut division between social rented housing in the public sector and the private rented sector.

In many respects housing conditions in Scotland are better than at any time in the past, as long-standing problems of shortage, slums and substandard dwellings have been largely overcome. But new problems have emerged to take their place. There is the disrepair of the housing stock, which is found in the owner-occupied and council sectors as well as in private rented property. There is difficult-to-let council housing, characterised by shortcomings such as poor environment, remote location and dampness. There is homelessness. It is a fallacy to believe that a single housing problem exists or has ever existed which can somehow be finally solved; there is rather a changing agenda of needs and problems. If they are to be tackled, flexible and evolving policies are required. The government is introducing important new policies, but it remains to be seen how effective they will be in improving the quality of housing enjoyed by Scottish people.

References

1. *Report of the Royal Commission on the Housing of the Industrial Population of Scotland, Rural and Urban*, Cd.8731, HMSO, 1917.
2. Scottish Special Housing Association, *A Chronicle of Forty Years 1937-77*, SSHA, 1977.
3. Data on the housing stock are from: Scottish Development Department, *Scottish Housing Statistics*, HMSO, annual; and Registrar General for Scotland, *Census 1981: Housing and Household Report*, HMSO, 1984.
4. City of Glasgow Housing Department, *House Condition Survey 1985: Volume One: The Condition of Glasgow's Housing*, Housing Department, 1987.
5. Cmnd.3598, HMSO, 1968.
6. See for example: L. Needleman, *The Economics of Housing*, Staples Press, 1965.
7. Scottish Development Department, *Statistical Bulletin: Housing Trends in Scotland: Quarter Ended 31 December 1987*, Scottish Office, 1988.
8. M. Foulis, 'The Effect of Sales on the Public Sector in Scotland' in D. Clapham and J. English (eds.), *Public Housing: Current Trends and Future Developments*, Croom Helm, 1987.
9. Scottish Development Department, *Statistical Bulletin*.
10. *Housing: The Government's Proposals for Scotland*, Cm.242, HMSO, 1987.
11. J. English, 'Access to Public Sector Housing' in M. Pacione (ed.), *Social Geography: Progress and Prospect*, Croom Helm, 1987.
12. Cm.242.
13. Scottish Development Department, *Scottish Homes: A New Agency for Housing in Scotland*, SDD, 1987.

FURTHER READING

H. Aughton, *Housing Finance: A Basic Guide*, Shelter, (2nd edition) 1986.
A brief introduction to an important topic.

D. Clapham and J. English (eds.) *Public Housing: Current Trends and Future Developments*, Croom Helm, 1987.
This book focuses on tenure change and the evolving role of public sector housing.

P. Malpass (ed.), *The Housing Crisis*, Croom Helm, 1986.
The contributions discuss a variety of current housing problems.

P. Malpass and A. Murie, *Housing Policy and Practice*, Macmillan, (2nd edition) 1987.
The best general textbook on housing policy which is currently available.

Roof, Shelter, bi-monthly.
This magazine has interesting articles often written from a radical standpoint.

Scottish Housing Statistics, HMSO, annual.
A valuable source of data on housing produced by the Scottish Development Department; publication ceased after the 1986 edition.

Statistical Bulletin, Scottish Office.
Housing statistics are covered in one series of bulletins with regular quarterly numbers and occasional additional ones on particular topics. In future these will be the only regular source of data on housing from the Scottish Development Department.

6
PERSONAL SOCIAL SERVICES

The personal social services are not so readily identifiable nor so widely familiar an aspect of the welfare state as, for example, the national health service or the social security system. Satisfactory definitions are difficult to find in the literature but Eric Sainsbury has written that 'personal social services are ... concerned with needs and difficulties which inhibit the individual's maximum social functioning ...; needs which have traditionally been dealt with by personal or family action'. These are needs, he goes on to say, 'which call for a high level of adaptability in the helping process, rather than a uniformity of provision'.[1] The personal social services are the statutory responsibility of social work departments (and social services departments in England and Wales) but they encompass not only the advice, guidance and support which are provided by 'field' social workers but also a wide range of other provisions including residential care, day care and domiciliary services such as home helps and meals-on-wheels.

The personnel involved in making these services available therefore include not only professionally qualified social workers, but also other professionals such as occupational therapists as well as residential and day care staff and home helps. Although voluntary organisations, such as Dr. Barnardo's, the Women's Royal Voluntary Service and Age Concern, play an important role in providing many of these services, often with support from public funds, we will be primarily concerned in this chapter with local authority social work departments.

Social work departments were created to implement the Social Work (Scotland) Act, 1968. In order to understand the organisation and role of these unified departments it is necessary to look briefly at their historical roots. One of the most important was the poor law, which was eventually abolished by the National Assistance Act, 1948. Welfare services for elderly, homeless and handicapped people were then transferred to local authority welfare departments, while the Children Act, 1948 created new children's departments to care for children who were 'deprived of a normal home life'. The probation service had developed independently from the turn of the century in response to separate legislation (and in England and Wales it is still a separate service). In hospitals and clinics, medical social workers (originally lady almoners) and psychiatric social workers were colleagues of medical and nursing staff. But they were never required by law, like probation and child care officers, and though they were able to develop a fully trained service it was at the price of being relatively few in number. Education and training developed separately for each of these groups and it was not until the 1950s that the identification of common areas of knowledge and skill, and therefore training, was taken seriously and 'generic' social work courses began to be introduced. Another important contribution to the development of the personal social services was the work of charitable organisations which increasingly began to employ trained staff.[2]

Progress in Scotland was, however, slow in terms of both training and the provision of services. Until the late 1950s and early 1960s the only courses for probation and child care officers were provided south of the border while Edinburgh University alone in Scotland had pioneered training for psychiatric and medical social workers. In England and Wales the Mental Health Act, 1959 required the involvement of social workers when people were admitted to hospital on a compulsory basis and the number of appropriately trained staff employed by local authority welfare departments rose rapidly as a consequence. The equivalent legislation for Scotland (the Mental Health (Scotland) Act, 1960) was somewhat different in its requirements, however, and did not result in a comparable increase in trained personnel. By the late 1960s, shortly before the Social Work (Scotland) Act came into force, there were only some 100 qualified workers employed by local authorities and about 180 in the probation service. In addition there was a small number of qualified psychiatric and medical social workers in hospitals throughout Scotland but a large part of the work of the personal social services, particularly in welfare departments, was carried out by staff without formal training or qualifications.

During the 1960s, social workers throughout the United Kingdom became increasingly interested in identifying the common elements of social work practice in the different settings described above; the conclusion was reached that the similarities were more important to the provision of appropriate personal social services than were variations of practice between the different services.[3] The development of these ideas led to an increase in the number of 'generic' training courses mentioned earlier, and a coming together of the different professional associations which culminated in the formation of the British Association of Social Workers in 1970 and in a reorganisation of the services provided by the state. This reorganisation, with its recognition of generic principles, came about in Scotland both more comprehensively and earlier than south of the border.

THE ESTABLISHMENT OF SOCIAL WORK DEPARTMENTS

The establishment in 1961 of the Kilbrandon Committee on Children and Young Persons is described elsewhere (see chapter 7) as are the main features of the committee's report. The report[4] was little concerned with theoretical principles of delinquency and penology or with more general problems of the social services. It was limited almost exclusively to setting out in some detail an original set of proposals for dealing with children 'in need of compulsory measures of care'. A key feature of these plans was the establishment in each major local authority of a lay children's panel which would reach decisions on appropriate measure of care, while responsibility for providing supportive social services to the new panels was to be in the hands of a group of specialist social workers attached to the local authority education department. The committee considered the suggestion put to it by some witnesses that the social work service for children and their families ought to be incorporated in a comprehensive welfare and social services agency. They rejected the proposal, principally because it fell outside their terms of reference, but possibly also because they were not wholly convinced of its practicability. But within a couple of years a white paper, *Social Work and the Community,*[5] had, in a sense, reversed the priorities. The government was aware, not only of the growing sense of unity among social workers, but also of the many criticisms that had been expressed – though not specifically in a Scottish context – of the wasteful and possibly even harmful effects of dividing responsibility for family care between different specialists. They were also conscious of the absence of preventive work when existing personal services were geared to dealing with crisis and breakdown. It was therefore argued that, instead of implementing the Kilbrandon proposals in isolation, the opportunity should be taken to reshape quite fundamentally the personal social services of Scottish local authorities. The comprehensive social work departments that would emerge from these changes would take on responsibility for the provision of supportive services to the proposed children's panels, together with a wide range of other duties that had previously been carried out separately by children's departments, welfare departments, public health departments and the probation service.

By the mid-1960s the movement towards unification of the personal social services was well ahead of that in England and Wales, where consideration of the future of the juvenile courts had not been linked with wider issues. The white paper, published in 1966, is the fullest statement available of the government's intentions. The Social Work (Scotland) Act, 1968, which gave legislative expression to most of these proposals, deals only with formal structures, powers and duties, so that the white paper is important as a statement of policy objectives.

The defects of the prevailing organisation of local authority social work and welfare services were seen in the white paper as arising from their piecemeal development in response to the 'identification at different times of certain groups of people who needed social help'. But the interrelatedness of human problems, the body of expertise common to all social workers, the shortage of trained and experienced staff and the bewildering array of agencies all pointed to one conclusion: 'the local authority services designed to provide community care and support, whether for children, the handicapped, the mentally and physically ill or the aged, should be brought within a single organisation'.[6] The white paper contains a sensible if superficial discussion of the importance of co-operation between the proposed new social work department and other statutory and voluntary agencies and of the value of preventive work. The areas of responsibility of the proposed new departments are briefly summarised. The main increase in cost, it was concluded, would be due to the appointment of directors of social work and some regrading of other posts, balanced by savings resulting from more efficient deployment of staff. It is perhaps unfortunate that the government did not commission some background studies. There is a complete lack of statistical information or research findings, and no sign of any analysis either of the social and economic context or of possible lines of future development.

Perhaps the most important change between the white paper and the 1968 act was the decision to increase the number of social work departments. The original intention had been for the then counties and four cities to form the new social work authorities. Political pressure rather than considerations of principle dictated the inclusion of the large burghs, some of them smaller in population than a Glasgow housing estate, bringing the number of new departments to 50. A specialist branch, the Social Work Services Group, had been established within the Scottish Education Department in the previous year. The new social work departments came into being in 1969, although the implementation of Part III of the act (that is the operation of the children's hearings system) was delayed until 1971.

The principal objective of the new departments was expressed in somewhat global terms in section 12(1) of the act: 'to promote social welfare by making available advice, guidance and assistance on such a scale as may be appropriate for their area'. Social work departments were made responsible for social work in the sense of personal, professional involvement with individuals and families with problems ('fieldwork'), and also for a wide range of other services. These include residential services, of which homes for children deprived of a normal family life and for old people unable to live on their own in the community account for the greater part; day care services, such as day nurseries and special centres for disabled or mentally disordered people; and domiciliary services, such as the provision of home helps and meals-on-wheels. Few qualified social workers were employed outside the fieldwork services, although the other responsibilities of the new departments involved substantial staffs and large numbers of clients. One notable feature of the act was the duty it gave to social work departments (under section 12) to provide assistance in cash. Cash payments had previously been permitted under child care legislation, but they now became more widely applicable as one of the ways in which social welfare might be promoted. It is interesting to note that neither the general power to promote social welfare nor the general power to give financial help is provided for in English legislation.

PROBLEMS OF THE NEW DEPARTMENTS

One early but recurrent problem was that of an unforeseen level of demand for personal social services. The act had been seen – in spite of the generous terminology of section 12 – as essentially a tidying-up operation, providing a new service that would cater more efficiently for the existing pattern of needs at little additional cost. Not for the first time in the history of welfare legislation, little serious consideration was given to the possibility that the very creation of a new service might itself help to influence the way in which people thought about their problems and the demands they would consequently make. Behind the assumption that the new departments would discharge responsibilities not very different from the sum total of those of the former specialised ones that they replaced lay the notion of needs and demands as somehow existing in fixed quanitities within the community. In fact, the demand for social services is extremely elastic, since the concept of need is largely a subjective one and very variable over time. What at any given time people think of as needs which justify a demand for services depends on the state of public awareness, which is itself influenced by both professional opinion and the nature of service provision.

It was certainly the case that, in urban-industrial districts in particular, the new service brought to light areas of need not previously recognised, which created very heavy demands. Much of the new demand stemmed from problems in which financial and environmental factors played a large part. Although local authorities quickly began to improve their staffing levels, these always seemed to fall short of the level of demand. There was no easy way of drawing boundaries and excluding certain areas of work. The almost inevitable consequence was a heavy emphasis on work in crisis situations as they arose, rather than the carefully planned long-term preventive work to which the white paper had looked forward.

The white paper had also stated the case for close collaboration between the social work department and other statutory agencies, and had seen the social work director functioning as an adviser on 'social' matters to housing and planning authorities. Whether social work training and experience provide the ideal foundation for such consultative functions is debatable; but in any case there was nothing in the tradition of local government to facilitate such trans-departmental alliances. In practice, in most areas separate departments pursued their own and sometimes conflicting ways.

The introduction of children's hearings in 1971 involved important new responsibilities for social workers, who were required to provide social background reports for reporters and panel members and to undertake the supervision of young people when an order was made at a hearing. The priority necessarily accorded to these statutory responsibilities inevitably reduced still further the scope for that careful assessment and long-term intensive work with vulnerable individuals and families that had been seen as a major objective of the unification of the personal social services.

The creation of unified departments imposed heavy demands on their staff, who were expected to lose old allegiances, to overcome inter-departmental suspicions, and to adapt their specialised skills to the needs of client groups with which they were not familiar. To create a new sense of unity and cohesiveness was a challenge to which not all social work directors could respond effectively. In the end the problem was not so much solved as swamped, as the rising demand for new staff resources led to enlarged training programmes and an influx of young professionals into the beleaguered departments.

A new dimension of uncertainty was added when it became clear that existing social work departments were soon to be amalgamated as a consequence of the reorganisation of local government in the early 1970s (see chapter 1). The location of social work was seriously debated but the arguments of those who saw it as essentially a community-based service, responsive to local needs, and therefore more appropriately defined as a district responsibility, were outweighed by the claim that the amalgamation of resources at the regional level would make for a more comprehensive range of provision and access to more high-powered specialist services. In addition to the regions the three all-purpose islands authorities also became responsible for social work. Thus after little more than five years of existence 50 social work departments were reduced to the present twelve.

THE ORGANISATIONAL STRUCTURE OF SOCIAL WORK DEPARTMENTS

Both before and after local government reorganisation the new social work departments grew rapidly. The recurrent demands for additional staff were met to a substantial extent – at least as far as field social workers were concerned – by the creation of new training courses and the expansion of existing ones. The work of the Central Council for Education and Training in Social Work, established for the whole of the United Kingdom in 1971, gave a powerful impetus to the promotion of training.

Figure 6.1 shows the number of staff (on a whole-time equivalent basis) employed by social work departments between 1971 and 1986. The total almost doubled between 1971 and 1981, but the proportion of different kinds of staff changed little except for the growing importance of fieldworkers. The overall rate of growth was, however, by no means consistent; during the first three years of the period the increase in staff numbers ran at about twelve per cent per annum, but between 1974 and 1979 annual growth was on average about seven per cent (though that for fieldwork staff was in excess of ten per cent). Particularly since the change of government in 1979 there has been strong pressure on local authorities to restrict expenditure, but except in 1981 the total number of staff has continued to rise, albeit at a slower rate.

The organisation and professional responsibilities of the various staff groups are considered later in this chapter. Before examining these it is useful to review briefly the current staffing pattern of social work authorities.[7] It is important to bear in mind that although social work gives its name to the departments concerned, social workers in the strict sense account for only a relatively small fraction of the total staff complement. The 'practitioner' grades (main grade social workers and senior social work staff) amount to only some 13 per cent of all full-time staff (and no more than half that figure if part-time staff are also included). The category 'fieldwork staff' also includes community workers and welfare rights officers – whose responsibilities many would see as

FIGURE 6.1 Staff of Social Work Departments, 1971-86

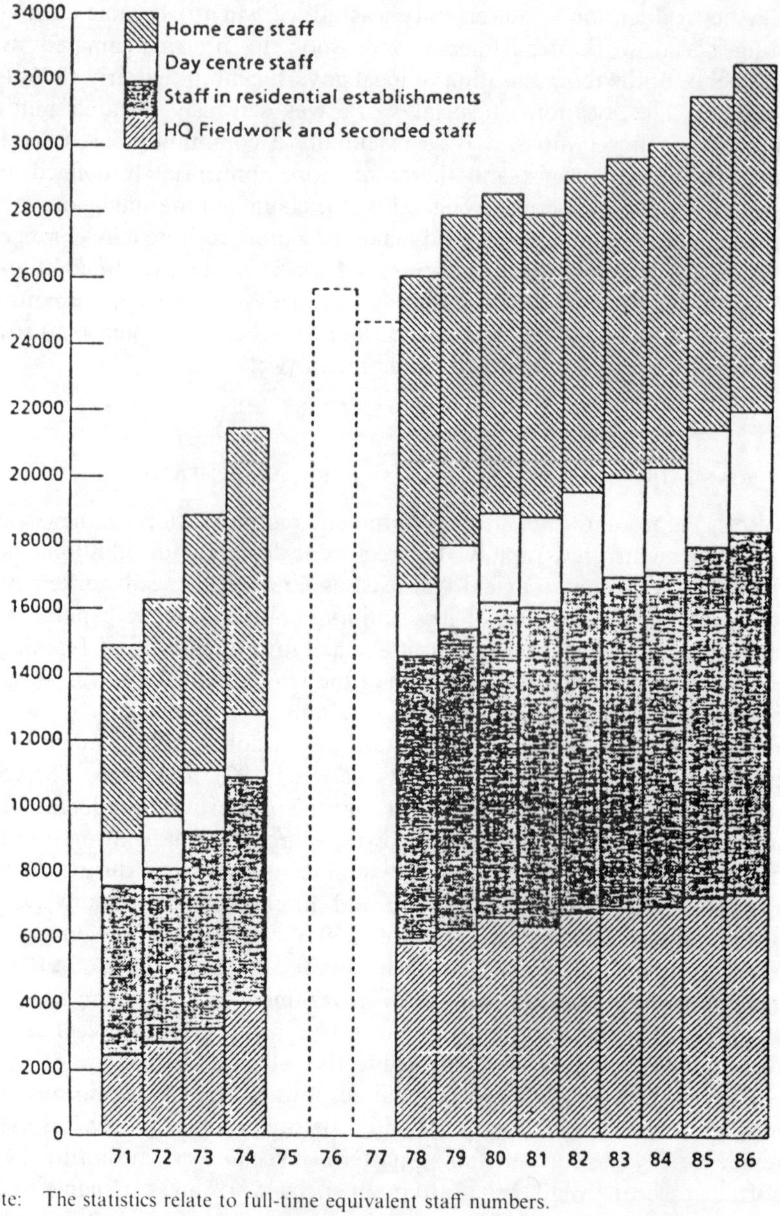

Note: The statistics relate to full-time equivalent staff numbers.

an integral part of social work practice – as well as occupational therapists, whose profession is generally classified as supplementary to medicine.

The personal social services do not give the impression of being top-heavy with managerial and administrative staff; indeed it could be argued that a more substantial investment in the forward planning and development of services would be beneficial. The 'managerial and administrative' category includes all staff responsible for research and training. These are comparatively few in number (less than 500) given the complex and constantly changing problems confronting the personal social services, the prevailing uncertainty about the effectiveness of various forms of service provision, and the large numbers of wholly untrained staff, particularly in the residential sector.

Furthermore, not only do social workers (that is those who hold the Certificate of Qualification in Social Work or its equivalent) form no more than a small proportion of social work department staff, but staff with formal qualifications of any kind are very much in the minority. Qualified social workers, occupational therapists, teachers and nurses taken together amount to only about one-quarter of the work-force. Home helps are by far the largest single group, and to these should be added domestic workers and unqualified care staff in day centres and residential establishments, as well as secretarial and clerical staff.

The Scottish personal social services on their present scale are obviously a far cry from the modest redeployment proposed in the mid-1960s. They employ more than 40,000 people (well over half of them on a part-time basis), control nearly 250 residential establishments, just over 200 day centres and about 200 day nurseries and pre-school playgroups. For public resources of this scale to be deployed with even a minimum of effectiveness or accountability, it is essential to have formal structures which allow for the formulation of policies and their implementation as well as for the oversight of more or less routine activities. Since the personal social services are a responsibility of local government, both political and administrative processes must be involved.

Each regional and islands authority is required by the 1968 act to appoint a social work committee, and in principle it is that committee which has the ultimate responsibility for the oversight of the authority's social work services. In practice, as is the case throughout local government, the position is a good deal more complex.[8] The elected members of local authorities almost always have other occupations or interests, and very rarely have either the time or the detailed knowledge that would be necessary if they wished to familiarise themselves with the workings of a complex and many-sided service. Inevitably, committee members are heavily dependent on the director of social work and his senior colleagues for a regular appreciation of current trends and emerging problems. It is after all the director and his staff who largely shape the agenda of committee meetings and prepare the papers that present committee members with policy choices. In keeping with the strong tradition of professionalism among local authority principal officers, the director of social work maintains a high degree of autonomy in the management of the service. The committee tends therefore to be concerned with broad questions of staffing levels and budgetary requirements and with major policy decisions such as a shift away from residential child care. There are, however, some important exceptions to the general dissociation of social work committees from the specifics of practice. Most noticeable is the rapid response of elected members to unfavourable publicity. If, for example, there are allegations in the press of malpractice in any of the local authority's own establishments, or if the death or serious injury of a child at the hands of his parents brings out the suggestion that this might have been prevented by closer supervision or more rapid intervention by a social worker, elected members tend to be galvanised into action. Searching enquiries are set in train and new guidelines rapidly drafted, but the wider implications of such events for management and the maintenance of professional standards often go unconsidered.

Another and more positive type of exception is exemplified by the creation in Strathclyde Region of a series of working groups made up jointly of social work committee members and senior departmental staff. These groups have tended to concentrate on the problems of client groups whose needs are admitted to have been inadequately met (for example alcoholics or the mentally handicapped). Initiated at least in part as a means of conveying to elected members a deeper sense of specific social problems, most of these groups have generated considerable enthusiasm and produced reports containing many practical recommendations for the improvement of services. In some instances 'monitoring groups' have been set up to check and report on the implementation of recommended changes.

At the administrative level, the pattern for management and delivery of personal social services depends on considerations such as the size and density of the population served. The regions with large concentrations of population and large social work departments need fairly complex management structures. On the other hand, a region such as the Highlands, with a population no bigger than that of Dundee but covering an area as large as Strathclyde and Grampian combined, faces special organisational problems in ensuring the delivery of services. While it is difficult to generalise about the structure of social work departments, it is safe to say that the key unit in the delivery of field services is the area, served by an area office.

Differences in patterns of organisation arise from regional policy, historical accident and population density, but most area offices serve populations of between 30,000 and 60,000. The area officer in overall charge is in turn accountable to higher authority within the regional department. In a typical area office there may be a dozen or so qualified social workers, organised into two teams each with a senior worker and one or two social work assistants, a small group of occupational therapists and assistants, a home help organiser and a fairly large team of home helps. Area offices may also provide bases for community workers and welfare rights officers. And, of course, in order to function with even minimal efficiency, an area office will need assistance with correspondence, maintaining records, taking incoming telephone calls and receiving members of the public.

There are several different ways of deploying social work services for the population of a particular district. The most common practice is for the district to be divided into a number of areas, each of which is served by its own team. In recent years there has been increasing interest (although perhaps to a greater extent in England than in Scotland) in the division of an area office's territory into several small 'patches', with a very small sub-team of social workers assigned to each.[9] It has been claimed that the 'patch' method enables professional workers to understand their territory intimately, and puts them in a better position to mobilise local resources and make more effective use of volunteers and of less highly trained staff. Like most innovations in social work, the method is forcefully advocated by some and sharply criticised by others, without the benefit of much objective research evidence concerning its advantages and shortcomings. One might speculate that the patch approach is most effective in areas with a strong sense of community identity, long-established families and well-developed informal supportive networks, and may be less appropriate where there is a good deal of population turnover and few social bonds between households.

There is too a professional dimension to be considered. If a particular area is to be served by two or three social workers, they will need to have a high degree of general professional competence. In a large team there may be opportunities for individual social workers to develop some degree of specialisation in the use of a particular social work method (such as group work or family work) or in work with a particular client group (such as the elderly or mentally handicapped people), whereas in a very small team the concept of the multi-purpose social worker is carried to an extreme. Nevertheless, the difference is one of degree, for it is very unusual anywhere to find social workers in area teams with clearly defined and formally recognised specialist roles.

In a number of offices, however, there is to be found an interesting variant which cuts across both the traditional specialist divisions and the differentiation by geographical boundaries. This is the use of an 'intake team' and a 'long-term team'. The former deals with all new referrals and retains cases which appear to be capable of being carried through within perhaps three months. The long-term team takes over cases where there is an initial expectation of protracted work – including those (for example, supervision orders made by children's hearings) where there is a continuing statutory obligation – and others which, whatever the original forecast, turn out in practice to require social work involvement over a lengthy period. In addition to statutory cases, a long-term team would inevitably have on its books a considerable number of families with multiple problems and complex needs.

The area office is an extremely important unit in the structure of the social work department, and the social worker in charge has both a very influential management role and some direct professional responsibilities, although not having his or her own caseload. It normally falls to the area officer to decide, for example, when to call a case conference in cases of suspected child abuse, and to chair the proceedings when one is convened. Much of what the social work department provides, however, is not generally organised through area teams. Residential and day care services are usually controlled from departmental headquarters.

As was pointed out above, social work authorities in Scotland vary considerably in the size of population and area served, so that there are differences in their management structures. In a small region the area officers may be directly responsible to the director of social work, while at the other extreme Strathclyde Region was originally made up of five divisions which in their turn were broken down into more than 20 districts and into over 60 areas. Following some years of discussion, in the 1980s there has been a major restructuring of the department, creating twelve larger districts and eliminating the divisional layer. District managers in Strathclyde have always had a considerable measure of operational autonomy, including responsibility for residential as well as community services. New ways of organising management responsibility for services have also been introduced with the needs of client groups, rather than types of provision, being the basis for allocating responsibility. At the time of writing the process of restructuring has not yet been completed and it will be some time before the value of the new structure can be adequately assessed.

To most front-line practitioners, especially in large and organisationally complex authorities, 'management' seems remote and largely irrelevant. Such judgements, though understandable, should not be taken at their face value. By no means all styles of management are equally constructive or imaginative, but given the scale of public resources involved and the vulnerability of most social work clients there are essential roles for management to play in ensuring accountability, monitoring the implementation of major policy decisions and providing specialist advice. In view of the shortage of workers with advanced training it is usual for the social work department to include in its staff a small group of specialist advisers, for example in mental health or in social work with offenders. However, because such advisers tend to be few in number and located at headquarters it is easy for them to become heavily involved in providing guidance to directors and committees at the expense of consultation and advice to practitioners.

THE WORK OF THE PERSONAL SOCIAL SERVICES

It is difficult to obtain precise information about the size and make-up of the clientele of social work departments. Maintaining detailed records and compiling statistical returns are not always highly valued activities and despite the continued efforts of the Social Work Services Group to implement a comprehensive system of statistical information there are still significant gaps. On the whole, as might be expected, firmer statistics are available for residential services and areas of work where local authorities have statutory responsibilities (for example children in care) than for non-statutory services.

Residential Care

Residential services account for a large share of local authority expenditure on the personal social services and for a high proportion of the staff employed (over 10,000 people). Residential care for children who are permanently or temporarily deprived of a normal home life is a significant component of this work. About 150 children's homes are provided, with an increasing tendency towards smaller units; the average number of places in each is now about 15. The occupancy rate in 1985 was 73 per cent, with some 1,700 children in residence at any one time. Local authorities also operate a number of residential assessment centres, mainly for children referred through the hearings system. These provide several hundred places, and deal with about 2,000 admissions each year. Ordinary children's homes also have a high proportion of short-term and medium-term admissions; more than half of children have been in residence for less than a year.[10]

Local authorities, however, do not take direct responsibility for the whole of residential child care; voluntary organisations such as Barnardo's and Quarrier's Homes also have large numbers of children in their care, nearly all of whom are maintained with the financial support of local authorities. It is noticeable, however, that while the total number of children in residential care has been falling steadily since 1976, the reduction has been much more marked in the registered voluntary homes than in those directly controlled by local authorities. Changes in social attitudes and in child care policies, discussed later in this chapter, have led to reductions in the demand for residential places, and local authority social work departments have preferred to see empty beds in voluntary homes than in their own. In 1985 there were under 500 children in care with voluntary organisations compared with over 1,500 in 1980. This has led to new and imaginative intiatives on the part of many voluntary organisations such as fostering and adoption services for children with physical or mental handicaps.

Concurrently with the decline in the numbers of children in residential care there has been an upsurge in the numbers of elderly people needing residential places. In 1985 local authorities provided just over 160 homes catering for nearly 9,000 elderly people who cannot satisfactorily look after themselves or be cared for in the community, but whose condition is supposed not to warrant hospital admission. There are also over 200 registered voluntary homes for the elderly, many of them run by the churches, the clients of which account for more than one-third of all old people in residential care. A new development in the 1980s has been the massive increase in the numbers of private-for-profit nursing and residential homes for the elderly (see chapter 10).

Unlike the other services of the local authority, residential care operates on a round-the-clock basis. Its potential impact on the quality of life of its clients is therefore very great, and it is perhaps the more surprising that it employs such a low proportion of qualified staff.[11] Furthermore, although there are now fewer children in residential care, the proportion with emotional or behavioural problems has increased substantially as have the numbers of physically handicapped or mentally confused residents of old people's homes. It is all the more disturbing therefore that approximately one in three of the officers in charge of both children's homes and old people's homes, and about one-half of their deputies, have no professional qualifications of any kind. While nursing qualifications are fairly common, social work qualifications are distinctly unusual. The emphasis on training for field social work staff has been accompanied until very recently by a neglect of the training needs of the residential services. Salaries and conditions of service are considerably less attractive in the residential and day care sectors so that there is virtualy no inducement for those with a qualification which includes the possibility of fieldwork to move into, or remain in, residential work.

Services for Children

Child care service must figure prominently in any account of the personal social services. The residential provision referred to above is of course a significant component of child care, though most social workers would hold to the view that taking a child into residential care should generally be thought of as a last resort. A considerable amount of skilled social work activity is therefore devoted to efforts to prevent family breakdown with a consequent need for children to be taken into care. Even when a residential solution becomes unavoidable, it is generally hoped that this will be temporary rather than permanent, and a period of intensive work with the parents may be required in the hope of making it possible for the child to return home. Increasingly when children are 'taken into care' they are placed with foster parents whether on a short or long-term basis. If it is clear that a child will not be able to return home, adoptive parents may be sought even for older children. This in turn has meant that residential services are increasingly reserved for children and youngsters whose difficulties, which may well include violent behaviour, make it virtually impossible to find foster families which are able to take them. Clearly this adds to the strain and the demands, both personal and professional, on staff and emphasises the need for the improved training and conditions of service discussed above. A further complication for social work departments is the increase in the numbers of single-parent families as a consequence of higher rates of marital breakdown and divorce, and the growth in the numbers of single mothers who prefer to bring up their own children. Such families often require a good deal of help of many kinds, though it would be optimistic to assume that these needs are always met.[12]

In the most extreme cases children need to be actively protected from one or both of their parents. There has in recent years been an intense development of interest in what is now usually referred to as non-accidental injury or, less euphemistically, 'child abuse'. Every year a number of children die and very many more are injured at the hands of their parents. Social work departments have powers to intervene in cases where it is clear that children are seriously at risk and to take them compulsorily into care. Such cases can be referred to the reporter to the children's panel and brought before a children's hearing. For social work management the problem of child abuse is an extremely sensitive political issue, and there is a tendency to seek safety in laying down elaborate procedural arrangements. Social workers involved in such cases sometimes face real moral dilemmas and they require high levels of professional judgement. This area of work also requires the sharing of information between several agencies – the social work department, health visitors, general practitioners, hospital specialists, the police and voluntary bodies – and the co-ordination of decision-making.[13]

Between 1,500 and 2,000 adoption orders are made each year by the Scottish courts, and in a large proportion of cases important responsibilities fall to the social work department. Investigating applications from prospective adoptive parents, and handling the doubts and guilt feelings of the natural mother, demand both human understanding and professional expertise. In recent years there has been a rapid growth of interest in finding 'new families' for children who have been in residential care. Making suitable arrangements for older or 'hard to place' children – often with physical or mental handicaps – is a complex professional task. In this field, as in many aspects of child care, Barnardo's have been pioneers.

Social Work and Children's Hearings

The children's hearings system is the subject of chapter 7, but here our concern is specifically with the social work contribution to it. Scotland is unusual in having a juvenile justice system that is controlled by social work legislation. Indeed, as has been explained, the proposal to reorganise Scottish social work services on the lines with which we are now familiar was originally a by-product of the Kilbrandon proposals for the replacement of the juvenile courts by a system of children's hearings. Since the latter have as their goal the promotion of the interests of the children who appear before them, and since they deal equally with children in need of care and protection as with those who have committed offences, it would be perfectly justifiable to discuss this aspect of social work practice under the heading of services for children rather than in the context of the justice system. However, it would be hypocritical to pretend that children's hearings have no connection with law enforcement; children who make their appearance there do so under compulsion, and the decisions reached by panel members carry legal force.

Social workers have a number of extremely significant responsibilities in relation to young offenders. When such children are brought to the notice of the reporter he will usually ask the social work department to provide a preliminary social background report; we know from research findings that these reports have an important influence on the reporter when he decides whether or not to bring a child before a hearing. If the reporter decides that the child does indeed appear to be in need of compulsory measures of care, either the same or a new, fuller social background report will be provided for the guidance of the panel members, generally with a recommendation about the disposal of the case. These reports in their turn help to shape discussion in the hearing and also have a good deal of influence on the outcome.

When that outcome is a supervision requirement (as is more often than not the case) social workers are given a central role. The great majority of such supervision orders allow the child to continue to live at home, but social workers may also have to maintain contact with the minority of young people who are required to spend perhaps a year in a List D school. A supervision requirement differs in many ways from a probation order, although the two are often confused. Essentially it is an opportunity for a young person to form a relationship of trust with a social worker, and for the latter to use that relationship to help bring about greater self-awareness and a move towards more mature attitudes and more responsible behaviour. There has in the last few years been a marked interest in developing programmes for young offenders which are somehow more exacting than supervision alone but do not involve removal from home. Many social work departments and voluntary agencies have begun to construct schemes of 'intermediate treatment', as it has come to be called, always involving group activity and ranging from discussion and drama to camping and climbing.[14]

Social Work and the Adult Offender

Social work connections with the sheriff courts are more limited than with children's hearings. When probation orders are made it falls to social work departments to carry them out, but such disposals account for only a very small fraction of sheriff court cases. Some sheriffs regret the demise of a specialised probation service, and are reluctant to involve social workers in duties that many may find uncongenial. The preparation of reports for the courts is, however, a large-scale activity, mainly because the Criminal Justice (Scotland) Act, 1980 requires the courts to obtain reports about young adult offenders (that is under the age of 21) in order to decide whether any method other than detention is appropriate, as well as about older offenders who have not previously been sentenced to imprisonment or detention.[15]

In the search for alternatives to imprisonment, the concept of the community service order has attracted widespread interest. Offenders – usually young adults – may be required to spend a fixed number of hours on some practical, socially constructive task. Several pilot schemes have been established in Scotland. The supervision of community service orders falls to the social work department, and the staff undertaking this work generally specialise in it.

One of the more neglected areas of social work practice is the after-care of discharged prisoners. Once the responsibility of the probation service, it is perhaps a field of work that has suffered more than most from the elimination of a corps of specialists. It is an area of practice with even more than the customary level of disappointment and frustration, and it is not altogether surprising that it receives little priority. Useful work is done by a voluntary body, the Scottish Association for the Care and Rehabilitation of Offenders (SACRO), though inevitably its scale of operation is comparatively small.

Health-Related Social Services

Medical social workers (or almoners as they were previously called) began to be appointed to the staffs of major hospitals before the 1914 war. They were at first largely concerned with the assessment of patients' ability to contribute towards the cost of their treatment, but they became increasingly involved with a wide range of social and domestic problems associated with illness – exclusively so after the creation of the national health service. After the training of psychiatric social workers commenced at the London School of Economics in 1929, some were employed in psychiatric hospitals (which also became part of the NHS) although initially most worked in the newly developing child guidance clinics. For some years social work within the NHS remained separate from the local authority services, and when the latter assumed responsibility in 1975 there was some anxiety that the hospital-based practitioners would all be absorbed into area teams. This has not happened although in most authorities hospital-based workers do have responsibility to their area officer and in many instances share some general duties with area team based staff. They also have responsibility to the medical or psychiatric team within the hospital to which for some their primary sense of loyalty (as opposed to organisational accountability) may well lie.

One setting for social work which many writers believe to have considerable potential but which has not been very highly developed is in health centres. A number of studies have indicated that social workers attached to primary care teams do more than provide a valuable ancillary service for general practitioners; they build up caseloads of individuals with often substantial personal and family problems who are not known to the area social work office and would be unlikely to approach it.[16]

Not all patients leave hospital cured. Many have varying degrees of disability, and usually become the responsibility of the local area social work office rather than of the hospital-based service. The responsibilities of local authorities for people with long-term handicap were strengthened by the Chronically Sick and Disabled Persons Act, 1970 and the Chronically Sick and Disabled Persons (Scotland) Act, 1972. Within the limits of available financial resources social work departments can meet the cost of various adaptations in the home and provide aids to daily living (from handrails to ramps for wheelchairs) as well as pay for telephone installations. The assessment of clients for 'aids and adaptations' is essentially the responsibility of occupational therapists and their aides, with social workers being drawn in only when there seem to be serious housing, financial or domestic problems. Some social workers have become particularly knowledgeable about the complex rules governing the various types of benefits to which disabled people may be entitled.[17] The Disabled Persons (Services, Consultation and Representation) Act, 1986 originated as a private member's bill which was supported, though with significant amendments, by government. This act aims to increase the accountability of local authorities for service provision, encourage consultation with consumers and permit representation when people question the level or quality of services received. The act has still not been fully implemented, however, and it seems unlikely that sufficient resources will be made available to enable local authorities to achieve what is demanded of them.

The role of the personal social services in provision for the mentally ill and mentally handicapped is discussed more fully in chapter 4. Here we may note that although the slower rate of rundown in hospital provision for these client groups in Scotland than in England might have been expected to provide a better opportunity for a compensating build-up of community services, this is not in fact what has happened. The development of community-based mental health and mental handicap services has in reality been extremely slow; it was not until 1981, for example, that an attempt was made to launch the first multi-disciplinary service in Glasgow for severely mentally handicapped children and their families, or that the first hostel for discharged psychiatric patients was opened. Until very recently social work departments had little to offer either the mentally ill or the mentally handicapped, whether as alternatives to institutional care, or by way of supportive services for those leaving hospital or other residential institutions with some degree of residual disability. Considerable strides have been made in a number of areas in recent years, however, particularly with regard to community-based services for mentally handicapped people. Voluntary organisations have also contributed to the development of services; examples include the Richmond Fellowship hostels for psychiatric patients discharged from hospital (although there is only one in Scotland), and Barnardo's Fred Martin project in Glasgow which works to help severely mentally handicapped people move from long-stay hospitals and settle satisfactorily in the community.

Other Aspects of Social Work Practice

Elderly people make up a substantial proportion of the clientele of social work departments, principally when they are isolated, frail or disabled, though frequently they are also poor. Residential provision by local authorities for the elderly has already been mentioned; in addition they are major beneficiaries of the home help service, of various day care services and of the community occupational therapy service. It must be said that they are not the favourite client group of many social workers, who perhaps tend to see them – erroneously – as offering only limited opportunities for achieving significant change. It is striking that when elderly clients become involved with area teams they are generally allocated to untrained social work assistants. Another important reason for this, however, is the overall pressure on limited social work resources, particularly in areas of acute deprivation. When there are not enough staff to respond effectively to all expressions of need, in most if not all departments priority is given to children suffering, or at risk of suffering, physical or sexual abuse. As the numbers of elderly people have increased, however, both in total and as a proportion of the population as a whole, there has also been an increase in resources and interest in work with them. As with provision for mentally handicapped people there have been some imaginative developments over the past few years.

There remains an area of work which is substantial, inevitably poorly defined, and overlapping in varying degrees with the other categories outlined above. It is made up of the miscellaneous requests for advice and assistance that come the way of social work departments. Some of these are misdirected and need only to be rerouted to another agency (for example, the local housing department or DSS office). Others require information or advice, or a straightforward form of help which need not involve any long-term relationship. In other cases, however, the problem may turn out to be complex; it may involve, for instance, negotiations with housing departments or public utilities to stave off eviction or the withdrawal of fuel supplies, some direct financial help in meeting arrears and, where appropriate, the beginning of rather more protracted professional work with the client in the hope of preventing similar crises in the future. Just how frequently the various client groups figure in the collective caseload of local authority social work, what is the time-scale of the services provided in response to their needs, and what proportions of available staff resources are absorbed by each group, are questions that cannot be answered until better statistical information becomes available. Still further questions about comprehensiveness of coverage and about the consequences of social work intervention must remain unanswered until major research studies are undertaken.

Community Work

Most of the activities of social work departments reviewed in this chapter have involved the provision of personal services, whether simple or complex, to individual clients or families. The professional activities usually brought together under the heading of 'community work' do not conform to this pattern, or indeed to the general public image of social work, and therefore merit some special comment. The community worker's focus of interest is most commonly the neighbourhood, with the object of encouraging residents to identify their collective problems and to try and find ways of resolving them. Most community workers – of whom there are now over 200 employed in Scottish social work departments – operate in either run-down inner city areas or deprived council housing schemes. Environmental, economic and personal problems tend to be widespread in these areas and there is little natural sense of interdependence and community identity. Around 1970 community work attracted a number of people with unrealistic, at times almost messianic, expectations of achieving far-reaching changes in the social order. The accumulation of experience, sometimes painful, has made clear the limitations of what can be achieved at the local level, but has also drawn attention to the possibility of bringing about comparatively modest but significant advances in community development. The skills and persistence required are considerable. Although community workers and 'traditional' caseworkers have often seen their respective priorities polarised, there are in fact parallels between their objectives. Both aim to help their clients – whether individuals or community groups – to attain greater insight into the nature of their problems and to mobilise their resources so as to deal more effectively with them. In community work this commonly involves patient discussion with and support of local groups (such as tenants' associations) to assist them to initiate campaigns, for example for housing or environmental improvements, or to establish community industries. While it would be absurd to suppose that most of the problems of deprived areas can be solved within their boundaries, the gains in community integration, self-esteem and self-confidence that good community work can help to bring about may notably strengthen their capacity for survival, even development, in the face of adversity.[18]

THE FUTURE OF THE PERSONAL SOCIAL SERVICES

While many social services, such as health care and social security, are used almost universally, the personal social services directly affect only a minority of the population. It is a minority made up largely of people with the lowest incomes and worst living conditions in our society. If social workers often seem overly passionate advocates of their clients' cause, it is partly because they know that such people do not elicit a great deal of sympathy from within the community at large and command virtually no social or economic power. The personal social services, which grew rapidly in a time of economic expansion and tolerant, liberal attitudes, are particularly vulnerable when the political context changes, public expenditure is closely scrutinised and the level of social generosity may decline.

Yet there is nothing to support the view that the volume of demand is likely to diminish. Indeed, the very shifts in our national economic fortunes that put pressure on local authority and voluntary agency budgets can be seen to generate more problems for the personal social services: more disaffected youths, more offenders, more broken families. The changing age structure of the population is also important and can be predicted with some certainty. The number of people aged over 65 will not vary greatly between now and the end of the century, but within that total the number aged 75 and over in Britain will go up by half a million. Yet the prospect for more than a very modest growth in the personal social services during at least the next few years seems remote.

Perhaps the largest single problem in these circumstances is that of delineating boundaries. In the days before the 1968 act, the specialised departments dealing with different aspects of social welfare were criticised because of their segregation and limited conception of their respective responsibilities. The situation was not without some counter-balancing advantages: specialist workers gained deep experience in their particular areas of responsibility, and lines of communication tended to be well defined. It might be argued that we have now gone to an opposite extreme, and that we have no clear sense of where the responsibilities of the personal social services begin or end. This has made it very difficult to determine priorities rationally in circumstances where demand outstrips the availability of resources, to lay down realistic objectives for social work training courses in terms of the knowledge and skills that newly-qualified workers should possess, or to provide any systematic basis for decisions about appropriate staffing levels. In addition, new legislation has required that additional duties be undertaken; for example, the Mental Health Act, 1983 required that social workers be involved in the process of compulsory admission to hospital and that they undergo additional training. Furthermore, the expectations of society at large seem more pressurising and in some ways more conflicting; for example, social workers should ensure that children at risk of ill-treatment at home should not be left there, while they are also seen as monsters who remove children from their parents.

One particular aspect of the problem of boundaries is that of the relations between the personal social services and other social services. However wide-ranging and ill-defined the role of the personal social services, they remain a departmental function of regional local government. They are therefore clearly separate from the NHS which is outside local government, from housing which is the responsibility of districts rather than regions, and even from education. Although education is also a regional service it may well find itself in competition with social work departments for influence and resources, and possibly at variance with social work in its values. Inescapably, it seems, provision for client groups tends to be considered and planned within the limits of each established service, even though it is impossible to imagine a pattern of comprehensive care for deprived children, the mentally ill, the mentally handicapped, the physically disabled or the high-risk elderly that does not cut across at least one existing service boundary. Exhortations to collaborate are common; examples of successful joint planning and collaborative practice are a good deal harder to find. Central government itself does not set a very good example. Co-operation between services at the local level might be easier to achieve if it could be carried through in the framework of co-ordinated national plans which recognised the interdependence of the separate services. To take a simple example: the home help service makes it possible for many elderly people to remain in their own homes, so that a reduction in that service is very likely to lead to an increase in demand for expensive hospital facilities. No one disputes this, but the different bases of financing make it seem quite reasonable for the social work committee to reduce its costs by throwing an additional burden on the NHS. The government has, however, introduced a system of 'support finance' (joint funding between the health and personal social services) for particular projects. One such project is in the Glasgow area where psychiatric patients are moving out of long-stay hospital to live in the community with, it is to be hoped, sufficient accommodation and supportive services so that their quality of life is enhanced rather than diminished.

Uncertainty about the scope and limits of the social work department is reflected in uncertainty about the knowledge and skills that the individual social worker should possess. Social workers are engaged in tasks that vary greatly in complexity and in the demands made on their expertise and depth of understanding. The mix no doubt varies from area to area, but there are probably few basic grade workers who work only at the high level of professionalism for which their training was intended to equip them.

We need to move towards a more explicit recognition of the fact that the social work department is a multi-purpose social service agency, and that as far as fieldwork is concerned a fair proportion of the public's demand for services can be met by less highly trained personnel. Indeed, the current moves towards 'community social work'[19] in some authorities, and on some training courses, is an attempt to involve residents with professional workers in assessing local needs and finding ways of meeting them. A contribution from local people must not mean simply shifting the burden of care on to them as can happen when such a strategy is attempted without sufficient preparation, skill or resources.

Social workers practise not only at varying levels of sophistication, but also with a considerable variety of client groups. Inevitably, the practice skills, theoretical understanding and legal knowledge needed to work effectively with a client will not be the same in the case of a neglected child, an adolescent persistent offender, a middle-aged housewife with a serious depressive illness or an isolated old man. The temperament and talents of the social worker may also greatly influence preferences for one client group or another. There have been criticisms from many quarters of the lack of that knowledge and experience in depth which collaborators in other professions claim that they used to be able to count upon in the days before it came to be assumed, quite incorrectly, that generic training should necessarily lead to generic practice. Talk of specialisation is now no longer taboo in social work circles, although there are very few within the profession who would seek to return to an era of segregated training and employment. Basic social work training is likely to be seen increasingly as a necessary foundation for practice, but one on which many social workers will wish to build specialist training after acquiring sufficient experience to find out where their own specific talents and interests lie.

At present, however, the Central Council for Education and Training in Social Work has plans to increase the length of basic social work training, requiring a minimum of three years, to ensure more active collaboration between social work authorities and training establishments and to introduce an accreditation requirement for practice teachers. Clearly this would necessitate significant additional resources and in 1988 the government refused to make them available. Many fear that, although the intention is to improve the basic level of training for all workers in an increasingly complex and demanding field, lack of sufficient funding will result in a less effective programme even if it is longer. The plan is that the increased length will allow some specialisation within the basic training. Post-qualifying training is still claimed to be important although it is increasingly being undertaken on an in-service basis. An important reason for this is that it is difficult for potential students to obtain funding to enter an educational establishment or for employers to second them for the necessary period owing to constraints on staffing levels.

Finally, it is worth considering the effectiveness of the personal social services. This is not a simple question. First, there needs to be agreement about objectives. The promotion of social welfare is an aim which may well be interpreted differently by different people. Some, for example, might place a premium on social order and aim for a quiescent populace who accept their place in society as long as they have sufficient to supply basic needs (although even here there can be disagreement as to what constitutes 'basic'). Others, however, might see it as more important that people should be active in social and political life, helping to shape the development of society and of their own lives even though this might lead to more debate and conflict. The same outcome, therefore, would be judged desirable (and therefore effective) by one group and not by the other. Second, there is the question of whose views about effectiveness should be sought. The most obvious group might appear to be those who receive the service but here too there are problems. A child removed from home, for example, might miss her family dreadfully but genuinely benefit in the long run if otherwise she would be sexually abused by her father. On the other hand, someone in very poor circumstances may be so grateful for any alleviation of her circumstances that she may fail to be critical of very real shortcomings in the service provided. In attempting to evaluate outcomes it is only feasible to focus on a small number of factors, but their selection can also have a crucial influence on conclusions about effectiveness. If someone in danger of eviction is helped to pay off her debts, for example, it may be at a very high price in terms of family relationships or even of adequate diet. Investigation of the first factor alone would rate the work done a success whereas such a judgement might be less straightforward if other considerations were taken into account as well.

In spite of these and other problems, considerable progress has been made in developing appropriate research methods.[20] It is arguable, however, that far more systematic investigation is needed into which methods of social work and social care are most likely to achieve intended results. It is difficult to justify the planning and organisation of services on a large scale without a basis of information about how such services work when they have been tried. It is arguable, too, that research findings which are available have not been disseminated or read as widely as would be useful either by practitioners or managers. In response, of course, many social workers would argue that the pressure of day-to-day tasks precludes the pursuit of wider perspectives.

It is clear, however, that, in spite of substantial remaining gaps, enormous strides have been made during the two decades since the personal social services were reorganised with the creation of social work departments. The growth in numbers of staff has been accompanied by the provision in many areas of new and imaginative services. But restrictions on public expenditure place limitations on the expansion in service provision, training and research. It remains to be seen in what ways the personal social services will evolve during the next two decades. Future developments will depend not only on the priorities of central and local government in distributing resources between alternative uses, but also on the skill and imagination exercised by social work departments and their staff in using the available resources to the best advantage of their clients.

References

1. E. Sainsbury, *The Personal Social Services*, Pitman, 1977, p.3
2. For the history of personal social services see: K. Woodroofe, *From Charity to Social Work*, Routledge and Kegan Paul, 1962; and P. Seed, *The Expansion of Social Work in Britain*, Routledge and Kegan Paul, 1973.
3. See for example: E. Younghusband (ed.), *New Developments in Casework*, Allen and Unwin, 1966.
4. *Report of the Committee on Children and Young Persons, Scotland* (Kilbrandon Committee), Cmnd. 2603, HMSO, 1964.
5. *Social Work and the Community*, Cmnd. 3065, HMSO, 1966.
6. *Social Work and the Community*, para 8.
7. For staffing figures see: Social Work Services Group, *Statistical Bulletin: Staff of Scottish Social Work Departments*, Scottish Office, annual.
8. See, for example: R.G.S. Brown, *The Management of Welfare*, Fontana, 1975.
9. R. Hadley and M. McGrath, *Going Local: Neighbourhood Social Services*, Bedford Square Press, 1981.
10. Social Work Services Group, *Statistical Bulletin: Residential Accommodation 1985*, Scottish Office, 1986.
11. See, for example: P. Brearley, *Residential Work with the Elderly*, Routledge and Kegan Paul, 1977; and L. Davis *Residential Care: A Community Resource*, Heinemann, 1982.
12. J. Packman, *The Child's Generation*, Basil Blackwell and Martin Robertson, 1975.
13. C. Hallett and O. Stevenson, *Child Abuse: Aspects of Inter-professional Co-operation*, Allen and Unwin, 1979.
14. F.M. Martin and K. Murray (eds.) *The Scottish Juvenile Justice System*, Scottish Academic Press, 1982 (especially V. Hiddleston, 'Using Reports' and R. Ford 'Consequences').
15. G. Moore and C.J. Wood, *Social Work and Criminal Law in Scotland*, Aberdeen University Press, 1981.
16. J.H. Barber and C.R. Kratz (eds.), *Towards Team Care*, Churchill Livingstone, 1979 (especially J. Ford, 'The Social Worker').
17. See, for example: J. Casserley and B. Clark, *A Welfare Rights Approach to the Chronically Sick and Disabled*, Strathclyde Regional Council, 1978.
18. P. Henderson and D.N. Thomas, *Skills in Neighbourhood Work*, Allen and Unwin, 1981.
19. *Social Workers: their Role and Tasks* (Barclay Report), Bedford Square Press, 1982.
20. E.M. Goldberg and N. Connelly (eds.), *Evaluative Research in Social Care*, Heinemann, 1981.

FURTHER READING

J.D. Cooper, *The Creation of the British Personal Social Services, 1962-74* Heinemann, 1982.

An account of the emergence of unified social services departments in England and Wales and social work departments in Scotland.

M. Davies, *The Essential Social Worker*, Heinemann, 1981.

An interesting and pragmatic review which is described as 'a guide to good practice'.

E.M. Goldberg and R.W. Warburton, *Ends and Means in Social Work*, Allen and Unwin, 1979.

One of the few attempts to analyse systematically the transactions of a social work agency.

C. Hallett, *The Personal Social Services in Local Government*, Allen and Unwin, 1982.

The personal social services are placed in the political and administrative context of the local authority.

E. Sainsbury, *The Personal Social Services*, Pitman, 1977.

A useful general introduction to the personal social services with references to the Scottish situation.

7
CHILDREN'S HEARINGS

The emergence and development of a separate juvenile system may be seen simply as one strand in a growing recognition of social welfare objectives in public policy during the late nineteenth and twentieth centuries. Changing beliefs about the nature of youth and its problems have been, however, an important set of specific influences. Within early industrial society children were viewed as miniature adults and those who broke the law were subject to adult procedures and penalties. Their cheap labour was a source of wealth, and protection by the state from abuse and neglect was virtually unknown. Gradually children came to be seen as individuals with needs and rights of their own, and as personalities still in the process of development. Society's increasing concern for their welfare was reflected in new approaches to child offenders, while new theories of criminality also influenced penal policy. The emphasis on adverse life experiences as predisposing factors gave added impetus to the move away from punitive attitudes and towards an increased recognition of the scope for reform and prevention. The new disciplines of psychiatry and psychoanalysis highlighted the importance of childhood experiences in the development of the personality and redrew the picture of the child offender as someone needing help and support.

Changing policy towards juvenile delinquents was gradually reflected in the segregation of children from adults in prisons, in the provision of separate institutions where children would receive appropriate training and education, and in the scaling down of certain offences committed by juveniles to a less serious category. But the most significant development was the provision in the Children Act, 1908 for a separate system of juvenile courts. Clearly the emphasis on punishment was beginning to shift towards a policy aimed at reform or, considerably more recently, prevention.

CHANGES IN LEGISLATION 1908-87

While the creation of juvenile courts proved an important landmark, it gradually became clear that children were not receiving the special consideration which their situation demanded. The 1908 act made no provision for the selection of special justices to sit in juvenile courts and by the 1920s this had come to be regarded as a major weakness. Following their review of the treatment of young offenders, the Morton Committee[1] recommended that jurisdiction over children and young persons be transferred to separately constituted juvenile courts conducted by justices with knowledge and experience of juvenile cases. The committee also recommended that the age of criminal responsibility, which under common law was seven years, be raised to eight. These recommendations were given effect in the Children and Young Persons (Scotland) Act, 1932. The welfare of the child was expressly stated to be one of the major objectives of the juvenile court. Separate juvenile courts were introduced in the counties of Ayr, Fife and Renfew and in the city of Aberdeen but they covered only 16 per cent of the juveniles coming before the courts of Scotland.

During the 1940s social reforms were aimed increasingly at the welfare of children and the improvement of relevant public services. The reports of the Clyde Committee[2] in Scotland and the Curtis Committee[3] in England resulted in the Children Act, 1948 which created local authority children's departments with an obligation to consider the needs of children in their care. The problem of the neglected child and of the young offender were seen as being rooted in broadly similar circumstances, and it was felt that efforts to prevent neglect could also lead to the prevention of delinquency.

During the 1950s the incidence of social problems generally and of crime and delinquency in particular became a matter of increasing public concern. Successive governments set up a series of committees to look into the problems of youth, the management of delinquency and the need for personal social services. The work of the Ingleby[4] and McBoyle[5] committees was followed by the Children and Young Persons Act, 1963 which placed a duty on local authorities to give such advice, guidance and assistance as was necessary to keep young offenders out of court; but no changes were made to the structure and procedure of the juvenile court.

The Kilbrandon Committee

In 1961 the Secretary of State for Scotland appointed a committee under the chairmanship of Lord Kilbrandon to review the arrangements for dealing with juvenile delinquents and juveniles in need of care or protection. The committee's remit was:

> To consider the provisions of the law of Scotland relating to the treatment of juvenile delinquents and juveniles in need of care or protection or beyond parental control and, in particular, the constitution, powers and procedure of the courts dealing with such juveniles, and to report.

The findings were published in 1964. The committee began with the assumption that children appearing before the juvenile court, whether for offences or as being in need of care or protection, were all exhibiting symptoms of the same difficulties. These were felt to arise from a failure in the upbringing process – in the home, in the family environment and in the school. The committee chose to approach these problems by 'social education' which would involve working closely with the parents in order to strengthen 'those natural influences for good which will assist the child's development into a mature and useful member of society'.[6]

The committee found that the existing juvenile court arrangements failed to give full effect to the educational principle. They proposed instead a separate structure for each of the court's dual functions – determining guilt or innocence and making decisions about treatment. This would involve removing all juveniles under the age of 16, except those who committed serious offences, from the jurisdiction of the criminal courts and bringing them before 'juvenile panels'. (The term 'panel' was used to describe both the lay body authorised to deal with juvenile offenders, and the group of three persons drawn from an area list on any given occasion.) Disputed issues of the fact would be settled by a court of law and not by panels.

The White Paper and the 1968 Act

In 1966 a series of proposals for legislation was set out in a white paper.[7] While this accepted the principles of the children's panel system and most of the Kilbrandon Committee's detailed recommendations on machinery, it did in one important sense reverse the priorities. Instead of a specialised family casework service set up within the education authority, the white paper proposed the creation of a comprehensive social work department which would among many other functions provide support for the children's panels (see chapter 6).

The white paper also significantly broadened the basis of panel membership. The Kilbrandon Committee had intended this non-legal body to be comprised of 'persons who either by knowledge or experience were considered to be specially qualified to consider children's problems'. The white paper advocated drawing members from a wide variety of occupation, neighbourhood, age and income groups as well as those whose circumstances had hitherto prevented them from taking a formal part in helping and advising young people.

The new method of dealing with children in need of compulsory measures of care proposed by the Kilbrandon Committee and endorsed in the white paper appeared as Part III of the Social Work (Scotland) Act, 1968. The reformed system came into force in 1971. It thus took an entire decade from the time the Kilbrandon Committee was appointed to the inception of the new system. A few amendments have been made by subsequent legislation but the legal and administrative framework remains in all important respects that of the 1968 act (and the Children's Hearings (Scotland) Rules, 1971 made under it). A continuing oversight of the system is exercised by the Secretary of State for Scotland through the Social Work Services Group, a specialised sub-department of the Scottish Education Department.

Developments in England and Wales

At this point it may be interesting to note the changes that were occurring at the same time in England and Wales. The Children and Young Persons Act,

1969 also endorsed a social welfare approach to children who offend. This was preceded by a number of committee reports. First, the Ingleby Committee was set up in 1956 to inquire into the operation of the juvenile court and to make recommendations for its improvement. The committee recognised the conflict between the court's judicial and welfare functions but still argued in favour of its retention. It recommended raising the age of criminal responsibility from eight to twelve and below that age replacing criminal proceedings with care and protection proceedings. These recommendations did not become law except that under the Children and Young Persons Act, 1963 the age of criminal responsibility was raised to ten in England and Wales.

While in opposition the Labour Party set up a study group which produced radical proposals with some similarity to Kilbrandon's ideas. As an alternative to the juvenile court this suggested a 'family service' in which the child, family and social worker would discuss the treatment of the child and only where agreement could not be reached or where the facts of the case were disputed would the child be referred to a new 'family court'. Shortly after the formation of the 1964 Labour government a white paper[8] was published which followed the ideas of the study group except that the 'family service' was replaced by a 'family council' consisting of social workers and other persons selected for their understanding and experience of children. This was strongly opposed by the lay magistrates and the probation service. The family council was itself abandoned by the 1968 white paper[9] which retained the juvenile court and formed the basis of the Children and Young Persons Act, 1969.

Had the 1969 act been fully implemented criminal proceedings for offenders under the age of 14 would have been prohibited, and for those between 14 and 17 would have been possible only after mandatory consultation between the police and local authority social services departments. The minimum age qualification for a borstal offence would have been 17 rather than 15, while detention centres and attendance centres would have been phased out. Because of a change of government in 1970 these features of the act never came into operation. However, social workers were given the power to vary, as well as responsibility for implementing, orders made by the courts. Magistrates were no longer involved in detailed decisions about the kind of treatment appropriate for the child. Thus, although the composition and constitution of the juvenile court were virtually unchanged, its jurisdiction was radically altered.

Both policies and practices in England and Wales have been repeatedly under attack since the 1970s. A major phenomenon has been the increase in the number of juveniles sentenced to custody in detention centres and borstals. Between 1965 and 1979 the number so sentenced rose five-fold. Less than a fifth of the rise can be attributed to increased offending; the remainder was caused by an increased tendency to give custodial sentences for almost all types of offence. This outcome of the 1969 act as much as any other factor prompted a general rethinking of the problem of juvenile offending. When the Conservative administration came into office in 1979 they immediately made plans for firmer measures to deal with young people who break the law. They were particularly alive to the fact that the criminal justice system was not responding well to the problem of young offenders, and that the judiciary did not feel they had the right powers to deal with those coming before them. The result was the 1980 white paper[10] which was followed by the Criminal Justice Act, 1982. This increased the range of custodial measures available to magistrates for children over the age of 15, restored their power to commit children to residential care and also gave them additional powers in relation to supervision.

An issue currently under discussion in England and Wales is the possible creation of a unified 'family court', first proposed in 1974 by the Finer Committee.[11] This was the subject of a consultation paper from the Lord Chancellor's Department in 1986.[12] While it is generally felt that the unification of all family and domestic matters is long overdue, some concern has been expressed about the fate of juvenile offenders if care and criminal proceedings were to be separated. However, in the present political and economic climate it is thought unlikely that changes will be made to the criminal proceedings of the juvenile court.

THE STRUCTURE AND OPERATION OF THE CHILDREN'S HEARINGS SYSTEM

Three agencies can be identified as the principal components of the hearings system: the reporter, the children's panel and the social work department. Of these the office of reporter and the children's panel itself were created solely as instruments of the new system. The police are of course quite independent of the hearings system but it need scarcely be said that the functioning of the system is heavily dependent on their co-operation.

The Reporter

The reporter is the administrator of the hearings system, its adviser on matters of law and procedure, and also a decision-maker with considerable discretionary powers. The 1968 act provides that 'Where any person has reasonable cause to believe a child may be in need of compulsory measures of care he may give to the reporter such information about the child as he may be able to discover'. Referrals come from police and procurators fiscal (80 per cent), from education departments (11 per cent) and social work departments (6 per cent) of local authorities, and also from other sources such as voluntary bodies and private individuals. Children are referred if they are alleged to have committed an offence, on grounds of truancy, if they are believed to have been neglected or harmed by their parents, because of solvent abuse, or if they are in the care of the local authority and special measures of care and control are needed. (The last was introduced under the Health and Social Services and Social Security Adjudications Act, 1983 which brought in provisions to safeguard the rights of a child placed in secure accommodation.)

After investigating the referral by inviting reports from the social work department and from the child's school the reporter can decide:

1. to take no further action; or
2. to ask the social work department to advise, guide and assist the child and family on a voluntary basis; or
3. to bring the child before a children's hearing if (i) he is satisfied that there is sufficient evidence of at least one ground for referral, and (ii) it appears to him that the child is in need of compulsory measures of care.[13]

The reporter refers only about a half of all juvenile offenders to a hearing, and of those reported to him for the first time the proportion referred is only 25 per cent. His effectiveness as an intake official depends on his skill in assessing social and other evidence, on his links with statutory and voluntary agencies and on his legal abilities. In the 12 regional and islands authorities the 93 posts for reporters and their deputies are filled largely by personnel with legal or social work backgrounds. No official requirements are laid down: the Secretary of State is empowered to prescribe the qualifications necessary for reporters but has not so far chosen to do so.

The Children's Panel

The children's panel exists to provide the members of children's hearings. It is a striking example of voluntary activity which currently involves some 1,700 people, ranging from approximately 800 in Strathclyde to nine in Orkney. In each region and islands authority members of the children's panel are appointed by the Secretary of State from a list of applicants who have been nominated by the children's panel advisory committee (CPAC), a committee created for the main purpose of recruiting and selecting panel members, although more recently it has started to monitor the standards of practice in hearings. Each CPAC can consist of up to ten members (15 in Strathclyde Region): at least half, including the chairman, are nominated by the Secretary of State. Generally appointments to a panel are made for a five year period but a few regions make them for two or three years. Appointments may be renewed on the recommendation of the CPAC but rarely continue beyond a total of ten years.

The aim of the recruitment and selection process is to achieve within each panel a blend of members with appropriate personal characteristics and a proper mix of community representation. There is an approximate balance of the sexes and an age range from about 20 to the maximum of 60. In the early stages there were some criticisms about the composition of panels. True community representation is difficult to achieve, lower income groups and manual occupations being particularly hard to recruit. Considerable efforts have been made to increase panel membership among manual workers. It may, however, be unrealistic to suppose that perfect representativeness can ever be achieved.

It is at least equally important that the selection procedure identifies people with the personal qualities needed to meet the heavy demands made upon them. They must be able to maintain an informal atmosphere during hearings while keeping to the detailed rules of procedure that have been laid down; they must deal responsively and coolly with information that is often sensitive and sometimes disturbing; and they must be competent to take decisions that can have serious implications for the lives of the families concerned. It is therefore essential to recruit people with a genuine concern for the welfare of children and who are free from extreme attitudes of either punitiveness or permissiveness.

Since the inception of the system considerable importance has also been attached to the training of panel members; all are required to attend a period of part-time training before commencing service and are encouraged to undergo regular in-service training thereafter. Training is at present organised by four university-based tutors, who are each responsible for a local authority region or group of regions. Over the years there has been an increasing emphasis given in training to the development of practice skills which will enable panel members to communicate more effectively with the family in the hearing and to make constructive use of professional advice in their decision-making.

The Social Work Department

The social work department was also created by the 1968 act. In each local authority area it took over responsibility for the personal social services formerly provided under the auspices of health, welfare and children's committees and for the work of the probation service (see chapter 6). Since the children's hearings system was initiated one of the major commitments of the department has been to work in close conjunction with hearings. It provides background reports on children and undertakes the supervision of those judged by the hearings to be in need of 'compulsory measures of care'. This responsibility applies whether the child is under supervision at home or in a residential establishment. Some children are also supervised on a voluntary basis. Reporters currently send about five per cent of all children referred to them to the social work department for voluntary supervision. It is possible that reporters would make more frequent use of voluntary supervision if social work departments were under less pressure; as matters now stand it often seems unlikely that active supervision can be expected unless a compulsory order is made by a hearing.

The number of qualified social workers has increased very substantially since the inception of the children's hearings system (see chapter 6) but so have competing demands on their time. Whether there has been a corresponding improvement in the quality of the services provided to children's hearings is not a matter on which there is any evidence.

JURISDICTION

Jurisdiction is limited to children under 16 years who commit offences, truant, fall into bad associations or whose environment is deemed to be unhealthy. Care and protection cases between 16 and 18 years remain within the jurisdiction of children's hearings if they are already the subject of a supervision requirement. Before 1982 this provision also applied to offenders but the Lord Advocate instructed procurators fiscal to take steps to bring all offenders over 16 before the courts unless there are special circumstances indicating that they should be dealt with by hearings. The Lord Advocate retains the power to direct the prosection of children of any age in serious cases. These cases are taken in the sheriff court or High Court and generally involve offences against the person except where a court hearing is technically necessary for proof (as in some cases where offences have been committed jointly with adults).

The children's hearing cannot proceed unless jurisdiction is established. If the grounds are not accepted by the child and parent, or if the child is unable to understand the grounds, the case must be dismissed or sent to the sheriff court for proof. The reporter has authority to abandon the referral but should he proceed and the sheriff finds it established the case will return to a hearing for consideration. Before reaching a decision the hearing considers the grounds for referral and reports obtained from the social work department and other sources. After careful discussion with the family, the hearing must decide on the course of action which is in the best interests of the child.

Challenges to the jurisdiction of a children's hearing are relatively infrequent. The Kilbrandon Committee was encouraged to develop the concept of a decision-making body which did not concern itself with guilt or innocence by the fact that some 95 per cent of children who appeared before the former juvenile courts entered a plea of guilty. Since the establishment of the hearings system, the proportion of children who deny the grounds for referral has generally been in the region of ten per cent. In the majority of such cases the matter is referred to the sheriff. Broadly speaking, sheriffs have agreed in about two-fifths of all such denials that the grounds for referral should be abandoned.

STATISTICAL PATTERNS

Statistics relating to the children's hearings system are published annually by the Social Work Services Group from records submitted by reporters. Table 7.1 shows, for each of the fourteen years 1972-85, the number of children coming into the system, the number of reports received by reporters in respect of these childen, the percentage of reports referred to hearings and their subsequent disposals.

Referrals to Reporters

Since a child may be referred to the reporter on more than one occasion in any year, the number of reports is greatly in excess of the number of separate children reported. The number both of children and of reports shows an increase between 1972 and 1974, followed by a marked decline over the period

TABLE 7.1:

Children Dealt with by Reporters and Hearings, 1972-85

	Total children reported*	Number of reports received	Reports referred to hearings %	Home supervision requirements (in relation to cases referred) %	Residential requirements (in relation to cases referred) %
1972	17,950	24,219	52	50	14
1973	21,017	29,566	51	47	12
1974	21,907	31,876	48	48	11
1975	22,207	30,022	49	42	13
1976	18,638	29,514	53	38	16
1977	18,537	28,551	53	39	16
1978	17,308	26,583	53	38	16
1979	16,924	25,842	53	38	16
1980	19,035	28,950	53	38	25
1981	20,111	30,786	51	37	14
1982	19,017	29,226	49	35	13
1983	19,365	30,071	46	38	13
1984	19,529	31,595	47	39	14
1985	21,108	34,151	45	42	13

* Children (of all ages) in respect of whom one or more reports were received during the year.

Source: Social Work Services Group, *Statistical Bulletin: Referrals of Children to Reporters and Children's Hearings, 1985.*

1975-79 and by a further increase during 1980-85 (except for 1982 when there was a slight decrease). The number of referrals recorded in 1985 (34,151) was the highest figure since the system began, and the rate of referral per 1,000 population of children in that year (19.4) was also well above previous levels. When there has been a decline in the number of children referred it has been rather more rapid than the decline in the number of referrals in the same year, while increases in the number of children referred have been less rapid than increases in the number of referrals. This implies a steady increase in the average number of referrals per child in a calendar year.

While the police continue to be the main source of reports, the proportion of cases referred by them decreased from 88 per cent in 1972 to 59 per cent in 1981 where it has since remained. This fall has to some extent been balanced by a corresponding increase in the number of referrals being routed through procurators fiscal rather than coming direct from the police. Offences are the grounds of referral to reporters in as many as 74 per cent of cases, while truancy grounds amount to 11 per cent of the total, grounds where the child is alleged to be beyond control or to be in moral danger to three per cent, grounds of solvent abuse to two per cent and those relating to non-accidental injury to ten per cent. The number of non-offence referrals shows the greatest increase in recent years: since 1982 these have risen by 39 per cent compared with an increase of 11 per cent in offence referrals.

Boys very substantially outnumber girls, and about 60 per cent of all referrals to reporters concern boys in the 12-15 age group. The predominance of boys is largely confined to offence referrals.

Referrals by Reporters to Hearings

When cases have been referred to reporters, they must decide whether to refer them to hearings. Between 1972 and 1974 the rate of referral of cases by reporters to hearings for Scotland as a whole fell from 52 per cent to 48 per cent, it then rose slightly and from 1976 to 1980 remained steady at 53 per cent. Since 1981 the rate has fallen steadily, reaching in 1985 the lowest rate (45 per cent) since the system started. There are, however, considerable regional variations, which may be explained by differences between reporters in the use made of informal supervision arrangements and of police warning schemes.

Striking differences are also recorded in the use made by hearings of different dispositions. During the first three years of operation the proportion placed on compulsory home supervision remained constant while residential requirements decreased. After 1974 a decrease in home supervision was accompanied by an increasing proportion of residential requirements until 1978 when the latter began to fall; this downward trend in the use of residential supervision has continued, particularly in care and protection cases for which community provision is favoured.

As mentioned above, not all young offenders find their way to hearings. In 1985 more than 700 children were prosecuted in court. Sheriffs have the power and, when a child is already on supervision, a duty to ask for the advice of a hearing on the disposition of a case although they are not obliged to take it. In 1985 Scottish courts made 643 references to hearings for advice and remitted 192 cases for disposal by a hearing.

POWERS

The powers of children's hearings are strictly limited. They are not empowered to send the child to prison or a detention centre, or to impose a fine or any other financial penalty. The decisions open to a hearing are:

1. to discharge the referral which means that the child goes home and no further contact is made;
2. to make a supervision order which means that the child is not taken away from home but is required to remain under the supervision of a social worker; or
3. to make a residential supervision order which requires the child to enter a specified residential school or home.

If a supervision requirement is made, whether in an institution or in the community, it must be reviewed within a year and can be reviewed at any time if this is requested by the social worker, the parent or the child himself.

The child or his parents may appeal to the sheriff against the decision of a hearing and, from him, on a point of law or irregularity, to the Court of Session. Between 20 and 30 appeals are heard in a typical year, and in these cases it is unusual – but not unknown – for a sheriff to overturn an order made by a hearing. It is important that child and parents should be advised of their right to appeal and of the availability of legal aid. (Since children's hearings are classified as tribunals legal aid is not available for the hearing itself.)

In 1981 the Secretary of State for Scotland announced the outcome of a major consultative exercise on the powers and procedures of children's hearings.[14] While rejecting the introduction of punitive measures he did suggest alterations with the intention of creating a broader framework for the activities of children's panel members. The changes which have been introduced are an extension to the grounds of referral so as to bring children who engage in potentially dangerous practices such as solvent abuse to the attention of the reporter (Solvent Abuse (Scotland) Act, 1983); and bringing all offenders over 16 before the courts unless there are special circumstances indicating that they should be brought before hearings. Other proposed changes have been ignored or abandoned, such as the suggestion that hearings should be encouraged to use voluntary reparation as a suitable method of treatment, and giving hearings the power to suspend the decision on a case for up to six months and to order the forfeiture of weapons used in the commission of offences.

Since 1984 children's hearings have been empowered to authorise a child's detention in secure accommodation either on warrant or as a condition of a residential supervision requirement.[15] Before making this condition the children's hearing must be satisfied either that the child has a history of absconding and is likely to continue to abscond unless kept in secure accommodation, and if he absconds it is likely that his physical, mental or moral welfare will be at risk; or, alternatively, that he is likely to injure himself or other persons unless he is kept in secure accommodation. When such a supervision requirement is made it must be reviewed at more regular intervals than normal supervision requirements and an automatic review must take place within three months of the last hearing. In 1985 there were 81 secure accommodation authorisations as a condition of a residential supervision requirement.

Under an amendment to the Children Act, 1975 made in 1985 the chairman of a children's hearing is empowered, in circumstances where he believes there to be an actual or potential conflict of interest between child and parent, to appoint a person - now identified as a 'safeguarder' – specifically to represent the interests of the child. In the first twelve months 89 safeguarders were appointed by the sheriff court and 40 by children's hearings but it is too early to say how this new provision is working out in practice.

None of these changes alters the welfare principles on which the hearings system is based but how effectively the new powers are used depends on the readiness of panel members to develop their practice skills and to deepen their understanding of the families they serve.

CURRENT ISSUES

The children's hearings system has, since its inception, given rise to extensive debate in Scotland and at the same time has aroused sympathetic interest on an international scale. In the early years, a good deal of adverse and often abusive criticism was expressed by people who were opposed to the whole idea of a non-punitive approach to young offenders, and any reported increase in the number of children referred to reporters was likely to be interpreted as evidence of the system's failure. Although by the late 1970s the hostility had abated, that did not mean that everyone in Scotland was fully attuned to or in complete sympathy with the welfare philosophy of children's hearings. But it does seem that 'the panel' had become a settled part of the scene, and even the return to power in 1979 of a Conservative government pledged to take firm measures in support of 'law and order' did not, in the event, lead to any significant changes in the structure or the powers of the established system.

During the first decade the discussion of the principles and practice of children's hearings was largely based on tentative knowledge gained by subjective and unrepresentative personal observation and experience. Thereafter, information derived from systematic research[16] has contributed an increased understanding of how the system works and a framework of empirical findings within which the case for development in policy, practice and training could be argued.

A number of the issues currently under discussion stem from new legislative or administrative decisions while others arise from the rapidly changing social and economic context in which the system operates.

The Best Interests of the Child

If the overriding concern of the hearings system is with the interests of the children who enter it, there are a number of complex questions to be faced about the best ways of identifying and advancing those interests. When the system was being planned, it was widely believed that it would bring as many children as possible before hearings; if what they had to offer was beneficial, it made sense for those benefits to be widely distributed. Fairly rapidly, however, an alternative viewpoint began to develop: that many early offenders had sufficient supports in their background to protect them from getting involved in a long-term delinquent career, and that in the cases of such children there was a lot to be said for keeping formal intervention to a minimum.

As indicated earlier, about half of all the offence cases referred to the reporter, and about three-quarters of those who come to his notice for the first time, have no further action taken. A substantial number of young offenders are thus being diverted from even the relatively informal proceedings of a children's hearing. The important thing to note about this is that three out of every four children so diverted do not come to the notice of the reporter on a subsequent occasion. It can be said therefore that reporters have developed considerable skill in identifying those children who have a good chance of getting through a patch of delinquent behaviour without recourse to compulsory measures of care.

When a child does come before a hearing, the sole concern of the panel members should be that child's need for care. The 1968 act defines care as including 'protection, guidance, treatment and control'. Unlike judges and English magistrates, panel members are not responsible for the protection of society in general. Neither are they supposed to be concerned with punishment. The aim of 'compulsory measures of care' is not to cause pain of any kind but to help the child develop more mature and socially constructive ways of living and of relating to others. The measures may indeed sometimes be experienced as restrictive, even as painful, but this is not the intention; the objective is to re-educate and rehabilitate, not to punish.

Of the alternatives open to children's hearings, only the residential supervision order, involving as it does compulsory removal from home, enforced intimacy with strangers and a more or less disciplined regime, could be seen as having punitive possibilities if punishment were the intention. The research evidence, however, leaves little doubt that with rare exceptions panel members see List D schools (formerly 'approved schools') as means of social education to be used sparingly, indeed reluctantly, as a last resort when home supervision has indisputably failed and parents are manifestly unable to cope. It is seen as a notable achievement that in 1987 the number of residents in List D schools was less than half the number recorded six years previously. Remarkably, the situation is different in England and Wales, where legislation intended to reduce the orientation of the juvenile court towards punishment appears to have led to a sharp increase in the number of children in custodial institutions.

The task of adapting the limited number of disposals available to panel members to the needs of individual children is a challenging one. Even when the members at a hearing are reasonably confident about a child's needs, they may be quite impotent when it comes to meeting them: 'no juvenile justice system, however sincere its commitment to welfare principles, can possibly meet all the needs of the children who come before it. Panel members cannot make poor children rich or substitute caring and competent for inadequate and neglectful parents'.[17] To a substantial extent this is also true of many other problems which may impede the satisfactory development of children. Since new, non-punitive powers are hard to come by there is a pressing need for greater inventiveness in the use of those powers that now exist. Home supervision in particular is too frequently identified in only the most general terms; it should often be possible to consider with the social worker in the case the specific objectives to be pursued and the styles of supervision to be employed. 'Intermediate treatment' covers a variety of group activities, and panel members should have sufficient knowledge of the provisions available to be able to recommend types of programme that they believe will be helpful in the individual case. Potential foster home placements should be carefully scrutinised and access arrangements checked. Residential establishments should offer, and be known to offer, a wide range of environments and opportunities, and be selected for their appropriateness.

It is clear that panel members in all their work with children depend heavily on the social work profession. Social workers are responsible for the preparation of reports on the children and their circumstances, and they also take on their supervision when the hearings decide that this would be an appropriate course of action. But reports vary greatly in quality. Important areas are sometimes omitted, and they seem too often to have been constructed with an insufficient awareness of the needs of those who will make use of them. Although there is very little systematic information about the quality of social work supervision, there is a widespread belief that its quality also differs from area to area and from one practitioner to another. Social workers tend to be burdened by heavy case loads so that new supervision orders or requests for reports must be weighed against competing demands on their time by a multiplicity of clients with needs that seem no less pressing.

Decisions and their Outcomes

Most panel members have a clear idea of what both home and residential supervision ought to achieve, but are astonishingly lacking in curiosity as to what extent the desired ends are in fact achieved. Although it is well known that more than 60 per cent of children placed on supervision make a subsequent entry into the system on new grounds of referral, and that over 70 per cent of those sent to List D school commit further offences, it remains a mystery why both forms of supervision are successful in some cases and not in others. Some styles of supervision may be more effective than others, or the differences in outcome may be related to particular aspects of the child or family, or to some interaction between the latter and factors in the supervision process. Perhaps changes occurred in the children as a consequence of the supervision process that might provide a better or at least an alternative criterion of success to the simple absence of recidivism. Such knowledge if it were available could provide an opportunity to improve the quality of decisions in future cases. Unless panel members know what they are trying to achieve in every compulsory intervention in children's lives, the 'best interest' principle is rapidly debased to the level of an empty and dishonest slogan.

Good intentions are necessary but not sufficient. There needs also to be a confident expectation that within the limits of uncertainty attached to all human enterprises they can be achieved. In addition, there must be a critical awareness of the possibility of unplanned and unintended consequences of a harmful nature. The first consideration raises the whole question of the professional resources available to the hearings system. This has almost always been treated simply as a quantitative issue. When panel members or others have complained about the quality or lateness of reports, the explanations offered have been in terms of the heavy pressure of demands on the services of the social work department and the need for additional resources. But there are more complex questions about the organisation and deployment of the human resources of a multi-purpose social work agency which are constantly evaded. The capacity to carry out effective supervision rests upon an understanding of the principles of the hearings system, a serious grasp of the problems of personal development in late childhood and adolescence in their social context, and not least on an ability to develop appropriate relationships with often difficult children and parents under compulsory conditions. By no means all social workers can meet these requirements; this is neither surprising nor shameful when one considers not merely the scale but the extraordinary variety of demands made upon them. The basic question is not whether children under supervision always receive services of high quality, but whether any group of clients does when the same workers are expected to respond to all of them. The time is ripe for serious debate on the limits of generic practice in social work and on possible alternative approaches to the training and deployment of practitioners.

There remains the matter of unintended consequences. This refers not so much to the question of labelling, in the sense of the development of a deviant sense of personal identity, as there is reasonably good evidence that children's hearings have minimally damaging effects of that kind,[18] but to the more obvious stigma resulting from the acceptance of offence grounds of referral and the subsequent hearing disposition. Most children believe they will be disadvantaged in their future relations with the police and with potential employers, and they may well be right. For the purpose of the Rehabilitation of Offenders Act, 1974 even a discharge decision by a hearing must be reckoned as a conviction, which may not be concealed from enquiring employers for a defined period (or in the case of certain categories of employment at any time in the future). The conflict between this ruling and the philosophy of the hearings system is intensified by the fact that children with trivial offences and serious family problems are more likely to be referred to a hearing than those with weightier offences and comparatively secure backgrounds.

The Rights of the Child

During recent years there has been increased concern over the definition and protection of the legal rights of children. As part of the post-war movement to codify international norms and to create mechanisms to encourage their observance, a variety of international documents addressing the issue of children's rights has emerged. These include treaties legally binding nations all over the world, such as the International Covenant on Civil and Political Rights (1976), and regional treaties like the European Convention on Human Rights (1950), as well as non-binding but highly influential instruments such as the United Nations Universal Declaration of Human Rights (1948), the Declaration of the Rights of the Child (1959), and the Standard Minimum Rules for the Administration of Juvenile Justice (1985). These and similar documents reflect an international consensus on children's rights in the administration of justice. In particular, the forthcoming

Convention on the Rights of the Child will create a new set of legally binding principles against which the hearings system may be tested.

There is a familiar argument that a lack of concern for legal safeguards is an inevitable corollary of a welfare-oriented approach to juvenile justice. According to this viewpoint, the temptation to assume control of young offenders' destinies, doubtless with benevolent intentions, is so powerful that legal protections are perceived as irritating and irrelevant obstacles, to be ignored or circumvented whenever it seems necessary. The most recent research evidence available[19] points to a significant proportion of hearings falling short of the by no means excessively demanding standards of procedure laid down in the 1968 act and the Hearing Rules. But the research evidence shows also that hearings are not incapable of maintaining the legal rights of children. Some hearings are impeccable in their adherence to the rules of procedure and, far from being stilted and formal, these same hearings are often the most successful in achieving a high level of family participation.

Full involvement of the child and his parents in the proceedings of the hearing is an important goal of the system. Research findings show clearly that a notable measure of success is achieved in involving family members in the hearing discussion, helping them to overcome their anxieties, defensiveness and lack of self-confidence, and occasionally even opening up sensitive and stressful areas of family life for honest examination. Children and parents in general respond very favourably, and see the panel members as genuinely interested in what they have to say, as trying to help them and as treating them with courtesy and respect. An honest exchange makes it easier for the hearing to assess what the child's needs are, and makes it possible to involve the family in the process of reaching a decision, so that at the end they too will agree that what is being done is in the child's best interests.

For the most part, however, discussion in hearings is contained within limits that exclude highly emotive areas. We know from research evidence that discussion is significantly influenced by the information contained in the social work, educational and other reports which are made available to the panel members in the case three days before the hearing. In general, references in reports to aspects of the child's home and school life provide conversational gambits; but when social background reports draw attention to specific domestic problems of a serious nature – psychiatric illness in a parent, a criminal record or a history of violent behaviour – the references act instead as danger signals. Anxious to avoid what they see as stressful and potentially damaging confrontation with parents, panel members shift rapidly to the firmer ground of the child's school attendance and leisure pursuits.

Entering into and maintaining a dialogue in which one participant is confronted with his own shortcomings calls for great skill and self-confidence, and we should not be surprised if panel members shrink from such a task, settle for superficial topics of conversation, and sometimes even appear to collude with parents against the child. Yet in doing so they are contradicting their own belief that parental failure and family breakdown are causal factors in delinquency. Perhaps most important, they may be missing an opportunity to prepare the way for the supervision process. Most social workers see supervision as requiring work with the whole family and not merely with the delinquent child, but few parents on emerging from the hearing would imagine that the process has any connection with them.

It is frequently asserted that since the publication of these research findings in 1981 there has been a marked improvement in the standard of procedural conformity in children's hearings. These claims, however, still need to be confirmed by the results of further systematic research.

Political Hazards

It is commonly assumed that the principal obstacle to reform of the juvenile justice system is the pressure of conservative opinion, both at the overtly political level and in the sense of a public opinion imbued with moral panic and heavily disposed towards rigorous law enforcement and harsh penalties. The possibility of a major assault on the children's hearings system from the assertive spokesmen for 'law and order' is not inconceivable. The outcome to the 1981 consultative exercise reflects a liberal climate which is less in evidence today. If high levels of unemployment continue, there might be a growth of disaffection and alienation among young people who see no future for themselves, with a consequent increase in law breaking. Economic pressures also tend to create intolerance and prejudice, and there is a distinct possibility that children's hearings could again come under fire from the exponents of harsh punishment. Some protection might be afforded if those identified with the hearings system were in a position to make an estimate of its overall impact on delinquency. It may be necessary only to demonstrate the effectiveness of hearings is no lower than that of other juvenile justice systems.

It would, however, be an error to suppose that courts and sentencing tariffs are preferred only by critics on the right of the political spectrum. The 'progressive' advocates of the 'Justice for Children' movement,[20] which embraces both libertarianism and formalism, have over the past decade expressed strong opposition to the employment of welfare principles in juvenile justice on the grounds that they lead inevitably to a degree of intervention that is excessive both in its scale and in its intensity. The very denial of punishment as an aim, so it is claimed, leads inevitably to a greater not a lesser volume of disposals indistinguishable from punishment. The movement has so far made little impact in Scotland but more could be heard of it in the future. Working within a framework of welfare principles has certainly resulted in far fewer children being brought before a tribunal and significantly fewer being removed from their homes. On the other hand, its casual attitude to procedural propriety, its reporters who lack specific training and its general assumption that good intentions are all that matter make the hearings system particularly vulnerable.

Future Prospects

In the next few years members may be given the opportunity to assume additional responsibilities in the aspects of their work that concern non-delinquent children. For example, making decisions about the custody of children affected by divorce rests currently with the sheriff court; many see a future role here for both reporters and panel members. Similarly, the assumption of parental rights might be the responsibility of the hearings system. This could prove to be an exciting although an immensely demanding extension of present responsibilities. Before the decision is made there would need to be some assurance of the competence of panel members and their ability to carry out the task.

Among the areas where research is needed are a sensitive study of the supervision process as well as a careful examination of the regimes, environments and social climates of residential establishments. While the reduced demand for List D school places is a matter for cautious congratulation, few believe that they have no future. The impact of community care requires sensitive evaluation. There is an urgent need for knowledge about the longer-term careers of children who have had contact with the hearings system: whether they come into conflict with the law as adults and, if so, at what age and for what reason.

Seen in international perspective, the principles embodied in the children's hearings system are not at present the height of intellectual fashion. So far as the processing of delinquents is concerned, there has recently been an emphasis on formalism, restriction of discretion and judicial structures. In penological circles, therapeutic nihilism has been quite widespread. 'Nothing works' is the current shorthand for what in even thoughtful discussion is referred to as 'the breakdown of the rehabilitative ideal'. Yet in Scotland, in developing a system which owes little to abstract theory and which wears its philosophical dilemmas openly, it has been shown that the generous use of discretion can reduce both the volume of formal processing and the number of children incarcerated; that the degrading ritual of court appearances can give way to open and constructive discussion; and that a large majority of the young people who come in contact with the system do so only once. The system also fulfils a unique and important role in the management of care and protection cases. Panel members function here as representatives of the community, whose task is to evaluate professional judgements – sympathetically but not uncritically – and determine to their own satisfaction how the child's interests are best served.

It is a widely held view that the potential of children's hearings is not yet fully developed and that an extension of their current jurisdiction to family and domestic matters is possible in the future. At the same time it is generally acknowledged that there are blemishes in practice that need to be remedied. It is only through education, critical self-examination and imaginative experiment with new approaches to treatment that it will be possible not merely to rectify present imperfections but to move forward towards fresh achievements.

References

1. *Report of the Departmental Committee on the Treatment of Young Offenders* (Morton Report). HMSO, 1928.
2. *Report of the Committee on Homeless Children* (Clyde Report), Cmd.6911, HMSO, 1946.
3. *Report of the Care of Children Committee* (Curtis Report), Cmd.6922, HMSO, 1946.
4. *Report of the Committee on Children and Young Persons* (Ingleby Report), Cmnd.1191, HMSO, 1960.
5. *Report of the Prevention of Neglect of Children* (McBoyle Report), Cmnd.1966, HMSO, 1963.
6. *Report of the Committee on Children and Young Persons* (Kilbrandon Report), Cmnd.2306, HMSO, 1964, para.17.
7. *Social Work and the Community*, Cmnd.3065, HMSO, 1966.
8. *The Child, the Family and the Young Offender*, Cmnd.2742, HMSO, 1965.
9. *Children in Trouble*, Cmnd.3601, HMSO, 1980.
10. *Young Offenders*, Cmnd.8045, HMSO, 1980.
11. *Report of the Committee on One-Parent Families* (Finer Report), Cmnd.5629, HMSO, 1974.
12. *Interdepartmental Review of Family and Domestic Jurisdiction: A Consultation Paper*, Lord Chancellor's Department, 1986.
13. See: Social Work (Scotland) Act, 1968, S.32(2)(a-i).
14. *Consultative Memorandum on Part III of the Social Work (Scotland) Act, 1968*, Social Work Services Group, 1980.
15. Health and Social Services and Social Security Adjudications Act, 1983, S.8.
16. F.M. Martin, S.J. Fox and K. Murray, *Children Out of Court*, Scottish Academic press, 1981.
17. Martin, Fox and Murray, *Children Out of Court*, p.319.
18. Martin, Fox and Murray, *Children Out of Court*, p.207.
19. Martin, Fox and Murray, *Children Out of Court*, p.103.
20. A. Morris, H. Giller, E. Szwed and H. Geach, *Justice for Children*, Macmillan, 1980.

FURTHER READING

S. Asquith, *Children and Justice: Decision-making in Children's Hearings and Juvenile Courts*, Edinburgh University Press, 1983.
A review of theoretical issues in juvenile justice drawing on the findings of an empirical enquiry.

N. Bruce and J.C. Spencer, *Face to Face with Families*, MacDonald, 1976.
An account of the hearings system based on studies of two urban and two rural areas.

F.M. Martin, S.J. Fox, and K. Murray, *Children out of Court*, Scottish Academic Press, 1981.
The findings of a major research study of the working of the hearings system.

F.M. Martin and K. Murray (eds.), *The Scottish Juvenile Justice System*, Scottish Academic Press, 1982.
A collection of essays drawing on research findings.

A. Morris and M. McIsaac, *Juvenile Justice?*, Heinemann, 1978.
The report of an early study of children's hearings in two districts.

P. Parsloe, *Juvenile Justice in Britain and the United States*, Routledge and Kegan Paul, 1978.
A comparative review of the juvenile justice systems in Scotland, England and the United States.

8
EDUCATION

Scotland, like all advanced industrial societies, has developed an extensive education system which is largely financed by the state and includes a wide range of schools, colleges and universities. While education must be understood in terms of its own aims and functions, it does not stand in isolation from wider society. It is closely related to the economic and social development of society and carries a responsibility to shape that process. Education occupies a higher position on political agendas than at almost any time since the second world war. None of the major parties is complacent about the role which schools are playing, while demands that they should be more efficient, accountable and sensitive to the needs of pupils are the common theme of educational debate. What is not so clear is how educational provision should be developed in order to achieve these goals.

Education has always had a prominent role in Scottish society. Its broad-based content and widespread availability to all classes of the population are generally well known, as well as how lack of wealth might be no barrier to the able 'lad o' pairts'.[1] Nevertheless, the extent of access to education in the past should not be over-emphasised.[2] But despite these strengths, a concern that the education system is not fully effective has gathered momentum among professionals, politicans and the public at large. Compounding factors over the last couple of decades have been large-scale demographic changes, economic recession and its impact on public expenditure, high levels of unemployment particularly among young people, acute social problems arising out of poverty and deprivation, rapid technological and structural change, and evolving social and political attitudes.[3] Current levels of criticism are unprecedented: Do schools and colleges achieve, as a minimum, an educated workforce? Do they give value for money?[4]

THE ORGANISATION AND CONTROL OF SCOTTISH EDUCATION

An important landmark in the development of public responsibility was the Education (Scotland) Act, 1872 and the introduction of compulsory education and a powerful central authority to raise and sustain standards. Even after 1872, however, it took some time for it to be generally realised that preconditions of educational success were good health and the availability of sufficient food and clothing. An expanding economy made these more widely available, but the Education (Scotland) Act, 1908 gave permissive powers to local authorities to provide them free where this was deemed necessary. It should be emphasised that from early in the present century until after the second world war educational equality was interpreted narrowly, mainly in terms of facilities and access to schools and courses.[5] This, together with an over-ready acceptance of the primarily genetic basis of human ability which was furthered by the growth of intelligence tests in the inter-war period, led to a belief that equality would be guaranteed by selection and streaming.

The present Scottish education system stems from the Education (Scotland) Act, 1946 (re-enacted in the Education (Scotland) Act, 1962 which is now the principal act). The 1946 act was the Scottish version of the Butler act of 1944 for England and Wales. The Scottish Office, through the Scottish Education Department (SED), has responsibility for all non-university education in Scotland. The main function of the SED is to formulate overall education policy and ensure that it is carried out by local education authorities (LEAs). Colleges of education and central institutions come under the direct responsibility of the SED while the universities are organised on a United Kingdom basis under the University Grants Committee.

The SED also carries out an important role through Her Majesty's Inspectors of Schools (HMIs). Originally, their main function was to ensure that educational standards were maintained, but over the years the emphasis has increasingly shifted towards a more collaborative approach with greater involvement in joint curriculum development and innovatory projects.

LEAs are responsible under the 1962 act for making educational provision in accordance with the policies laid down by the SED. The management functions of the LEA include the appointment of staff, administration of buildings and provision of school meals as well as the allocation of children to schools. The decrease of the school-age population during the 1980s resulted in spare capacity in schools, and a number of LEAs are opening them to the community and encouraging adults to take advantage of what they have to offer.

THE SCHOOLS SYSTEM

The 1962 act stipulates that all children must receive education appropriate to their age, aptitude and ability; about five per cent of children either go to private schools or receive education in other ways, for example by parents teaching their own children. Until 1974 the school leaving age was 15, when it was raised to 16, a change which was foreshadowed in the 1946 act. It has been argued, however, that another reason was to reduce youth unemployment.[6]

Following the Education (Scotland) Act, 1946 a bipartite system of junior and senior secondary schools was established to cater for the whole ability range from the age of 12. Senior secondary schools provided a more academic course for children selected on the basis of a qualifying examination (similar to the eleven plus south of the border) taken in the final year of primary education. The belief was that 'the aptitude and ability' of an individual child was best served by differentiated educational provision and in theory the two kinds of school were to be different but equal. No-one should be regarded as inferior or as a failure if selected for a junior secondary school. But this never really worked in practice, and the 1950s and 1960s saw an accumulation of research which suggested that the notion of 'parity of prestige' had not gained acceptance.[7] Influenced by these studies, the Labour government in 1965 requested LEAs to submit plans to move toward a fully comprehensive secondary system. An SED circular stopped the selection of children entering secondary schools as well as abolishing the distinction between the two types of schools.[8]

Another important document was also published by the SED in 1965, *Primary Education in Scotland*, which emphasised the need to achieve the fullest development of which a child is capable.[9] It suggested a move from a subject based curriculum to a more integrated and child centred approach.

Provision for Pre-School Children

Although the 1965 report concentrated mainly on primary education, by implication it acknowledged the importance of the pre-school stage in a child's life. This was reinforced by a body of knowledge emphasising the need for children to have an environment where their language and intellectual development could be fostered.[10] A similar view was also expressed by the Plowden report,[11] which will be discussed in the context of primary education.

A white paper, *Education in Scotland: A Statement of Policy*, published in 1972 gave a new direction to the provision of pre-school facilities.[12] As a result the number of children in nursery schools increased from some 10,000 in 1972 to nearly 38,000 in 1984-85. As well as this provision by LEAs, voluntary and church bodies also play an important part in pre-school provision. The Scottish Pre-school Playgroups Association has placed considerable stress on the principle that schooling for the under-fives should include the active involvement of parents, especially mothers, and should not be left entirely to professional staff. As Barbara Tizard has pointed out, 'Because parents and children have a shared life, stretching back into the past and forward into the future, parents can help the children to make sense of their present experiences by relating them to the past. Children's own intellectual efforts, and their persistent curiosity, are an essential part of this learning process'.[13]

In 1977 an interesting experiment was introduced as part of the Govan Project in Glasgow, reflecting its notion of 'total education'. Pre-school co-ordinators contacted all families in the area with a number of aims: first, to provide information about the significance of pre-school education for children, second, to seek support for the further development of this provision in the area and, third, to initiate new activities, for example a toy library.[14]

A number of LEAs are responding to the need of pre-school children by creating special under fives' units as well as collaborating with other agencies, such as social work, health and voluntary organisations. But the financial restrictions imposed on local authorities in recent years have meant that only a limited amount of money is available for new developments which is very thinly spread. More is expected from parents and communities in devising ways of providing stimulating environments for children.

Primary Education

The main educational objective for primary education between the ages of five and 12 has always been the mastering of the 'three Rs' of reading, writing and arithmetic, but there are now also broader aims such as the development of an understanding of the child's own environment. Over the last 15 years there has been a move away from the traditional approach of teachers giving instruction towards more emphasis on creating a classroom culture in which children can feel comfortable and secure. The idea behind this shift has been to foster a broad curriculum and its importance has been acknowledged by those LEAs which have set up specialist advisory units. The success of this approach varies considerably depending upon the locality and the support teachers receive through in-service training.

The 'rediscovery of poverty' in the 1960s (see chapter 2) introduced another kind of discussion to educational policy in general and primary education in particular. This drew attention to the need for special policies to assist with the intellectual development of children brought up in deprived and unstimulating backgrounds. The Plowden Report which was published in 1967 called for 'positive discrimination' in favour of Education Priority Areas (EPAs). There was one EPA in Scotland, in Dundee, as well as four projects in England.[15]

The notion of positive discrimination and its effectiveness in bringing about changes in educational outcomes have been a source of debate since the publication of the Plowden Report. Positive discrimination is concerned both with the distribution of material resources and with attitudinal changes. Distribution of resources is based on the principle that where inequalities exist a greater share of resources should go to the least favoured. The emphasis shifts from equality of inputs and opportunity to equality of outcomes. The Dundee project operated between 1968 and 1971, and its programme of action included not only primary schools but also the pre-school sector and secondary schools. In addition, there were formal links with other statutory agencies responsible for housing, health and social work. The project's conclusion was a telling one and is equally valid today: the report stated that 'we have come further to the more fundamental conclusion that educational deprivation, let alone societal or economic deprivation, can be tackled only in part through the educational service'.[16]

Secondary Education

State education from the age 12 is in comprehensive secondary schools. The debate about their effectiveness continues and there are educationalists and politicians who still argue that the best way to provide education for children is to segregate them according to their intellectual abilities. This argument stems from three broad assumptions:

(1) that levels of ability remain roughly constant, at least from the age of 11 or 12 onwards;

(2) that a small proportion of children, say a fifth or a quarter, are capable of benefiting from an 'academic' type of education; and

(3) that it is possible to teach pupils to higher educational standards when they are separated into different types of school.

A key choice in secondary education is whether society wants good education for everyone so as to give 'secondary education for all' real meaning, or whether it prefers to provide good education for some and a lower level of training for the majority. One of the main criticisms of comprehensive schools is that they have failed to improve educational standards and examination success.[17] However, this view has been challenged; one study carried out over eight years involving 40,000 school leavers in 1976, 1980 and 1984, for example, indicated that the proportion of pupils gaining at least one 'O' grade pass increased by nine per cent over the period, with a 5.5 per cent improvement among middle class and 12.5 per cent improvement among working class pupils.[18] The study concluded that the case against comprehensive schools could no longer be based on grounds of practicability or standards, but only on those of ideology and cost.

In 1977 two reports, on curriculum and assessment in secondary schools, were published. The Munn Committee,[19] which was set up to review the curriculum in the third and fourth years of secondary education, recommended a new structure based on a core of compulsory studies and an elective area, where the choice of the individual pupil would play a major part. Pupils would continue to study essential curriculum areas throughout third and fourth years while at the same time they would be enabled to develop their particular interests and abilities. This was to be done by studying two or three additional subjects chosen from a wide range which would be designed to provide a broader understanding of society.

The Dunning Report[20] recommended a new assessment system which would give all pupils the chance of a certificate at the end of the fourth year of secondary education. It argued that assessment should make a positive contribution to the teaching and learning process, and emphasised its importance for diagnosis and guidance. The committee proposed that one certificate, the 'Certificate of Education in Scotland', should be awarded to all pupils completing the last compulsory year of education. In most subjects there should be three levels of syllabus and award to cover the whole range of ability. The foundation level was intended primarily for pupils outwith the existing system of awards, while the general level would cater for the middle 50 per cent of the age group and the credit level was designed to challenge those pupils who would aim at Higher grade. For each subject there would be national guidelines for the syllabus and assessment together with school-designed syllabus components at all levels. The syllabuses for each level should overlap to ensure ease of transfer and to discourage premature categorisation of pupils. The assessment should be partly internal and partly external.

The SED accepted the main recommendations of both these reports in principle and the new curriculum and certification for all have been implemented, initially to cover three subject areas: English, mathematics and general science. Evaluation of the new system must wait until enough data are available but it may be asked how valuable certification will be to lower-ability pupils in the employment market.

Another important feature of secondary schools during the 1980s has been a fall in the school population as a result of decreased birth rates. Figure 8.1 illustrates the effect of these trends on the number of secondary school pupils between 1980 and 1985. Over-capacity has resulted and some LEAs, as mentioned earlier, have been using schools in new ways.

FIGURE 8.1 Local Education Authority Secondary Schools: Pupils, Teachers and Pupil-Teacher Ratios, 1980-85

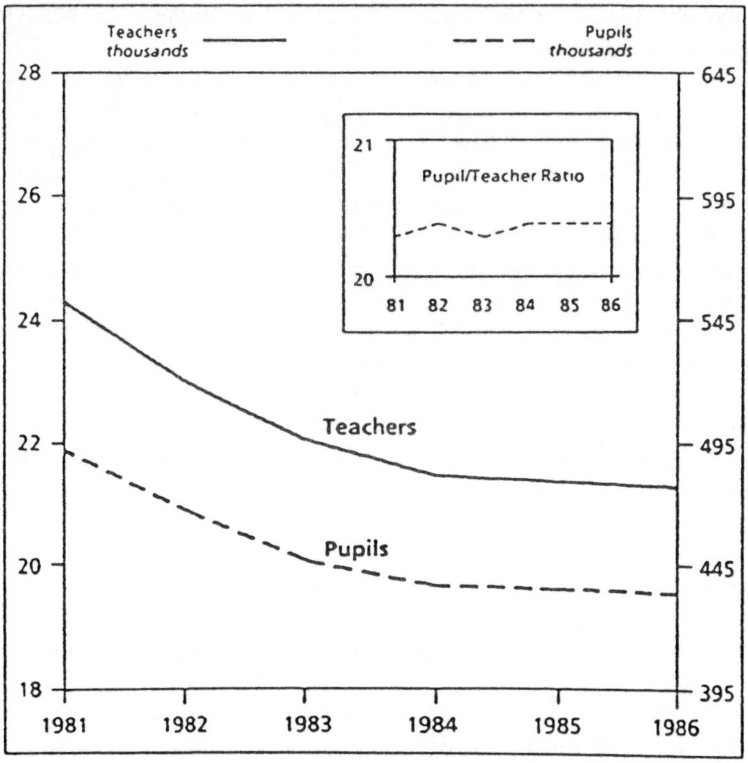

Schools for Special Needs

There are a number of other types of school which cater for children who require special educational provision. The Education (Scotland) Act, 1969 makes it obligatory for LEAs to provide educational support for children with special needs, such as physical handicap, mental disability, blindness and deafness. Most of these schools are day establishments but some, especially in rural areas, are residential. Over the last decade there has been discussion about the justification for special schools and these children are increasingly being integrated into ordinary schools.

PARENTS AND EDUCATION

Recent years have seen an increase in the interest of parents in the education system. This change may be seen as an aspect of consumer involvement and also as a reflection of an increasing awareness of the connection between education, social mobility and employment opportunities. There has been a development of interest in parental rights, especially over choice of school and the standard of education provided as expressed in examination results. Schools differ substantially in their organisation, their resources and certainly in their reputation. Recent research has confirmed the strong belief that, from the point of view of both attainment and behaviour, it matters very much which school a child attends.[21]

Parental choice has been promoted by the Conservative government since 1979. The Education (Scotland) Act, 1981 puts an obligation on LEAs to provide information for parents about a school's examination results, its facilities and choice of subjects. Parents now also have the right to send a child to a school outwith the local catchment area provided that there are no extra costs involved for the LEA.

It has been suggested that these rights should be further expanded and that parents should be given power in the actual running of schools. These ideas were incorporated in an SED discussion paper published in 1987 in order to have consultation with parents and other interested groups.[22] It proposed that there should be a school board for each primary and secondary school, replacing school councils. A school board would encourage a sense of identification with the life of the school and exercise a central role in its organisation and management. Parent members would have a majority on school boards.

The discussion paper suggested that the boards should from the outset assume responsibility for expenditure on books and other materials, that they should have the right to raise funds and dispose of them, and that they should oversee statutory attendance procedures and the letting of premises outside school hours. It also proposed that parent members of boards should be involved as voting members of appointment committees and that boards should have a right of veto over the appointment of head teachers.

Boards will be small in size so as to be effective management bodies and the membership will be elected by a postal ballot of parents with children at each school. The head teacher will have a duty to attend board meetings but without a vote, and the LEA will be entitled to nominate a representative but again without voting rights. There will be staff representatives as well as co-opted members representing the local community. Each board will be required to produce by a specific date a written constitution after consultation with local interests, and the Secretary of State will have the power either to accept it, to suggest alterations or to impose a different one.

Early in 1988 the SED published its conclusions following the consultation exercise and these included a number of changes from the discussion paper.[23] All schools regardless of size will have a board, and members will hold office for four years with half being elected every two years. Boards are not to have a veto over the appointment of head teachers, while the extent of their control over curriculum and staffing has been limited. They may request powers over the school budget from the LEA and if these are refused an appeal can be made to the Secretary of State provided that a majority of parents have supported this in a ballot. Legislation is expected to be passed during 1988 to implement the proposals.

It is now widely accepted that parents should have more say in the management of schools but the precise form this should take is under discussion and will probably be decided more on ideological than purely educational grounds. It has been argued by some parents' organisations that control over education which is intended to enhance parental choice is meaningless and unacceptably onerous unless several conditions are met, including an increase in both revenue and capital spending. Because staff costs account for some 70 per cent of a school's budget, a school board would have little room for manoeuvre. There is also often an urgent need for school premises to be brought up to an acceptable standard. There are, moreover, many schools where it may prove difficult to find enough interested parents with the necessary width of experience and expertise to provide effective management.

Very often choice means that parents support reputedly good schools to the neglect of schools with a poor reputation. Parental choice may provide an opportunity for the children of highly-educated and articulate parents to cluster in a minority of schools, and so weaken the pressure for improvement in schools at large.

A more radical approach to increasing the power of parents than the school board proposals would be a system of education vouchers. Parents would be given vouchers entitling them to buy education at the school of their choice. The schools might be able to charge what they like, although some proposals specifically exclude fees in excess of the value of vouchers. Advocates of vouchers claim that they would increase both parental freedom of choice and diversity of educational provision.

One of the difficulties with the notion of parental choice in general, and the voucher scheme in particular, is that both can be implemented in a variety of ways. Indeed, it has been suggested that a voucher system's flexibility is its strength. There are, however, a number of proposed voucher schemes which may not be satisfactory on criteria on equality and equal access. For instance, under Friedman's scheme[24] parents would be free to supplement the value of vouchers out of their own pockets but the travelling costs of children from poorer families would not be met. Since high-quality schools are not generally located in deprived areas, real choice for all would be difficult to achieve. Voucher schemes have not been implemented anywhere in the United Kingdom and only on a limited experimental basis in the United States.

HIGHER AND FURTHER EDUCATION

The majority of changes during the last two decades in higher education can be evaluated in terms of the proposals of the Robbins Report published in 1963.[25] The committee had the following terms of reference: 'to review the pattern of full-time higher education in Great Britain and in the light of national needs and resources to advise Her Majesty's Government on what principles its long-term development should be'.

The principle which should link the demand for higher education with its supply was made explicit by the committee: 'courses of higher education should be made available for all those who are qualified by ability and attainment to pursue them and who wish to do so'.[26] It recommended a substantial increase of the number of higher education places, from eight per cent of the relevant age group at the time of the report to one of 17 per cent by 1980-81. The increase in places was to be realised by the setting up of a number of new universities and by the expansion of technological institutions of higher education. The committee also recommended the creation of a Council for National Academic Awards (CNAA) to validate advanced courses in the non-university sector, and the introduction of degree courses for teacher-training students.

Universities

Although largely financed by the exchequer, universities are not strictly a part of the statutory education system as they are independent, self-governing institutions. The University Grants Committee (UGC) apportions their income, links central government with the separate institutions and attempts to define a national policy for higher education.

There were four universities in Scotland at the time of the Robbins Report – Aberdeen, Edinburgh, Glasgow and St. Andrews – and four more were created as a result of its recommendations. Dundee was divided from St. Andrew's, Heriot-Watt and Strathclyde were formerly major colleges of technology, while Stirling was a new foundation. The Scottish universities have been well known for their emphasis on broadly-based education, whereas their English counterparts have tended to favour more specialised courses. In Scotland a high proportion of students study for an ordinary, as opposed to an honours, degree. It is also easier in Scotland for students to incorporate a variety of subjects in their degree courses.

The universities have been subjected to severe financial restrictions since 1981-82 which have led to staff losses and cutbacks in student numbers. Like the rest of the education system their effectiveness has come under public scrutiny. There are some who argue that there should be two types of universities, one concentrating primarily on teaching and the other mainly on research. But what is often overlooked is that teaching and research are interdependent and that the former cannot be fully effective without the latter. On the other hand, some claim that the universities are elitist in their approach to education and in the values they hold. It is argued that they have very little contact with ordinary people and their local communities, while there has been over-emphasis on formal qualifications for entry. Critics would like to see wider access to universities, especially by mature students and those with working class backgrounds.

Colleges of Education

The colleges of education were formerly known as teacher training colleges. Their altered name, which was meant to symbolise a new status, was adopted following a recommendation of the Robbins Report. It proposed that they should present students for a new degree of Bachelor of Education (BEd) at the end of a four-year course. There are now seven colleges of education in Scotland, which are directly financed by the SED. Falling school rolls, mentioned earlier, have also affected the colleges. They are no longer solely involved in teacher training but have incorporated other types of courses such as social work, speech therapy and youth and community work, though their diversification has been more modest than that of similar institutions in England.

The General Teaching Council is a statutory body with a responsibility to carry out a number of monitoring functions and to advise the Secretary of State for Scotland about the required number of teachers. It awards registration after a two-year probationary period of teaching.

Central Institutions

These colleges are also directly funded by the SED and they fall into a number of categories. The five largest are Dundee College of Technology, Glasgow College of Technology, Napier College of Commerce and Technology in Edinburgh, Paisley College of Technology and Robert Gordon's Institute of Technology in Aberdeen. They provide courses mainly in science, engineering, and management and business studies. There are three colleges of art, while Queen Margaret College, Edinburgh and The Queen's College, Glasgow specialise in domestic science, para-medical and related subjects. The other central institutions are the Royal Scottish Academy of Music and Drama and the Scottish College of Textiles. The three colleges of agriculture are exceptional in that they are funded by the Department of Agriculture and Fisheries for Scotland. Many courses in central institutions are designed to prepare students for specific careers, and a greater emphasis on vocational education distinguishes them from universities.

In 1984 the Secretary of State appointed the Scottish Tertiary Education Advisory Council (STEAC) 'to consider and report on the future strategy for higher education in Scotland'.[27] The council took a broad and long-term perspective. The report recognised that falling numbers of school leavers in the 1990s would provide an opportunity for a renewed commitment to the principle of maximum access to higher education. Universities and colleges were asked to encourage students with a wide range of qualifications, mature students and continuing education.

The STEAC report called for a Scottish Higher Education Planning Council to be set up which would continuously review demand for places in higher education. It would also be expected to identify shortages of qualified manpower and provide guidance on the adjustments in provision which would be required to respond to them. There would also be a Scottish sub-committee of the UGC. A similar body would be charged with the distribution of funds among the institutions which are funded by the SED. The majority of the Scottish universities were opposed to these recommendations and they were rejected by the government, STEAC itself being dissolved.

Colleges of Further Education

LEAs provide vocationally oriented courses through further education (FE) colleges. Some of these courses are full-time and others are organised on a day-release basis. Many students study for Scottish and higher national certificates and diplomas of the Scottish Vocational Education Council. FE colleges have been the main source of SCE qualifications for mature students who intend to enter higher education. They also run courses for adults jointly with other organisations such as the Workers' Education Association and university-based adult and continuing education departments.

Other Local Education Authority Responsibilities

A careers service is provided by LEAs to offer vocational guidance to young people at school or college. It is particularly important for the majority of young people who do not enter higher education by assisting their transition to work.

Some LEAs run child guidance clinics for the treatment of emotionally disturbed children (in other areas this service is provided by the health board). Child guidance clinics employ a number of professions, including psychiatrists, psychologists and social workers, in dealing with problems of maladjustment. The school psychological service assesses children with learning and other educational difficulties as well as speech defects. Some general welfare facilities are also provided by LEAs such as school meals and milk in infant schools; many children in deprived areas are entitled to free meals although their availability was substantially reduced under the social security legislation which came into force in 1988 (see chapter 2).

EDUCATION AND DISADVANTAGE

Sir Keith Joseph, then Secretary of State for Education and Science, took the view in 1984 that a substantially higher standard of attainment at the age of 16 could be achieved by pupils of all abilities. He went on to outline ambitious plans to enable children to do better at school. But admirable though the government's aims may be, raising educational standards is unlikely to be easy. The factors that make for success at school are complicated and frequently have their roots outside the classroom.

If one wants to make a generalisation about the educational process it would be safe to pick out three predictors of success: social class, gender and skin colour. One of the most useful sources of information about the effect of social class on educational achievement comes from the recent work of the National Children's Bureau.[28] Research shows that achievement between the ages of seven and 11 in school varies a great deal. When the researchers divided children into high achievers, average achievers and low achievers, they found that a third of the top group at seven had dropped out of that group by the time they were 11; on the other hand, a third of the low achieving group had risen to a higher group. And social class was a major factor; those on the way down were the most likely to be working class.

Such differences have a profound effect on the school careers of children from different social classes, and as they move up the educational ladder these distinctions grow more marked. A statistical analysis by the SED found that children in social classes I and II are four times as likely to become 'qualified leavers' as are others.[29]

Class differences affect who goes on to higher education and who gets the best jobs, even when people are of equal intelligence. The Robbins Committee found that of children with a very high IQ (130 or more) born in 1940-41, those from middle class families were twice as likely as working class children to gain entry to a degree course. But the expansion of higher education as a result of the report benefited the middle class more than the working class. Halsey's research in England and Wales showed that, compared with their parents' generation, the proportion of working class boys entering university increased by two per cent, and the proportion of boys from the intermediate class (clerical workers, small proprietors and foremen) increased by six per cent, but the proportion of boys from the 'service' class (professionals and administrators) increased by 19 per cent. Halsey notes that when secondary education was made free 'the state may have tempted some parents of able children to forsake the private sector of education for the state one, and the extra competition from these children may thus have nullified any gains which the working class would otherwise have obtained from the reform. This point is an important and paradoxical one for social policy. A service is made free in order to enable the poor to take advantage of it, but this also makes the service more attractive to the rich'.[30] The same concern about the extent of educational disadvantage has been expressed by a number of studies in Scotland over the last 20 years, such as the work of the National Children's Bureau[31] and the EPA project in Dundee. The consistent message is that a socially deprived child is also likely to be educationally disadvantaged.

Educational disadvantage is in part a political issue. Halsey and others have shown that education can assist the creation of a more efficient, open and just society but there is a price in terms of public expenditure. Whether we are prepared to pay it depends on how high a priority we place on the fulfilment of educational potential. The struggle among interest groups within the education system is largely concerned with the competition for resources, and in recent years there has been increased central government control over not only how much should be spent but also on what it may be spent.

In terms of scale, organisation, control and content, Scottish education is in a state of more rapid change than for many years. The notion of equality of opportunity can only be real if there is a variety of routes to educational achievement, and if everyone who is willing to do so is able to attain his or her full potential through at least one of them. Although such an objective is widely espoused, it remains to be seen how much progress will be made towards it in the coming years.

References

1. J. Scotland, *The History of Scottish Education*, University of London Press, 1969.
2. M. MacIntosh, *Education in Scotland: Yesterday and Today*, Gibson, 1962.
3. N.D.C. Grant, *Crisis in Scottish Education*, Saltire Society, 1982.
4. C. Cookson, 'It's Where You Learn that Counts Most', *Times Educational Supplement Scotland (Scotland)*, 9 November 1977.
5. MacIntosh, *Education in Scotland.*
6. D. Raffe (ed.), *Fourteen to Eighteen: The Changing Pattern of Schooling in Scotland*, Aberdeen University Press, 1984.
7. G.S. Osborne, *Change in Scottish Education*, Longman, 1968.
8. Scottish Education Department, *Reorganisation of Secondary Education on Comprehensive Lines*, HMSO, 1965.
9. *Primary Education in Scotland*, Cmnd.3216, HMSO, 1965.
10. R.S. Peters, *Perspective on Plowden*, Routledge and Kegan Paul, 1969.
11. Department of Education and Science, *Children and Their Primary Schools* (Plowden Report), HMSO, 1967.
12. *Education in Scotland: A Statement of Policy*, Cmnd.5175, HMSO, 1972.
13. B. Tizard, 'What Joyce Learnt from Her Mother', *New Society*, 13 September 1984.
14. J.E. Wilkinson, D. Grant and D. Williamson, *Strathclyde Experiment in Education: Govan Project: Public Report*, University of Glasgow, Department of Education, 1978.
15. C.M. Morrison (ed.), *Education Priority: Vol.5: EPA - A Scottish Study*, HMSO, 1974.
16. Morrison, *Education Priority*, p.209.
17. M. Rutter, B. Monaghan, P. Mortimor, and J. Duston, *Fifteen Thousand Hours: Secondary Schools and Their Effects on Children*, Open Books, 1979.
18. A. MacPherson and D. Willms, 'Equalisation and Improvement: Some Effects of Comprehensive Reorganisation in Scotland', *Sociology*, Vol.21, No.4, 1987.
19. Scottish Education Department, *The Structure of the Curriculum in the Third and Fourth Years of the Scottish Secondary School* (Munn Report), HMSO, 1977.
20. Scottish Education Department, *Assessment for All: Report of the Committee to Review Assessment in the Third and Fourth Years of Secondary Education in Scotland* (Dunning Report), HMSO, 1977.
21. J.H. Goldthorpe, *Social Mobility and Class Structure in Modern Britain*, Clarendon Press, 1980.
22. Scottish Education Department, *School Management and the Role of Parents: Consultative Paper*, SED, 1987.

23. Scottish Education Department, *School Management: The Government's Conclusions*, SED, 1988.
24. M. Friedman, *Capitalism and Freedom*, University of Chicago Press, 1963.
25. *Higher Education* (Robbins Report), Cmnd.2154, HMSO, 1963.
26. *Higher Education*, p.15.
27. *Future Strategy for Higher Education in Scotland* (STEAC Report), Cmnd.9676, HMSO, 1985.
28. P. Wedge and J. Essen, *Children in Adversity*, Pan Books, 1982.
29. Scottish Education Department, *Statistical Bulletin: Higher Education Projections*, Scottish Office, 1983.
30. A.H. Halsey, A.F. Heath and J.M. Ridge, *Origins and Destinations*, Clarendon Press, 1980, pp.70-1.
31. P. Wedge and H. Prosser, *Born to Fail?*, Arrow Books, 1973.

FURTHER READING

J. Finch, *Education as Social Policy*, Longman, 1984.
A very useful account of the education system and its problems which has relevance to Scotland.

D.C. Grant and R. Bell, *Patterns of Education in the British Isles*, Allen and Unwin, 1977.
A description of educational provision which discusses differences between Scotland and the rest of Britain.

J. Karabel and A. Halsey (eds.), *Power and Ideology in Education*, Oxford University Press, 1978.
A collection of essays which concentrates on issues in the education field.

D. Raffe (ed.), *Fourteen to Eighteen: The Changing Pattern of Schooling in Scotland*, Aberdeen University Press, 1984.
A review of comprehensive schools in Scotland in the 1970s based on the performance of a sample of pupils.

9
EMPLOYMENT SERVICES

As the problems of unemployment have deepened and widened, employment services have become increasingly varied with some special programmes for the unemployed showing prodigious growth. Most employment services are operated by the Department of Employment. However, given the depth of the economic depression and its uneven geographical spread, many local authorities, voluntary bodies and, more recently, community groups have become involved in the provision of services for the unemployed.

In this chapter we concentrate on the activities of the Department of Employment as the major service provider, and begin by considering the impact of rising unemployment on individuals and households, before moving on to consider in detail the nature of the unemployment problem in Scotland. Here we will be looking at the changing extent of the problem as well as the nature of variations in unemployment experiences. Finally, the range of employment services available will be mapped out in detail.

WHY IS UNEMPLOYMENT A PROBLEM?

The fundamental problem with unemployment is that it is unevenly distributed within society. There are two senses in which this is true:

(1) a large proportion of the labour force never experience unemployment; and

(2) of those becoming unemployed a large proportion do not experience the most lengthy durations of unemployment.

As a consequence a relatively small proportion of the population account for a high proportion of the total amount of unemployment within our society. However, the problem is not just the uneven distribution of unemployment. The people who are most at risk of unemployment are often those who are the least well-rewarded even when they are in work. Thus the rates of unemployment for the unskilled are eight times greater than for professional workers.[1] Also unemployment rates in the prosperous south east of England are significantly below the rates in the depressed north of Britain. The rate in Scotland in 1988 is twice as high as in the south east.

Unemployment is therefore an experience which is distributed very unevenly within society. This still begs the question as to what damage is done by unemployment to those affected by it. Some of the reasons for being seriously concerned about unemployment are listed below.

(1) Unemployment reduces the incomes of the individuals and households affected and is an important cause of poverty. In 1985 it was estimated[2] that the net annual income of unemployed persons was on average £2,120 lower than their take-home pay when in work. This is a substantial loss of income for people who experience low levels of income even when in work.

(2) Unemployment exerts a damaging influence on the psychological well-being of those affected by it. There is a strong body of evidence to support the view that unemployment directly affects aspects of life experience such as self-confidence, concentration and feelings of depression.[3]

(3) Unemployment may have a damaging influence on the health of those directly and indirectly affected by it. This may operate through changes in diet, alterations to smoking and drinking behaviour, and increases in stress-related symptoms. Some argue that people die as a result of unemployment, either because of the longer-run effects of these changes or directly through higher rates of suicide.[4] It is important to note that this is a difficult area in which to carry out research and it is worth recalling that certain types of work are also bad for health.

(4) Unemployment may set up stresses and strains in families and households, and may lead, for example, to increases in the amount of wife battering and child abuse. These issues are not well researched although some recent work has clearly established a relationship between unemployment and deteriorating relationships between partners.[5]

(5) The problems raised above relate to individuals and families. However, unemployment also exacts costs on both local and national government, and ultimately on society at large. Localities characterised by high unemployment suffer reduced spending with knock-on effects on local traders. The local authorities may find increased demands being made on their services, such as social work and welfare rights advice. At the national level, the exchequer loses the tax formerly paid by the unemployed and at the same time has to meet the cost of unemployment benefits.

Having outlined some of the principal reasons why unemployment is such a major issue, we now look at some of the facts and figures relating to unemployment in Scotland.

STATISTICS ON SCOTTISH UNEMPLOYMENT

Before presenting statistical evidence on the nature and extent of the unemployment problem in Scotland, it is important to discuss briefly the way in which the statistics are compiled. For many years the standard method of counting unemployment was on the basis of the number of individuals registering as unemployed at their local jobcentre or employment office. However, in 1983 the basis of the count was changed to include only those claiming benefit at an unemployment benefit office. An immediate consequence of this was to reduce the count of the unemployed by excluding those who did not claim benefit, either because they were not eligible or because the amount of benefit involved would have been trifling.

Since 1983 there have been various other changes in the way unemployment is counted, generally leading to reductions in the published figures. Additionally, many thousands are on various special programmes which have been introduced in response to rising unemployment. They are not included in the count of unemployment. Strathclyde Regional Council has produced estimates for July 1986 of the difference between the official count of the unemployed and what they regard as the underlying level of unemployment in the region. The details are shown below:

Total officially unemployed (claiming benefit)	194,000
Numbers on special programmes	37,000
Unemployed not claiming or not eligible for benefit	26,000
Numbers deleted due to changes in count	23,000
School leaver non-claimants	9,000
Estimated true level of unemployment	289,000

These figures suggest that for every two people counted as unemployed there is a third person who does not feature in the unemployment statistics.

While bearing in mind the disputes which rage over the true figures for unemployment, we can consider some of the trends and variations in the published statistics relating to Scotland, starting with an examination of the overall position relative to the United Kingdom as a whole.

The figures in Table 9.1 are clear evidence of a massive rise in the official unemployment figures, notwithstanding changes in the counting procedure. In Scotland and in the UK as a whole the increase has been greater than threefold when considering the absolute numbers. The growth in the rate of unemployment, which expresses the unemployed as a percentage of the labour force as a whole (unemployed plus employed), has been a little less marked. The timing of changes in unemployment is also clearly visible. There was a very substantial growth in Scottish unemployment in the period 1975-79 followed by a near doubling of the numbers between 1979 and 1983. Unemployment reached a peak in mid-1986, and by mid-1988 it had fallen to less than 300,000

TABLE 9.1:

Unemployment Statistics for Scotland and the United Kingdom, 1975-86

	Total Unemployed (000s)		Unemployment Rate	
	Scotland	UK	Scotland %	UK %
1975	112	978	5.2	4.1
1979	182	1,391	8.0	5.8
1983	336	3,105	13.7	11.6
1986	361	3,289	14.3	11.9

Source: *Employment Gazette.*

TABLE 9.2:

Proportion of Scottish Unemployed in Particular Categories

	Women %	Long-term %	Under 25s %	School leavers %
1975	24	16	not available	5
1979	35	26	45	7
1983	31	37	42	6
1986	31	41	38	5

Source: *Employment Gazette.*

(11.5 per cent) in Scotland and to some 2.3 million (eight per cent) in the UK. But to some extent the reduction reflects changes in the methods of counting and the massive expansion of various special programmes.

The changing nature of Scottish unemployment is considered in Table 9.2 where we look at the position of women, under-25s, school-leavers and the long-term unemployed (that is, those out of work for over a year).

The figures for women are interesting in as much as they show two contradictory trends. Women grew in importance as members of the dole queues between 1975 and 1979, reflecting their increased importance in the labour market. However, there has been a drop in their share of unemployment since 1979, in part as a consequence of the move towards counting the unemployed on the basis of benefit claimed (because married women are often not eligible). One of the most dramatic changes has been the growth in the proportion of the unemployed out of work for over a year. This has risen from 16 per cent in 1975 to around 41 per cent in 1986. The underlying change is worse than the figures suggest because many of the special employment schemes are targeted at the long-term unemployed, so disguising the extent of the problem. The final issue considered here is the age structure of the unemployed. School leavers are an important component of unemployment, but when their position is evaluated over the year (instead of in the autumn when their numbers peak) we can see that their quantitative contribution to unemployment is not great. Of course this is largely a reflection of the major impact now being made on the numbers by the Youth Training Scheme. More generally, a critical problem group is the under 25s, who have taken the brunt of the economic depression since the mid-1970s. They are seriously over-represented among the ranks of the unemployed, although their share of unemployment has fallen over the last few years.

So far we have looked at the unemployment situation in Scotland as a whole. However, the experience of different parts of Scotland varies dramatically, as is illustrated in Table 9.3 which shows the position for the regions and islands areas. Restricting consideration to mainland Scotland, it can be seen that the rate of unemployment in Strathclyde is twice as high as the rate for the Borders. In effect, the variations in unemployment rates within Scotland are similar to the differences between regions of Britain.

TABLE 9.3:

Unemployment Rates by Regions and Islands Council Areas, 1987

	%		%
Shetlands	7.6	Highland	13.7
Borders	9.0	Tayside	14.4
Grampian	9.4	Fife	15.6
Orkney Islands	11.8	Central	16.2
Lothian	12.6	Strathclyde	18.1
Dumfries & Galloway	12.7	Western Isles	18.4

Note: Figures relate to July 1987.

Source: Manpower Services Commission, *Labour Market Quarterly Report, Scotland.*

When smaller geographical areas are looked at the variations become even starker. Table 9.4 shows the ten 'best' and 'worst' areas in Scotland on the measure of unemployment rates. Unemployment rates in the worst area (Cumnock and Sanquhar) are nearly four times greater than those prevailing in Galashiels and the Shetlands.

TABLE 9.4:

Unemployment Rates for 'Best' and 'Worst' Areas, 1986

Best Areas	%	Worst Areas	%
Galashiels	7.5	Dumbarton	21.3
Shetlands	7.6	Forres	21.4
Aberdeen	8.0	Irvine	22.6
Haddington	8.7	Girvan	23.8
Peebles	9.0	Cumnock and Sanquhar	23.9

Note: Figures relate to July 1987.

Source: Manpower Services Commission, *Labour Market Quarterly Report, Scotland.*

It is at the scale of variations within urban areas, however, that the greatest disparities in unemployment experiences occur, as the figures for male unemployment in the Glasgow area clearly show. The middle-class suburb of Bearsden has an unemployment rate for males which is only a fifth of that experienced in the most depressed electoral divisions within the area (Table 9.5).

The statistical information presented in the last few pages highlights a number of key points:

(1) unemployment has grown substantially since the late 1970s, and long-term unemployment has become a particularly severe problem;

(2) Scotland's position is worse than the average for the United Kingdom as a whole; and

(3) the experiences of different parts of Scotland are very varied, and these variations tend to be extremely marked within urban areas.

TABLE 9.5:

Male Unemployment Rates for Selected Electoral Divisions in the Glasgow Area, 1985

	%		%
Bearsden	7.0	Drumoyne-Govan	38.4
Milngavie-Kilmardinny	9.4	Central-Calton	38.7
Kings Park-Aitkenhead	13.0	Gartloch-Easterhouse	38.8
Pollokshaws-Newlands	13.3	Belvidere-Carntyne	40.4

Note: Figures relate to July 1985.

Source: *Strathclyde Economic Trends.*

There is not enough room here to discuss the various theories of unemployment. It is worth noting, however, that during 1986 there were on average around 17,000 vacancies notified to the Scottish jobcentres. As not all vacancies are reported (notification is voluntary) these probably reflect a true figure of around 50,000 vacancies. We saw earlier that the average number unemployed in 1986 was 361,000, which itself may be a serious underestimate of the true level of unemployment. Even if every vacancy had been filled this would still have left unemployment at substantially above 300,000. This simple comparison puts into context a number of the arguments brought forward to explain high unemployment, such as the generosity of benefit payments, the lack of mobility of the unemployed and their unwillingness to retrain. Fundamentally, the problem is lack of work.

SERVICES FOR THE UNEMPLOYED

For many years the services provided for the unemployed followed a well-tried pattern, with changes taking place at the margins. However, as unemployment began to rise from the mid-1970s, new developments came on stream in the fields of job creation and youth training. As the unemployment problem deepened into crisis in the 1980s these new initiatives expanded dramatically.

There was a dramatic growth in expenditure on the initiatives, and overall spending in cash terms rose almost threefold between 1980-81 and 1985-86. Scotland's share is roughly ten per cent of the total. Employment services (jobcentres, etc.) saw only a very small growth in expenditure and consequently a dramatic fall in their proportional significance. A similar story can be told for adult training. The high growth areas have been youth training and job creation. Expenditure on job creation rose by a factor of twelve over this period and has continued to grow since 1985-86.

Services for the unemployed can be categorised into three broad headings:

(1) placement and advisory services including the running of jobcentres;

(2) training services; and

(3) job creation services.

From the mid-1970s all these services were the responsibility of the Manpower Services Commission (MSC), but in 1987 the placement and advisory services were returned to the direct control of the Department of Employment. In 1988 the MSC was renamed the Training Commission but later in the year it was abolished following the refusal of the Trades Union Congress to participate in the new Employment Training Scheme (see below). All the services then became the direct responsibility of the Department of Employment.

Rather than discuss a long 'shopping list' of services it is helpful to look at these headings in turn, saying a little about the broad rationale behind each.

Placement and Advisory Services

In the 1970s the MSC began to replace and upgrade the existing network of employment offices with jobcentres. These were to be located in busy shopping areas, rather than up side streets. They were to have a brighter, more modern image, and the emphasis was to be on displaying vacancies in such a way as to facilitate a 'self-service' approach to job search by unemployed (and employed) people. During 1985-86, over 25,000 Scots were placed in jobs through the jobcentre network, including over 8,000 disabled people. Increasingly, however, the jobcentres have taken on a role much wider than the placing of people in jobs. They are now viewed as the 'gateway' to a full range of services on offer to the unemployed. At the jobcentre information and advice can be obtained on the plethora of schemes currently available.

One of the difficulties faced in providing employment services is that the inadequate volume of job vacancies severely constrains the capacity of jobcentres to help people find work. Jobcentres do not create jobs; rather they are a facility which helps bring together employers seeking workers and workers seeking jobs. The extent of the problem is illustrated by the fact that during 1986 there were roughly 20 unemployed persons chasing every vacancy notified at jobcentres in Scotland.

As a consequence of continued depression in the labour market an increasing number of the people placed by jobcentres have gone into part-time or temporary jobs, including the Community Programme (see below) which provided temporary jobs for the long-term unemployed. It is estimated that one-in-four of vacancies at Scottish jobcentres have been on the Community Programme; in other words the programme had become one of the major employers in many areas.

With the deepening problem of long-term unemployment the jobcentres became the focus of the nationwide *Restart* programme, launched during 1986. This programme of interviewing and counselling has been targeted at the long-term unemployed with a view to offering them one of seven alternatives:

(1) A job.

(2) A place on a job creation or related scheme.

(3) A place on a training scheme.

(4) A place on the job subsidy scheme – the New Workers Scheme.

(5) A Jobstart allowance of £20 per week if they take a job with a gross wage of under £80 per week.

(6) A place on a Restart course, lasting up to two weeks and concentrating on job search skills.

(7) A place in a Jobclub, where groups of the unemployed have access to telephones, stationery, etc. and to advice on job search.

The Restart idea was piloted in nine areas (including Dundee) prior to its introduction. The results of the exercise were not encouraging. For every 100 unemployed interviewed at their jobcentre the following results were obtained[6]:

	%
Placed in a job	1.0
Placed in the Community Programme	4.6
Placed in Restart courses	7.5
Placed in Jobclubs	1.0
Placed in training courses	1.0
Total assisted	15.1

More than four out of five of the claimants interviewed received no assistance, and of those assisted only a small proportion were placed in work or in programmes offering a high probability of a job at the end of the day.

Responsibility for jobcentres was transferred from the MSC to the Department of Employment in 1987. The latter has always been responsible for running unemployment benefit offices, and in the future benefit payment and placement services may once again be provided under one roof as they were before the introduction of jobcentres in the early 1970s. There is an argument that a closer association between the two functions would facilitate the monitoring of benefit claims.

Training Services

The development of the Youth Training Scheme was very significant and there have also been major changes to adult training, culminating in the Employment Training scheme set up in 1988. Youth training and adult training will be discussed in turn.

Youth Training: The first major expansion was in 1983 when the *Youth Training Scheme* (YTS) was introduced, building on many of the elements present in the earlier Youth Opportunities Programme (YOP). Although introduced as a one-year training scheme, YTS was expanded to a two-year scheme during 1986. In Scotland, in 1985-86, over 45,000 youngsters took part in YTS.

The key features of YTS can be listed as follows:

(1) It is targeted at unemployed 16 and 17 year olds and seeks to offer all eligible youngsters a place on the scheme.

(2) It combines work experience and formal teaching, although the balance varies from one type of scheme to another.

(3) The youngsters are paid an allowance rather than a wage as such, although some sponsors 'top up' the allowance.

The scheme has had its critics. A number of the criticisms date back to earlier schemes such as the Work Experience on Employers' Premises programme introduced in the 1970s. Work experience still plays a significant role in YTS. The key criticisms are that:

(1) Youngsters on schemes with a large work experience element may simply be used as cheap labour. There is no obligation on employers to top up the allowance paid to trainees.

(2) To the extent that there is an element of cheap labour, youngsters may be recruited at the expense of the people who would otherwise have been hired, for example unskilled adult workers, so leading to higher rates of unemployment among these groups. The problem of youth unemployment is thus in part being displaced into the problem of adult unemployment.

(3) Although the quality of training provided under YTS has almost certainly improved over time, it is still the case that a high proportion of youngsters leaving the scheme do not find jobs. The statistical returns suggest that only around 50 per cent of youngsters found work when they left the YTS.

(4) There is a distinction between YTS schemes where there is a high level of work experience with private or public sector employers and those which are based heavily on colleges, training workshops, etc. The former attract better qualified youngsters and are also more successful when measured against the proportion of participants finding a job at the end of the scheme. To some extent the inequalities which have developed in the schools continue through YTS and into the labour market.

(5) In the more depressed urban areas or parts of urban areas (for example peripheral housing estates in big cities) there are few local employers and so fewer places available on the more favoured employer-based YTS schemes.

On the credit side YTS has expanded rapidly to achieve a very significant scale of operation. Additionally, whatever the strategic thinking behind the development of YTS – that is, whether it is simply there to 'mop up' youth unemployment or an attempt to restructure Britain's training system – it is clear that something had to be done. In the late 1970s 44 per cent of Britain's 16 year olds entered a job which offered no training or became unemployed. The corresponding figures for West Germany and France were 19 per cent and six per cent respectively.[7]

Adult Training: Although the Employment Training scheme (ET) replaced the existing separate schemes in 1988, it will initially incorporate many of their features so that it is worth discussing them. Starting in 1985 the MSC organised the Adult Training Campaign to try and raise awareness of the benefits of training. This initiative followed a series of reports which showed how poor was Britain's training effort compared with that of our competitors.[8]

Adult training was reorganised into two broad programme areas. The *Job*

Training Programme (JTP) was oriented towards the needs of industry by providing occupational training for the unemployed, grants to employers and various types of enterprise training for new or small businesses. The *Wider Opportunities Training Programme* (WOTP) was aimed at improving the basic skills and employability of the unemployed. In large measure these programmes brought together individual schemes which were already in existence.

However, the balance of training effort altered: the old Training Opportunities Scheme (TOPS), which provided occupational training for the unemployed, had over 9,000 trainees in 1979-80; but its later equivalent, called the Job Training Scheme, in 1985-86 had only 4,300 trainees. Part of the rationale for this dramatic reduction was the collapse of placement rates (that is the proportions of trainees finding work after the end of their courses) during the late 1970s and early 1980s.

TABLE 9.6:

Proportion of Scottish Adult Trainees Finding Work

	1979 %	1981 %	1984 %	1985 %
Working/using skill	49	28	39	46
Working/not using skill	14	11	12	11
Unemployed	37	61	49	43

Source: Manpower Services Commission, *Annual Reports*.

The figures in Table 9.6 illustrate clearly the extent to which government training programmes are constrained by the performance of the economy as a whole. The increase in placement rates more recently has resulted partly from the closure of those courses with low rates. In the process, a number of Scottish skillcentres (where much of this type of training is carried out) have been shut down, including those at Dumbarton and Queenslie in Glasgow. There is a genuine dilemma here. Where there is mass unemployment should not the government seek to enhance the skills of unemployed people and so raise their employability? The problem is that training competes for resources with many other services such as education, health and the personal social services. If trainees are not getting jobs, questions are raised as to the effectiveness of continuing with training at existing levels. One rationale for maintaining high levels of training would be if the economy were about to begin growing in employment terms. Few forecasters take an optimistic view of the prospect for a significant and sustained growth in jobs in Scotland.

Although occupational training for the unemployed has been cut back significantly, the numbers receiving basic skills training and work preparation courses have increased. The objective of these types of courses is not the provision of high-level, vocational skills; rather, the courses tend to be short (lasting a few weeks at most) and may be the prelude to more sophisticated training. They range across practical job search and interview techniques, assessment courses where the unemployed may try out a series of activities, and work preparation courses (for example, for women coming back to the labour market after a break for family reasons).

A recent development in the field of training for the unemployed was the *Job Training Scheme*. Run on a trial basis in 1986 in nine areas (including Dundee) this scheme had, somewhat misleadingly, the same name as the existing occupational training scheme for the unemployed. In 1987 the scheme was introduced on a national basis. It was targeted at 18 to 25 year olds, offering them training courses lasting six months, starting with a one week period of assessment. The trainees were paid travel expenses together with an allowance which was equivalent to the individual's existing benefit. Basically, the individuals on the scheme were removed from the count of the unemployed at little cost to the government. Critics saw the scheme as the first step towards the development of the American 'workfare' system where the unemployed work for their benefit.

Whatever the rationale behind the scheme's introduction it appeared to have some positive features. The staff of the Dundee project responsible for running the pilot scheme in their area saw merit in the quality of the initial assessment course, the combination of work experience and off-the-job training, and free access to college courses.[9] However, the scheme attracted widespread criticism. In many ways it appeared to be the first stage in the development of an equivalent of the former Youth Opportunities Programme (YOP) for young adults. As such it faced the perils the YOP had to contend with, such as variability in the quality of training.

The major difficulty with training schemes lies in the old maxim 'training does not create jobs'. They can make it easier for some people to get jobs in competition with others. They can raise the effectiveness with which work is carried out, to the long-run benefit of the economy. However, unless there are vacancies that cannot be filled due to shortages of people with the necessary skills, training does not create jobs in the short term. In recognition of this much of the recent growth of employment services has gone into direct or indirect job creation.

Job Creation

The *Community Programme* (CP), which was incorporated in Employment Training in 1988, provided temporary jobs lasting up to a year and was targeted at the long-term unemployed. The *Enterprise Allowance Scheme* (EAS), which is still separate, gives a subsidy for one year to unemployed people starting up their own business. One programme removed people from unemployment by providing a large number of temporary jobs; the other is intended to effect a permanent transition from unemployment to self-employment by offering a temporary financial support. We now discuss each in turn.

Community Programme: The CP was in a long line of job creation schemes beginning in 1975. During 1986-87, the scheme catered for around 45,000 long-term unemployed in Scotland. The target groups for the scheme were: people aged 18 to 24 who had been out of work for at least six of the previous nine months; and people aged 25 or over who had been out of work for at least 12 of the previous 15 months. They must also have been directly or indirectly (through another member of the family) in receipt of benefit in relation to their unemployment. From October 1987 the minimum period out of work qualifying people for the CP became 12 months.

The jobs available under the CP were created by sponsors and agents, principally local authorities and voluntary organisations. Survey evidence shows that over 40 per cent of participants worked on environmental projects (for example landscaping, gardening and construction), most involving work of an unskilled nature. A further 16 per cent of jobs were described as 'manual'.

Unlike earlier job creation schemes, the CP was primarily a provider of part-time jobs. Over 80 per cent of the participants were part-time. In part this reflected a constraint placed on organisations involved in the scheme that the average wage paid to the worker could not exceed £67 per week (in 1987). In effect, by keeping a relatively low average wage and so creating a high proportion of part-time jobs the impact of the CP on unemployment was increased. It reflected a dilemma when unemployment is at very high levels. Is it better to offer a full-time (albeit temporary job) to a smaller number or a part-time job to a greater number of the long-term unemployed?

The spreading of the job creation effort thinly over a large number of the unemployed leads to a series of consequences in terms of the types of unemployed people benefiting from the scheme. Around 80 per cent of participants were single and 65 per cent under the age of 25. For older, married unemployed people the low part-time wages available on the CP were simply not financially attractive. Given the preponderance of the young, only 58 per cent of participants had been unemployed for over a year. Although not related to the issue of part-time jobs, it is important to note that only around 20 per cent of CP participants were female, reflecting the impact of benefit entitlement on eligibility for the scheme. Many unemployed married women are not eligible for unemployment benefit because they have exhausted their entitlement to it, or for income support because they cannot claim separately from their husbands. As a consequence they did not qualify for a place on the CP.

One of the main criticisms of the CP was the lack of a proper training component. When taken together with the relatively low level of many of the jobs available under the scheme, this was used to explain the modest percentages of participants who found work when they finished with the scheme. A survey of people leaving the CP found that nearly eight months after leaving only around 30 per cent were in employment.[10] However, it has to be remembered that the long-term unemployed are one of the most difficult groups to place in work. Once an individual has been unemployed for even a relatively short period of time his or her chances of finding a job deteriorate rapidly. The experience of people leaving the CP has to be compared with the very low proportion of the longer term unemployed who would have found a job if they had not gone on the scheme.

Employment Training Scheme: As already mentioned, in September 1988 the Community Programme, both Job Training Schemes and most other facilities for adults (except the Enterprise Allowance Scheme) were amalgamated in the new ET scheme. A key change from the CP is that participants are paid an allowance equal to their benefit plus about £10 a week. This is intended to make the scheme more attractive to the unemployed with dependants than the CP which paid a fixed and relatively low wage.[11]

Enterprise Allowance Scheme: The EAS offers unemployed people an allowance of £40 per week for a period of one year to assist them to set up their own business. The potential viability of businesses is not assessed but recipients of the allowance must establish at the outset that they can raise £1,000 to put into the business start-up. The scheme is very simple to administer and cheap to run.

During 1986-87 around 8,000 unemployed people in Scotland benefited from the scheme. However, this is one scheme where Scotland's share of national places is less than would be anticipated in relation to its share of unemployment. The scheme depends on demand from the unemployed, and just as Scotland has a relatively small share of Britain's self-employed, so its unemployed are not as willing as their counterparts south of the border to take part in the EAS.

The scheme appears to be relatively successful when evaluated from the perspective of businesses surviving beyond the subsidy period. Survey evidence suggests that three years after entering the scheme 50 per cent were still trading. Furthermore, for every 100 businesses surviving there were an average of 99 additional employees, roughly half of whom were working full-time.

The difficulties with the EAS are basically twofold. First, the MSC has estimated that around 50 per cent of the businesses would have been started without a subsidy. This problem is known as 'deadweight' and refers to a situation where a grant or subsidy is paid to individuals or organisations, for doing something they would have done anyway. Second, a very large proportion of the businesses set up provide services to essentially local markets. Around 75 per cent of the businesses are in small retail premises, miscellaneous services (mainly garage repairs) and the building trades. The problem is quite straightforward: unless markets for these services are growing the influx of new businesses will simply lead to increased competition and lower profits all round. To the extent that the EAS businesses have a good survival rate this may be at the expense of other businesses in their local areas. In effect, part of the benefit of the EAS will be lost as some existing small businesses go bust, leading to unemployment for their owners and employees. In these circumstances unemployment is redistributed rather than reduced.

CONCLUSIONS

Over the last decade unemployment has become a major social problem on a scale as great or possibly greater than the experience of the 1930s.

Employment services have responded to this massive problem in two ways: they have expanded substantially in quantitative terms and have diversified significantly with the introduction of a battery of new measures. There are various perspectives which can be adopted in evaluating these developments. The most cynical interpretation is that the developments have been directed principally towards reducing the published statistics of unemployment rather than tackling the problem itself. This view is supported by the numerous changes in the methods of counting the unemployed which have in the main reduced the measured level of unemployment. In addition, participation in employment schemes has increasingly been restricted to benefit recipients, that is the people who appear in the official count of the unemployed.

There can be little argument about the basic accuracy of this perception. It must also be stated, however, that in a very short period of time the MSC developed a richly varied portfolio of schemes, directed at different groups of the unemployed and offering them a variety of supports. The operating environment has been difficult. No sooner was the one-year YTS in place than the government moved the MSC towards a two-year scheme. The number of participants on programmes has been increased dramatically in very short periods, with the CP being a particular case in point.

The schemes which have been developed are by no means perfect, and a number of criticisms have been voiced in this chapter. However, a large amount of commitment has gone into many of these schemes, from MSC operational staff and from sponsors (such as local authorities, voluntary agencies and community groups). The MSC was allocated the role of patching up a problem which has deep-seated economic and social causes. Employment services cannot really cure such a problem. They certainly made it less visible and at best they also made it more bearable for the unemployed themselves.

References

1. M. Wicks, 'The Decade of Inequality', *New Society*, 6th February 1987.
2. N. Fraser and A. Sinfield, 'Can We Afford High Unemployment?', *Unemployment Bulletin*, July 1985.
3. P. Warr, 'Twelve Questions about Unemployment and Health' in B. Roberts *et al.* (eds.), *New Approaches to Economic Life*, Manchester University Press, 1985.
4. M.H. Brenner, 'Mortality and the National Economy: A Review of the Experience of England and Wales, 1936-76' *Lancet*, 1979, vol.2, pp.568-73.
5. J. Burgoyne, 'Unemployment and Married Life', *Unemployment Bulletin*, November 1985.
6. *Unemployment Bulletin*, Autumn 1986.
7. *Outlook on Training: Review of the Employment and Training Act, 1973*, Manpower Services Commission, 1980.
8. NEDC, *Competence and Competition: Training and Education in the Federal Republic of Germany, the United States and Japan*, NEDO, 1984.
9. *Glasgow Herald*, 16 January 1987.
10. P. Turner, 'After the Community Programme: Results of the First Follow-up Survey', *Employment Gazette*, January 1985.
11. *Training for Employment*, Cm.316, HMSO, 1988.

FURTHER READING

Employment Gazette, HMSO monthly.
Produced by the Department of Employment, this journal contains statistics, news of developments and articles on employment topics. The perspective is generally supportive of government policies.

Unemployment Bulletin, Unemployment Unit.
This journal is published regularly by the independent Unemployment Unit and provides a critical perspective on employment issues, backed up by good statistical information.

N. Fraser and A. Sinfield, 'The Scottish Labour Force in Recession' in D. McCrone (ed.), *The Scottish Government Yearbook 1987*, Unit for the Study of Government in Scotland, University of Edinburgh, 1987.
A useful general discussion of employment problems in Scotland.

10

SERVICES FOR THE ELDERLY AND FOR THE PHYSICALLY DISABLED

INTRODUCTION

In this chapter attention is focused on two large groups in the population and the assistance they receive from the services discussed in earlier chapters of the book. Various cash benefits and services have grown up within these systems to meet the particular needs of the elderly and of people with physical handicaps: policies of 'positive discrimination' to use the term originally coined by Richard Titmuss. The result is a bewildering array of provisions made by central and local government, and also by voluntary and private-for-profit organisations. Likewise professionals from many disciplines are concerned, together with the very important 'informal carers' – families, friends and neighbours. This is often referred to as the 'mixed economy of social welfare'. Inevitably there is some overlap between the two sections of the chapter, for many services cater for both elderly and disabled people who have many needs in common; moreover, two-thirds of the disabled are also of pension age.

Some of the consequences of this diversity and complexity of provision, which runs throughout the social services, have already been touched on elsewhere in the book. There may be wasteful duplication of services. Potential beneficiaries may not be fully informed of their entitlements or may be put off by the complexities of the application process. While some benefits are universal, others are available only on a test of means which may act as a further deterrent. Individuals may resent being categorised as 'old' or 'disabled' and be reluctant to accept differential treatment. Further, with the exception of cash benefits, the services available differ from area to area. For largely historical reasons there are considerable local variations in the inherited stock of hospitals and residential homes, and local authorities also differ in their political and financial commitments to the social services. Individuals with like needs may then receive different levels of service according to where they live, what is called in the social administration literature 'territorial inequality'. In Scotland there are particular difficulties in providing services for scattered rural populations, and the territorial inequalities tend to be greater north than south of the border.

A recurrent theme in any discussion of the social services is the scarcity of resources in relation to potential demand and the consequent 'rationing' of provision. The elderly already account for over a half of public expenditure on social security and the health and personal social services. If services need to be extended there is, however, no reason why government, at central or local level, should be the sole provider. Many individuals are able, and many prefer, to take some of the responsibility for themselves when, for example, they accumulate private savings for old age or purchase private domestic help. It may be more difficult to plan and save in advance for the less predictable needs of chronic illness or physical handicap. In the final analysis, of course, the money to pay for public social benefits comes out of the pockets of taxpayers and ratepayers. There may be limits to the extent to which taxpayers are prepared to sacrifice their current levels of consumption, and those of their families, in order to finance benefits for the elderly or disabled or to make forced savings for their own old age. Higher rates of economic growth and lower levels of unemployment than we have experienced in the 1970s and 1980s would make more resources available for the social services.

THE ELDERLY POPULATION

The 'problem' of old age is to a large extent a creation of the late nineteenth and twentieth centuries. The relatively small numbers who survived into old age before the nineteenth century revolution in public health and standards of living in the main worked on into old age or were cared for by their families. Others received alms from church or private charity; outdoor poor law relief or the hated poorhouse were the last resort of the least fortunate. The position has changed dramatically since the turn of the century. The size of the elderly population has increased threefold as a proportion of the total, and new policies of compulsory retirement have raised fresh problems of providing alternative incomes for large and increasing numbers of non-working old people. Nor do the elderly always take kindly to the fall in income and loss of status and occupation which retirement may bring, and too little attention has been given to preparation for the change in lifestyle. There are large class differences here: the middle classes have on the whole a wider range of interests to ease the transition to retirement and also the financial means to pursue them.

The elderly population is generally defined as people of retirement pension age, that is men over age 65 and women over 60, who together make up some 17 per cent of the population of Scotland. However, much of the data we will be using, in particular for the health and personal social services, relates to a smaller group, men *and* women of 65 and over. There are nearly three-quarters of a million people of this age, over 14 per cent of the population. The demographic problem of the next two decades, as Table 10.1 shows, will not be so much the increase in the total numbers of the elderly but rather the ageing of the elderly population itself. By the year 2000 more than two-fifths of the elderly – over 325,000 men and women – will be over the age of 75, and one in ten – 74,000 individuals – will be 85 years of age and over. It is these older age groups, in which women outnumber men by two to one, who

TABLE 10.1:

Size and Composition by Age of the Elderly Population (65 and over) in Scotland, 1983-2000

	Persons	65-74 %	75-84 %	85+ %
1983	729,021	60.0	33.0	7.0
1990	748,681	57.2	34.2	8.5
2000	739,355	55.9	33.5	10.4

Source: Figures supplied by General Register Office for Scotland in July 1986.

make the greatest demands on the health and personal social services. A further complication is the uneven spread of the elderly population between different parts of Scotland, to a large extent the result of the emigration of younger people from the remoter, rural areas in search of employment in the central belt, in England or overseas. People of 65/60 years of age make up about 16 per cent of the population in the Central and Strathclyde regions but over 20 per cent in the Borders, Dumfries and Galloway and the Western Isles. Within the regions there are also wide variations: in a post-war housing estate like Drumchapel West on the outskirts of Glasgow, 5.7 per cent of the population are of pension age, whereas in a long-established seaside resort like West Kilbride, favoured by the retired, the proportion is 17.8 per cent.

The elderly are, of course, a cross-section of society from all social, occupational and income groups who have little in common except that they have reached a certain age. Too often they are stereotyped in negative, 'ageist' terms as very old, in poor health and poverty-stricken, and much is written of the 'burden of dependency'. But the great majority are active, in reasonable health and able to live independent and satisfying lives. Many give as well as receive help – a point too often overlooked – in assisting children and grandchildren, neighbours and friends, or working for voluntary organisations. Nearly 95 per cent live in their own homes or those of their families and of these only 15 per cent receive any assistance from the local authority personal social services. Even among severely disabled elderly people three times as many are being cared for at home as in institutions. However, about one in four people over age 75 have no spouse or surviving children and the capacity for self-care declines with advancing years. Thus a small number – between five and six per cent – are living in residential homes or hospitals.

Community care is the stated objective of official policies for the elderly, and in that more than nine out of ten elderly people live outside institutions this objective would appear to have been largely achieved. What generally happens, however, is that they live completely independent lives and the bulk of such assistance as may be required comes from their families. In so far as the community, however that may be defined, is concerned the involvement tends to be marginal and confined in the main to near neighbours, the local authority personal social services or voluntary organisations. In the 1980s there have been some signs of a wider community participation in the growth of good neighbour, street warden and similar schemes but they are still very limited in scope. Contrary to much talk of family neglect, most families, in particular daughters and daughters-in-law, have continued to show a strong commitment to their older members, albeit under increasing strain.[1] In extreme cases psychological or even physical abuse of a difficult old person may result. Families now have fewer members to share the caring and about one in two married women are employed outside the home whether from choice or necessity. With greater longevity many of the carers are of pension age and may be in need of assistance themselves. The increase in single parenthood, and in divorce and remarriage rates, may raise still further problems, while the ability of families to care for growing numbers of very old parents is a matter for concern.

THE FINANCIAL CIRCUMSTANCES OF PENSIONERS

An adequate income is of course basic to a satisfactory life in old age. State benefits for the elderly have been discussed in chapter 2. Here we take an overall look at the incomes of the elderly from all sources, occupational as well as state pensions, income from investments and private savings as well as indirect income from benefits in kind, in particular the national health service. The picture often painted of the financial circumstances of the elderly is one of sharp falls in income after retirement, leading to standards of living far below those of the working population and implying widespread poverty. There is some truth in this but the real position is very much more complex and, overall, less sombre.

The great majority of people retire at or before the official retirement age and an immediate fall in income is inevitable, particularly as earnings tend to peak towards the end of working life, at least for non-manual employees. Information, however, is not available to compare incomes before and after retirement for such a large section of the population. The usual convention, which is followed here, is to look at the incomes of the retired population in relation to those of the current generation of workers. In doing so, it must, of course, be borne in mind that, while heating costs are in general higher in old age, family commitments have in most cases been completed, national insurance and occupational pension contributions no longer have to be met, income tax is lower and work expenses are a thing of the past.

For today's pensioners taken as a whole, the state retirement pension, supplementary benefit (income support), housing benefit and various disability allowances make up about 60 per cent of gross incomes, occupational pensions another 22 per cent, and income from earnings and from investments nine per cent each. The most important of these is the national insurance pension which all but a very few people of pension age receive. The pension is the equivalent of about a third of average net male earnings, after the deduction of income tax and national insurance contributions, in the case of a single person and about a half in the case of married couples. This compares with about a fifth and less than a third respectively in the late 1940s, demonstrating how the incomes of the elderly have improved over time in comparison with those of the average worker. The majority of pensioners also have a second income, although in many cases it is small, from the state earnings-related pension scheme (SERPS), an occupational pension, earnings or private investments. Fiegehen in his very useful article on 'Income after Retirement[2] estimates that *per capita* disposable income, that is income after the payment of taxes and contributions, of pensioners in 1984-85 was nearly 70 per cent of that of non-pensioners, or 75 per cent if account is taken of benefits in kind, notably the national health service of which the elderly make much greater than average use.

These are average figures and conceal wide inequalities of incomes within the pensioner population. Fiegehen has made an analysis of these inequalities using data from the Family Expenditure Survey. From this he concludes that: first, 'many pensioners are as well off as workers and their families'; second, 'pensioners are in general a quarter better off than people below pension age who are not in work (the unemployed, the disabled, lone women, etc.)'; third, 'few pensioners are very well off (only one in ten has an income above the average for working families)'; and, fourth, 'few workers and their families have incomes as low as most pensioners' (only one-fifth of working families are below the average pensioner income). Although the overall income position of pensioners has improved very considerably, many still have relatively low incomes. Most pensioners rely on the state pension as their largest single source of income and this makes up 60 per cent or more of their total gross incomes. Over 20 per cent are having these pensions supplemented by means-tested income support. Significant numbers are living below the supplementary benefit (income support) level, the 'official' poverty line, because they are not claiming all the benefits to which they are entitled, through ignorance of their rights or dislike of the means test. The amounts unclaimed are, however, in most cases small. Particularly badly off are very old lone women – widows and spinsters – two-fifths of whom were drawing supplementary benefit in 1982. In the case of widows, their husbands' occupational pensions, if any, may have died with them or been much reduced. Unmarried women are less likely than pensioners as a whole to have occupational pensions, and any savings they may once have had have been used up with advancing years.

The *wealth* (or capital assets) of the pensioner population should also be taken into account, although in the main it receives relatively little attention in the social administration literature. Taking the wealth of the pensioner population as a whole, Fiegehen estimates that in 1982 net marketable wealth was about a quarter higher per head than for other adults. By net marketable wealth is meant total assets – homes, savings and investments, cars and consumer durables – after the deduction of debts such as mortgages, hire purchase commitments and bank loans. For the large numbers of pensioners who are owner occupiers – one in three in Scotland and one in two in England – their houses are often the most important single asset and, unlike the majority of the non-pensioner population, the mortgages have in most cases been repaid. Maintenance and repairs of their properties may, however, be a heavy drain on income, and some of the most acute poverty is to be found among elderly owner occupiers, particularly those living in old property in decaying inner-city areas. There are very large inequalities of wealth as of income within the pensioner population and with increasing age wealth declines as savings get used up and are not replaced.

THE ELDERLY AND THE NATIONAL HEALTH SERVICE

Although the majority of the elderly enjoy reasonably good health, as we have noted already, the incidence of sickness and disability does increase with age. Expenditure on health care and personal social services per head for persons over age 65 is 2.5 times the average for all ages and for people over 75 it is 5.5 times.[3] Geriatric and psychiatric patients occupy about half of all NHS hospital beds at any one time, and people over 65 make disproportionate use of general practioners and domiciliary services like home nursing and chiropody. (GPs receive higher capitation fees for patients over 65 and over 75.)

Scotland has taken the lead over England, and internationally too, in the development of geriatrics as a medical specialism; the University of Glasgow was the first university in the UK to found a chair of geriatric medicine. Scotland is also relatively well provided with geriatric hospital beds, with 15 per 1,000 people over age 65. Even so there are elderly patients in some areas unnecessarily occupying expensive beds in acute wards, while there are others in geriatric hospitals who would be more appropriately cared for in nursing or residential homes. Only two per cent of the elderly, however, are in hospital beds of any kind at any point in time and in many cases they need only short spells of in-patient care for surgery or other treatment. Geriatrics remain even in Scotland one of the less prestigious and less sought-after areas of medical and nursing practice, and staffing levels and standards of amenity in geriatric hospitals or wards are often inferior to those provided for other patients.[4]

In other ways, too, the elderly may not always be receiving all the medical attention they need. Some of the responsibility here rests with the elderly themselves. Many are reluctant to consult their GPs with what they mistakenly accept as the inevitable and untreatable health problems of old age; nevertheless, their right to take responsibility, if they are fit to do so, for their own health must of course be respected. The GP is the central figure in the health services for the majority of the elderly, and performs an important 'gatekeeper' role in controlling access to other health and personal social services. It has been suggested by some critics, however, that GPs and health personnel might well make more regular home visits to frailer patients to check up on their health and, in particular, to detect early signs of hypothermia, senile dementia or problems of incontinence. As it is, preventive and rehabilitative geriatric medicine are particularly neglected areas of medical practice. The elderly may benefit from the move towards primary health care teams based on group practices or health centres and providing a range of facilities including a health visitor, a home nurse and perhaps a chiropodist. The closure on grounds of economy of many local pharmacies may also deprive the elderly of easy access to simple advice and medication as well as causing inconvenience in having prescriptions dispensed.

The community health services play an important role in helping the elderly remain in their own homes when ill. The home nursing service was used by one in five people aged 65 and over in 1984, compared with one in 25 of the population under 65. The NHS chiropody service is used almost exclusively by the elderly, treating nearly one in four old people in 1984. Minor foot complaints, if untreated, may seriously affect mobility and the capacity for self-care. More old people would benefit from the service, and many patients need more frequent treatment than they receive at present, but there is an acute shortage of trained chiropodists. Elderly people, however, make less than average use of the dental services and this may have adverse effects on their eating habits. Many may not see the need for preventive dentistry but for others transport problems can make visits to the dentist difficult, particularly in rural areas.

An important component of the community health service are day hospitals which provide diagnostic, medical and rehabilitative services on an out-patient basis with the aim of keeping the elderly out of hospital. The number of day hospitals has been growing, if slowly, but there are wide variations in provision between health districts and only one in three have any special day facilities for elderly people with psychiatric problems. Transport may again raise difficulties. Day hospitals should not be confused with the local authority day centres mentioned below. The role of one is primarily medical, of the other primarily social, but they perform complementary functions in the spectrum of community services.

A case has been made by the Scottish Home and Health Department and the Social Work Services Group for the extension of the health services for the elderly to include the provision of NHS nursing homes. This, it is claimed, would relieve pressure on hospital beds and also provide more intensive care for the increasing numbers of very frail, and in particular mentally confused, inmates of residential homes.[5] A similar case has been made for England but without much hope of success.[6] Overall, Scotland does not have as wide a range of residential facilities for the elderly as are available south of the border. Opinions are, however, divided as to whether a further tier of provision would be useful or would only add to the difficulties of deciding the appropriate placement for the frailer old person, whether in sheltered housing, residential accommodation, nursing home or hospital. There has, however, been a large expansion during the 1980s in private nursing and residential homes in response to the increasing numbers of very old people, the shortfall in local authority facilities and the revised arrangements operated by the DHSS from 1983 for meeting the costs of nursing home or residential care. The standard of amenity and quality of care in some of these private homes is, however, a matter for serious concern.

THE HOUSING CONDITIONS OF THE ELDERLY

Financial assistance is available to help cover rent, certain costs incurred by owner occupiers, and rates. However, the housing which many elderly people occupy is below average in standards of amenity. The majority live in ordinary mainstream housing, usually the family home. But as the children move away and the occupants age these houses may become too large, difficult and expensive to run and heat and, if owner-occupied, costly to maintain. Grants are available from the local authorities towards the cost of insulation and other home improvements but elderly people may not be well informed about their entitlements and may be unable to cope unaided with the complexities of applying and with the upheaval of building work. If they should wish to move they may have difficulty in finding suitable smaller houses they can afford to buy or alternatively in obtaining a council tenancy. Nearly half of the elderly already live in council housing but this too may not be satisfactory as to size and amenity. There may be difficulties in obtaining a transfer although this would release a large, family-size unit. The poorest conditions are to be found among those elderly people – one in five – who live in privately rented accommodation, much of it in decaying inner-city areas. This section of the housing market is notorious for the lack of basic amenities and for poor standards of maintenance. Rent controls may deter landlords from carrying out improvements and the elderly occupants may in any case prefer to stay on in low-rent accommodation particularly in areas with which they have had long associations. Progress has, however, been made in the 1980s in the rehabilitation of such accommodation by housing associations in housing action areas where many of the residents are elderly.

In the light of evidence from the 1971 census of the unsatisfactory housing in which many elderly people lived, the Scottish Development Department drew up guidelines for a more flexible approach to meeting their needs. Three types of housing were distinguished: 'mainstream' housing, that is ordinary housing stock; 'amenity' housing, that is small dwellings (usually flats) with central heating and various built-in facilities such as easily reached cupboards and switches; and 'sheltered' housing, that is amenity housing with a resident warden, a call-system and possibly communal dining, laundry or recreational facilities. It was envisaged that the majority of the elderly would continue to live in small mainstream dwellings but that the supply of amenity and sheltered housing would be greatly increased either by conversion of existing properties or by new building. In recent years there has been a marked increase in the construction of owner-occupied housing designed for the elderly, but in the absence of the same tradition of home ownership in Scotland as in England fewer old people have a house to sell to finance the purchase of a new dwelling. A target of 25 local authority or housing association sheltered units per 1,000 of the population over 65 seemed reasonable in the early 1970s but subsequently this target was doubled.[7] Table 10.2 shows the considerable progress that was made between 1979 and 1985 in such public provision.

TABLE 10.2:

Local Authority and Housing Association Dwellings for the Elderly and the Disabled in Scotland, 1979 and 1985.

	Shelt'd Housing	Shelt'd W'chair	Amenity Housing	Other W'chair	Ambulant Disabled	Other Adapted	TOTAL
1979	6,877	154	2,544	443	1,641	911	12,570
1985	18,673	630	6,389	999	3,178	7,784	37,654

Source: Figures supplied by the Scottish Development Department in May 1986.

By 1986 there were 47 places in sheltered housing for every 1,000 people over 65 and it is estimated that by 1989 this figure will have risen to about 61. In the meantime, research has been commissioned by the Scottish Development Department with the object of refining the measures used to assess applicants for the various types of special housing. A number of other questions have been raised about the validity of the claims that are made for sheltered housing. Are the appropriate mixes of ages and states of dependency achieved in selecting residents so that they can be of mutual assistance to each other? What happens to tenants as they become frailer and more dependent? What role is the warden expected to fulfil? Would it be better if small numbers of sheltered units were included in ordinary housing schemes rather than, as is more generally the case, being concentrated in segregated developments? Is sheltered housing an unnecessarily costly answer to the needs of the elderly? Small one-storey houses, perhaps built on infill sites in residential areas, or suitably converted flats in older property, might be less costly and equally suitable.

CARE IN THE COMMUNITY

The official objective of policies for the elderly, as we have seen, has been to enable them to remain in the community for as long as possible. Increasingly both professionals and lay people are coming round to the view that care should be seen as a continuum from completely independent living to acute hospital treatment. Ideally, a whole range of domiciliary and residential options should be available to older people for use as and when necessary. The elderly may, of course, need guidance in making choices, which is not always available or well-informed, and there is much evidence of inappropriate use of resources, involving unnecessary expense to the social services and with possible distress to the individual. The great majority of elderly people do in fact manage on their own or with support from their families. So far, however, while much has been spoken and written about community care the outcome has been disappointing. The Audit Commission in a report published in 1986, *Making a Reality of Community Care*, was highly critical of the slow and uneven development of services in the community, particularly in view of the large-scale closure of geriatric and psychiatric wards, and it held both hospitals and local authorities responsible.[8] Nor have informal community initiatives been any quicker to get off the ground.

The core of the community care services are those personal social services which it is the responsibility of local authorities to provide, either as a mandatory duty, as in the case of the home help service, or as part of their general duty 'to promote social welfare' under section 12 of the Social Work (Scotland) Act, 1968. In most cases the client is directed to these services by a general practitioner or other health personnel; only rarely are elderly people in contact with a social worker. On the whole the elderly are not popular with social workers, nor is working with the elderly given the attention it merits in social work training. Goldberg and Connelly, from their review of research into the effectiveness of social care for the elderly, stress the need for a much larger contribution from social workers in supporting the elderly and their families and in promoting community initiatives.[9] Undue priority is perhaps given to their statutory responsibilities for the welfare of children and the mentally ill.

Nevertheless, the elderly make very substantial use of the resources of social work departments. Residential care for the elderly accounted for over half of their total expenditure in the mid-1980s, and as many as 90 per cent of the clients of the home help service were over 65. Even so, only two per cent of the elderly are in residential care at local authority expense and less than 15 per cent are receiving any of the domiciliary services. The home help service is the most widely used and most costly of these services. About one in eight or nine people over age 65, in the main old people without family support, were receiving the service in the mid-1980s. It provides invaluable social contacts as well as help with cleaning, shopping and cooking. However, provision has not kept pace with, and in some areas has fallen behind, the growth in the numbers of elderly. Consequently, the service is 'rationed', both as to the number of clients and the amount of assistance each client receives, which may be as little as one or two hours per week. Moreover, very few authorities will provide a home help when a female relative is on hand, however hard-pressed she may be. Local authorities may make a 'reasonable' means-tested charge for the service, except to people in receipt of income support. The means tests and the charges may deter some old people from applying for a home help or restrict the amount of assistance they are willing to purchase. The domiciliary meals service and luncheon clubs come next in popularity. Potential demand again exceeds supply both as to the number of recipients and the frequency with which meals are provided, which in the main is limited to between two and four a week. The meals are generally supplied by the school meals service and there are doubts as to their suitability for old people. The meals service is an important example of collaborative practice between the statutory services which supply the meals and volunteers (generally members of the Women's Royal Voluntary Service) who deliver them or run the lunch clubs. A new development is the supply of meals in residential homes to local non-residents.

Small numbers of elderly people – about 13 per 1,000 – attend day centres run by social work departments or by voluntary organisations which provide chiropody, meals and recreational facilities as well as useful social contacts for the old person and some relief for the caring family. Attendance may, however, only be possible on a few days per week because of excess demand while transport often presents problems. In all these services there are very wide differences between regions in the level of provision, as Table 10.3 demonstrates. A variety of other services, such as home visiting, laundry and library services, outings and holidays, may also be made available though here the differences in local practice are even greater. Such variations can be accounted for only in part by differences in needs or in local geography; local authorities interpret their responsibilities in very diverse ways.

TABLE 10.3:

Day Care and Domiciliary Services by Region, 1985: Recipients per 1,000 Population 65 and Over

	Persons attending day centres	Home Help clients	Persons receiving meals-on-wheels
Borders	8.9	61	19
Central	16.0	98	26
Dumfries and Galloway	17.7	60	24
Fife	0.9	107	24
Grampian	7.1	85	19
Highland	6.7	58	37
Lothian	24.3	91	23
Strathclyde	14.2	89	18
Tayside	10.7	69	15
Orkney	0.0	96	0
Shetland	19.4	139	75
Western Isles	0.0	123	0
Scotland	13.5	87	21

Notes: Day centres include registered voluntary centres as well as local authority provision.

Source: Social Work Services Group, *Statistical Bulletin: Home Care Services, Day Care Establishments and Day Services 1985*.

RESIDENTIAL CARE FOR THE ELDERLY

Unsuitable housing, inadequate domiciliary services or lack of family support rather than physical infirmity may precipitate the need for residential care. It is the statutory responsibility of the social work department to make provision for alternative accommodation for persons who for reasons of age or infirmity are unable to receive adequate care in their own homes. If a person is in need of care but refuses to enter residential accommodation the department may exercise compulsory powers of admission. Such cases are rare but they raise important questions of individual liberty. What level of damage to self and inconvenience to neighbours can be tolerated before an old person is moved against his or her wishes? A balance has to be struck between the risks of remaining independent and the risk of becoming institutionalised if committed to care.[10] Social work departments may either themselves build and run residential homes or sponsor elderly people in voluntary or private homes. The latter are built and operated by voluntary bodies or on a commercial basis but are inspected and registered by the departments. There is accommodation in local authority and voluntary homes for only 21 per thousand persons over age 65, with wide local variations, although as early as 1963 central government set a target of 25 places. In fact, there have been cuts in the 1980s in the rate of expansion of local authority homes in spite of ageing populations, and social work departments are now looking for more flexible and economical ways of using resources, such as day care or short periods of rehabilitative residential care. Purpose-built homes may have built-in provision for day care or short-term residents and some regions, for example Strathclyde, are endeavouring to ensure that such facilities are available in every area. Staff, however, are already under strain given the rise in recent years in the average age of residents and the increasing incidence of physical handicap and mental confusion.

There are two ways in which elderly people may be helped, according to their financial means, with the heavy costs of residential care. If they are placed in local authority homes, or in voluntary or private (commercial) homes with local authority sponsorship, the minimum charge is set so as to equal, together with an allowance for personal expenses, the basic retirement pension. If an elderly person has little or no other income the social work department meets the difference between the minimum charge and the actual cost. If, on the other hand, an elderly person enters a voluntary or private nursing or residential home on his or her own initiative, the DHSS has, since 1983, taken responsibility on a means-tested basis for meeting the home's fees through supplementary benefit (income support). The fees which can be met are, however, subject to a maximum level laid down nationally. This development in DHSS policy, together with the rise in the numbers of very elderly people and the shortfall in local authority accommodation, has led to a massive growth in private-for-profit homes. In Strathclyde, for example, there was a ninefold increase in the number of private homes in the first half of the 1980s with a particular concentration in the seaside resorts of Argyll and Ayrshire. The phenomenal growth, which is paralleled in other parts of Scotland, has led to widespread concern. Social work department staff have been hard-pressed to inspect homes before registration and to monitor the quality of care provided. General practitioners and other health and social services in the popular areas are not equipped to cope with the massive increase in the elderly population, and distances are often such as to make visiting by relatives difficult. Nor, it is claimed, are the maximum fees which the DHSS (now the DSS) is prepared to cover high enough to provide adequate standards of care, and staff are often poorly paid and overworked.

Local authority and voluntary homes had already come under criticism for the hospital-type regimes they operated, the lack of privacy and stimulation for residents, the absence of opportunities for resident participation in management, and the disregard of rehabilitation for return to the community. Doubts have been expressed by the Health Advisory Service for England and Wales about the quality of care provided in private homes and there is no reason to suppose that the position is any better in Scotland.

Furthermore, the easier access to residential care which is now possible highlights the problem of 'misplacement'. An elderly person, or relatives on his or her behalf, may choose to enter a nursing or residential home without undue financial burden and without professional assessment of the need for such care. Some people may then give up independent living before they need to and thus accelerate the ageing process – as well as adding to the cost to the social services. Even before the vast expansion in private homes various studies carried out both north and south of the border of the elderly in residential homes or geriatric hospitals had already provided evidence of large numbers of people who could have continued to live in their own homes with some support from the social services.[11]

The recent growth in the private market for residential care also raises renewed interest in the debate about 'welfare for profit'. A case has been made for the increased privatisation of other welfare services, such as home helps, domiciliary meals and the like, on the grounds that this would enhance supply, cut back on public expenditure and give the consumer greater freedom of choice. Conversely, it has been argued that economies of scale can be expected from public provision and that there are ethical objections to profits being made from the needs of dependent sections of the population.[12]

COMMUNITY CARE AND THE VOLUNTARY SERVICES

The new concern with a wider and more imaginative community involvement in caring for the elderly underlines the importance of the voluntary sector, which has had a long tradition of service in this field. The churches have provided and still provide a very considerable part of the residential care and their local congregations have shown their Christian concern in home visiting and in providing a variety of social and recreational activities. Large national organisations like Age Concern, Help the Aged and the National Council for the Care of Old People have provided services, support and advice for individual elderly people and their families, and have undertaken research into the needs of old people as well as playing an important advocacy role in pressing on government the need for improvements in state provision. Others, such as the Women's Royal Voluntary Service, have worked in collaboration with the social work departments in running meals-on-wheels, luncheon clubs, laundry and library services. In some cases the local authorities pay on a fee-for-service basis for facilities provided, in others they make grants to the general funds of the voluntary agencies.

New developments in voluntary activity are in the main more informal and varied in nature, and more local in scale such as Good Neighbour and Street Warden schemes. Their objectives are to substitute for family care by performing simple but important tasks like shopping and home visiting or keeping a watch on elderly people to detect early signs of a need for help. Others aim to help relatives to keep old people out of residential care by providing services like night-sitting. The Crossroads Care Attendant Scheme is a more formalised example of such assistance. The part-time care attendants, who relieve relatives by day or night, at weekends or for holiday breaks, receive some training and are paid. By 1986 there were three dozen Crossroads schemes operating in different parts of Scotland, including the Highlands and Islands. Different again are projects which concentrate on advising elderly people on the repair and improvement of their homes, processing applications for local authority grants and supervising building work.

Most of the work involved in running and operating these new services is given on a voluntary basis and some of the funds required come from voluntary donations, but central government, social work departments and health authorities may also provide finance. Many of the new ventures are in the nature of pilot projects and for their full potential to be reached careful monitoring and evaluation are essential, the resources for which Age Concern, for example, considers should come from central and local government.[13] Other new developments are self-help initiatives, such as the stroke groups and the Alzheimers Relatives Support Group, whose primary aim is to provide mutual support and advice for the victims and their families.

The work of the voluntary organisations has sometimes suffered from inadequate financial and other support from local authorities, many of which have had doubts about the reliability and standards of service given by untrained volunteers without themselves always being willing to provide adequate training and continuing support. The voluntary organisations for their part have often been jealous of their independence and resentful of local authority supervision, even if they were receiving financial help from public funds. The longer-established voluntary agencies, local authorities and the new innovative projects will have to work together closely to bring about a greater community involvement in the welfare of the elderly. The younger elderly, who are retired but active, are one of the largest reserves of voluntary labour, but stronger efforts need to be made to bring them into the volunteer workforce.

THE PHYSICALLY DISABLED AND THE SOCIAL SERVICES

The definition of physical disability, and the enumeration and identification of the disabled population, present major difficulties. This information is, however, essential, at national level for planning services and at local level for pinpointing the individuals who require assistance. The last national investigation of the extent of handicap, defined in terms of the reduction in capacity for self care, was sponsored by the DHSS and other departments and carried out by the Office of Population Censuses and Surveys (OPCS) in the late 1960s; it was published in 1971 as *The Handicapped and Impaired in Great Britain*.[14] A new survey was commissioned by the DHSS but the results are not expected until the end of 1988. At the individual level there are a number of registers of people with particular disabilities or needs. Local education authorities keep registers of children with special educational needs, the Department of Employment of disabled adults requiring assistance in obtaining employment, and voluntary organisations of individuals with specific disabilities such as the blind, the deaf, spastics and epileptics. Local authorities have the responsibility to ascertain the numbers of disabled people in their areas and to make known to them the services available, such as home helps, adaptations to housing and aids to mobility. There is obviously considerable overlap between these registers and, more seriously, numbers of disabled people who need assistance do not appear on any register.

Recognition of the special needs of the disabled is a relatively recent phenomenon. Advances in medical science as well as environmental health improvements and higher standards of living keep alive many individuals who would formerly have died of congenital abnormalities or of diseases or accidents but can now expect normal life spans. When numbers were small the care of the disabled could be left to their families, charitable organisations or the poor law. The blind, with whose disability it is perhaps most easy to identify, were the first to benefit from both voluntary and later government activities and, with the deaf, they have continued to be the pacesetters for what are known as the 'general' classes of the handicapped. Two world wars drew attention to the needs of the war disabled, in particular for rehabilitation and retraining for employment, which was also in the national interest at times when labour was in short supply. In other fields – financial support, health and education – the disabled have on the whole benefited more from general improvements in the social services, and in particular the Beveridge reforms of the late 1940s, than from measures directed at their specific needs.

Attention did, however, turn more directly to the disabled in the 1960s and 1970s. They had not profited to the full from the economic growth or welfare reforms of the post-war years and were becoming more insistent in their demands for improvements in their benefits, encouraged by the increasing number of voluntary organisations concerned for the welfare of the disabled. This growing interest took shape in a private member's bill which became the Chronically Sick and Disabled Persons Act, 1970, extended to Scotland in 1971, and in the introduction by the government of various new cash benefits such as the attendance and mobility allowances. However, the local welfare services promised in the legislation were only beginning to get under way when the recession of the later 1970s slowed down such progress as was taking place. When in 1986 important social security legislation was passed which brought a number of changes in cash payments, the benefits for the disabled were held over for further consideration until the results of the new survey were available. In the meantime, the widespread dissatisfaction with the slowness in implementing the 1970 legislation found expression in another private member's bill which eventually reached the statute book as the Disabled Persons (Services, Consultation and Representation) Act, 1986. How successful the new act will be in hastening reforms it is too soon to say. Like its predecessor it lacks specific requirements and it did not bring any guarantee of new money to implement it.

The broad objectives of these policies is to rehabilitate the disabled, to integrate them into the community as far as is possible and to enable them to lead as near normal lives as their remaining impairments permit. By and large, this should mean living in their own or in their families' homes, with support when needed from community social services, earning their own livelihoods and taking a full part in social and recreational activities. In practice the living standards of the disabled are generally inferior to those of their able-bodied contemporaries, and families provide the greatest part of the caring, often under considerable strain. Again, as in the case of the elderly, the services available may vary widely according to where the disabled person happens to live and in this case also according to the type and cause of handicap. Thus the blind and the war-disabled enjoy preferential treatment over other sections of the handicapped population. It should not be overlooked, however, that many disabled people can manage on their own without outside assistance and do not wish to be categorised as handicapped, a choice which must be respected.

The OPCS report of 1971 made a distinction between *impairment*, which is the physical fact of 'having a defective limb, organ or mechanism of the body' (few people are without some impairment if it is only less than perfect eyesight, hearing or teeth); *disability*, which is 'the loss or reduction of functional ability' for self-care; and *handicap*, which is 'the disadvantage or restriction of activity caused by disability'. In practice, the borderlines between the categories are blurred and the terms are used interchangeably, although 'disability' and 'disabled' have become the more common usage. In 1971, according to the report, there were in Scotland some 108,000 severely or appreciably handicapped people over the age of 16 living in their own homes, and large numbers of these were elderly women living alone. These figures underestimated the handicapped population as they did not include people living in institutions or children under 16. The numbers have increased over the ensuing years as a result of continued medical advances, the ageing of the population, and the inadequate attention given to the prevention of handicap in, for example, ante-natal and peri-natal services. Nor are the disabled evenly spread throughout Scotland: there is an estimated range from 25 to 40 per 1,000 of the population between areas.

A further complication is the wide range of disabilities which have to be catered for. These include sensory defects of vision and hearing, disabilities like arthritis and muscular dystrophy which affect mobility, and conditions which may affect total functioning, such as strokes, cerebral palsy or heart and chest complaints. Some impairments, like limb amputations, are stable, some may improve and others may become progressively worse. Growing numbers of people have multiple handicaps, which may include both mental and physical disabilities. The type and amount of assistance required obviously varies from individual to individual, and from one disability to another. However, disabled people also have many problems in common: below-average incomes, the extra expense of living with a disability, difficulties of self-care and finding suitable education and employment. Attitudes are also important. The disabled may be regarded as inferior and this may reinforce self-images of inferiority in a society peopled by 'normal', healthy children and adults. In some cases this may strengthen their reluctance to seek assistance from the bewildering variety of organisations, statutory and voluntary, which exist to help them. Many handicapped people are therefore not known to the relevant agencies and are not receiving all their entitlements.

THE NATIONAL HEALTH SERVICE AND THE DISABLED

The NHS plays a very important role not only in keeping alive many disabled people but also in making available the continuing medical care which many require. General practitioners are central figures in diagnosing, treating and helping individuals to manage their disabilities. Health visitors, in their routine examination of young children, are often the first to pick up signs of impairment, and have an important role in screening for developmental delays and referring to community health teams, where such exist, for multi-disciplinary assessment. But access to the GP and the various services available depends, in the main, on self-referral by disabled people or by their families; many of the handicapped, particularly among the elderly, either find difficulty in visiting their doctors or are reluctant to trouble them.

The hospital services are responsible for acute treatment in the case of serious illness or accidents, for rehabilitation and for long-term in-patient care for the severely and permanently handicapped. Acute care is generally of high quality. There is, however, a shortage, more pronounced in Scotland than in England, of multi-disciplinary rehabilitation units which would give the disabled person the wide range of medical, paramedical, educational, employment and social services which may be essential for complete recovery or the management of any remaining disability. Rehabilitation is important not only in the more obvious cases such as young victims of road accidents but also for the elderly victims of, say, strokes in order to delay entry to a residential home or geriatric hospital. NHS prosthetic aids – artificial limbs, hearing aids and so on – are not always of the highest quality and sophistication, a problem which is the subject of investigation by the health authorities at the time of writing. The Scottish Hospital Advisory Service in its report for 1980 was particularly critical of the poor standard of in-patient provision for the young physically handicapped, who may find themselves in long-stay wards with geriatric patients. It pointed to the need for small wards in general hospitals providing active rehabilitation plus privacy and a stimulating environment.[15] Physical handicap and rehabilitative medicine are not, however, prestigious areas of medical practice. They have still not received the attention they merit, although they were singled out for priority treatment as early as 1976 in the plans put forward in *The Health Services in Scotland: The Way Ahead.*[16]

CHILDREN WITH PHYSICAL DISABILITIES: SOCIAL AND EDUCATIONAL SERVICES

There is no complete, national register of disabled children, although local education and social work departments keep registers of handicapped children known to them, as do various voluntary organisations. There are likely, however, to be numbers of disabled children who are not registered with any agency. On the other hand, parents may not wish a child to be labelled as handicapped, a decision that must be accepted if they are able to cope unaided. Provision by the personal social services of advice and facilities, such as special day nursery places and home helps, is not in any case sufficient to meet the needs of those children who are already registered. Without adequate support, however, family life may suffer and in extreme cases marriages may break up under the strain, or parents may find it impossible to keep the disabled child at home. The voluntary organisations, such as Dr. Barnardo's, have been pioneers in providing long-term residential care for disabled children in such cases and in recent years have taken a lead in finding foster or adoptive parents. More needs to be done to make parents aware of such help as is available; often their first contact with officialdom does not come until the question of their child's education arises when it is obvious that outside help is indispensable.

Lack of suitable education may be as much of a handicap as the disability itself. The responsibility to provide for the education of handicapped children rests with the local education authorities as part of the duties laid upon them by the Education (Scotland) Act, 1946 to provide for every child education according to his or her 'age, aptitude and ability'. Whenever possible the handicapped child was to attend an ordinary school but for severely handicapped children special schools were to be provided with high staff/pupil ratios, specially qualified staff and appropriate environmental conditions. The number of places in special schools grew steadily from 1946 onwards, and here voluntary organisations, with local education authority financial support, played a large part. In time, however, special schools attracted increasing criticism for their low academic standards and the segregationist policies on which they were based. During the 1970s the debate about the respective merits of integrated and special school education gathered momentum. The Warnock Committee appointed to report on the education of handicapped children gave a cautious welcome to the principle of integration, in the interests of the disabled and the able-bodied child alike. More importance, however, was attached to the quality than to the location of education and the committee saw a continuing role for special schools in catering for the severely handicapped and as resource and advice centres for ordinary schools coping with less handicapped children.[17]

Provision for children with special educational needs is now covered by the Education (Scotland) Act, 1980. The great majority of such children attend ordinary schools, in principle with such personal tuition and modifications to curriculum as required. The legislation is largely concerned with children having 'pronounced, specific or complex' educational needs. Local education authorities have the duty to assess such children, to keep records of their educational needs and how it is proposed to meet them, and to re-assess them before they leave school and record if they require continuing assistance as disabled adults. Parents may ask to be involved in the assessment and they have a right of appeal against any plans made for their children with which they are not in agreement. There are some 9,450 children in local authority special schools, 440 in grant-aided special schools and 675 in independent special schools. The numbers have been declining steadily and this trend will continue as more handicapped children are integrated into ordinary schools. Some very severely handicapped or chronically ill children cannot attend school at all and receive personal tuition on a part-time, and too often very limited, basis from a visiting teacher in their own homes or in hospital.

The transition from school to adult life and work presents particular difficulties for handicapped teenagers and their parents. If the teenagers stay on at school or take up further education they remain the concern of the education department, which is also responsible for careers advice, training and job placement. If they enter a local authority or voluntary training centre for the more severely handicapped they come under the oversight of the social work department or a voluntary agency. All too often, however, without adequate guidance, and with low expectations for the future, the young person falls through the educational net and out of the employment market altogether.

EMPLOYMENT SERVICES FOR DISABLED PEOPLE

Needless to say people with disabilities often have special difficulties in finding employment. Government policies to assist them in doing so date from the Disabled Persons (Employment) Act, 1944 which, with amendments in 1958, remains the relevant statute. In the light of experience with these policies, and in response to mounting criticism of their operation, the Manpower Services Commission (MSC) made a number of changes in their services in the early 1980s and issued in 1984, for the guidance of employers and trade unions, a *Code of Good Practice on the Employment of Disabled People*. Under the 1944 Act a register is maintained of people who are substantially and permanently disabled and require assistance in finding work. Any employer of more than 20 people has a duty to employ a three per cent quota of registered disabled people. Two occupations are reserved for disabled people and people so employed do not count towards the quota. The demand for car park and lift attendants has, however, declined and the jobs are poorly paid.

To assist employers the *Disablement Advisory Service* advises on the financial and other assistance available such as grants to help with conversion of premises and purchase of special equipment for disabled employees. The Department of Employment (DE) also operates a *Disablement Resettlement Service* whose disablement resettlement officers help those with particular difficulties in finding employment – very severely disabled people, the newly disabled and people who are not well adjusted to their handicap. Other disabled people are advised by the normal jobcentre staff. The four employment rehabilitation centres in Scotland have some 300 places, which deal with over 3,000 individuals a year. The centres assess employment potential and provide rehabilitation courses for working life and preparation for training. The training schemes for able-bodied unemployed school-leavers and older workers offer special assistance to the disabled.

Many severely handicapped people are unable to cope with normal jobs and the DE runs eleven Remploy factories in Scotland, where the pace and conditions of work are adapted to individual capabilities. In addition the DE gives financial support to eleven sheltered workshops run by local authorities and voluntary organisations. Together, these factories and workshops have places for about 2,000 severely disabled people. An interesting new development is the grant-aided Sheltered Placement Scheme which caters for 250 severely handicapped workers. A local authority sponsors and employs the disabled worker and pays him or her the full rate for the job whatever the level of output achieved. The host firm provides the job and pays the sponsor for the amount of work actually done. This scheme provides sheltered employment in areas where there are no Remploy factories or sheltered workshops, with the added advantage of integrating the handicapped person into the able-bodied workforce. For people too severely handicapped to cope even with sheltered employment, or if such is not available locally, some local authorities and voluntary organisations run adult training centres which provide occupational and recreational facilities.

The employment services appear at first sight to be fairly comprehensive but they have in fact been subject to increasing criticism, not least from the former MSC, in spite of the improvements introduced in the early 1980s. By no means all handicapped people choose to put their names on the disabled register; registration is voluntary. They may be ignorant of its existence, doubtful of its usefulness, especially in times of high unemployment, or may consider it a positive disadvantage to be labelled as handicapped. They do not in any case have to be registered to make use of the services available. However, if registration is incomplete this may make it difficult for willing employers to find disabled workers with the required skills. For many years large numbers of employers have failed to fill their quotas of disabled workers but there have been very few prosecutions for non-compliance. In times of high unemployment employers may be particularly reluctant to take what they see as the risk and trouble of employing disabled people. The two occupations which are reserved for disabled people have also been widely criticised.

Other criticism has centred on the training and employment facilities provided by the DE itself. Places in employment rehabilitation centres are too few and all are located, understandably, near large centres of population – Dundee, Edinburgh, Glasgow and Bellshill. Accommodation or travel costs might, however, be met to make them more widely accessible. Likewise, there are not enough sheltered workshop places and much of the work they provide is repetitive, unskilled and poorly paid. The Remploy factories in particular are expensive to operate and they have run into management problems and difficulties in finding outlets for their limited range of products. Furthermore, the most severely handicapped workers are virtually excluded, as it is unusual for anyone to be given a place who cannot reach 30 per cent of the output of an able-bodied employee.

Overall, the employment prospects of disabled people are poor; rates of pay are low and levels of male unemployment are double those of the able-bodied population. Nevertheless, employment, even if poorly paid, gives status and social contacts. Research in Scotland has shown that young people suddenly experiencing a serious disability, say as a result of a road accident, get a good deal of help from the DE services and job prospects, especially for non-manual and skilled workers, are reasonable. On the other hand, handicapped workers who have been unemployed for some length of time, people with congenital or childhood disabilities or chronic sickness, disabled school leavers and disabled women are poorly served.[18]

FINANCIAL CIRCUMSTANCES OF THE DISABLED

Earnings of disabled people from work are less than half average wages, and the great majority of the disabled who are unable to work or cannot find employment have to rely on a confusing array of state benefits which give very different levels of income to various sections of the handicapped population. These are discussed in chapter 2 and only a few comments are necessary here. The state benefits fulfil two broad sets of functions: first, income maintenance payments provide a basic income for those not in work; and, second, other payments help meet the additional expenditure incurred by people with disabilities irrespective of whether or not they work. The source and level of basic income depend primarily on the cause of handicap, while the extra allowances are related to need. There is a hierarchy of benefit levels ranging from those received by war and industrial pensioners, through national insurance payments for those previously at work, to benefits for severely disabled people without insurance rights. Many of those in the last category also claim supplementary benefit (income support). Benefits related to specific needs, like the attendance and mobility allowances, do something to make up for the inadequacy of certain income maintenance benefits but even these are in some respects more generous for war and industrial claimants than for other handicapped people.

As a matter of principle, it is open to question whether income should vary with the cause of handicap rather than with need. On the practical level the complexity of the benefit structure is such that many disabled people are imperfectly informed of their rights and do not claim everything to which they are entitled. If a claimant qualifies for and receives all the various benefits available it is possible for a severely handicapped person to manage reasonably well on his or her income from the state. The position is very different if the conditions of eligibility are not met or if the individual is not in receipt of all his or her entitlements. Various proposals have been made for reform. The Disablement Alliance, a consortium of pressure groups for the disabled, has proposed a single income for all handicapped people, part pension, part a needs-related allowance. Another suggestion is a universal disability benefit related to severity of handicap and paid irrespective of income. Some countries, Sweden for example, pay part pensions to the less severely disabled to encourage them to take up at least part-time employment. The government has promised a review of the arrangements for the disabled when the results of the new survey into the extent of handicap are available towards the end of 1988, but it appears unlikely that anything as costly as these proposals will be adopted.

HOUSING AND PERSONAL SOCIAL SERVICES FOR THE HANDICAPPED

Suitable housing may be the key to leading as near normal a life as possible in the community. The cost of housing (for tenants at any rate) is by and large taken care of by housing benefit; the type and quality of housing are different matters. Like the elderly, most disabled people live in ordinary houses or flats but these may have steps and stairs, no ground-floor bedroom, passageways and doorways too narrow for wheelchair access, and unsuitable kitchens and bathrooms. The OPCS Survey of 1971 found that over a quarter of the handicapped lived in very poor housing conditions. The responsibility for providing purpose-built housing where this is needed rests with the local housing authorities. The lead was, however, taken by voluntary organisations such as the Thistle Foundation and the Cheshire Homes, which pioneered various experiments in living patterns for the disabled. Overall progress was slow at first but Table 10.2 shows that there was a three-fold growth between 1979 and 1985 in the stock of local authority and housing association special dwellings for the elderly and handicapped. Sheltered housing for the elderly has been given the highest priority but many of the elderly occupants are also disabled.

Adaptations to mainstream housing – ramps, wider doorways, alterations to kitchens and bathrooms – may, however, be sufficient. The Chronically Sick and Disabled Persons (Scotland) Act, 1972 made it mandatory for housing or social work departments to undertake such adaptations. There has been some confusion as to the respective responsibilities of the two departments, which has contributed to the delays in assessing what adaptations are needed and in carrying out the work. Limits have also been set on the amount which may be spent on any one property. Many of those who can afford it have opted to have the necessary alterations done by a private contractor at their own expense.

Even if suitably housed, many handicapped people, especially if the disability is severe or they are advanced in years, may need help with self-care and domestic chores. In the majority of cases the family provides such care while the attendance and invalid care allowances make some recognition of the financial burden this may entail, especially if paid employment has to be foregone. If family care is not available or needs to be supplemented, responsibility then rests with the social work department under either the Social Work (Scotland) Act, 1968 or the Chronically Sick and Disabled Persons (Scotland) Act, 1972. The 1972 legislation laid upon local authorities the duty to obtain information about the numbers of handicapped people in their areas and to make known to them the services available. The home help service, which is so important for the elderly, does not normally provide the regular daily assistance with personal care which many disabled people require. Overall, the services have not been growing in proportion to the increase in the disabled population and there are also wide disparities between areas in the extent of provision.

The availability or otherwise of family or social service support may be one factor which determines how long a severely handicapped person can continue to live in the community. If residential care should be necessary, but hospital treatment is not required, then responsibility rests with the social work department. There are, however, no local authority homes for the disabled in Scotland, although numbers of disabled people, whether under or over the age of 65, are living in local authority residential homes for the elderly. Social work departments have delegated responsibility for providing residential accommodation for younger disabled persons to voluntary organisations such as the Cheshire Homes, the Red Cross Society, the Spastics Society and the Thistle Foundation, which together have places for some 660 people. The majority of residents have the charges met on a means-tested basis by the DSS which also pays them a personal allowance. While it would not be a rational policy for all individual local authorities to build homes for small numbers of disabled people in their areas, waiting lists for places in voluntary homes suggest that there is an overall shortfall in provision. The responsibility to increase the number of places rests with social work departments, which might usefully provide more financial support to voluntary organisations to enable them to extend their residential services. The Chronically Sick and Disabled Persons legislation requires the social work departments and health authorities to make annual returns to parliament of any disabled persons under the age of 65 living in residential homes for the elderly or in geriatric wards. Although the intent is commendable, it is questionable whether it is always in the best interests of non-elderly disabled persons to move them from familiar surroundings, especially when suitable places in voluntary residential homes or in special hospital wards are in short supply.

MOBILITY AND ACCESS

Walking frames, wheelchairs and so on which are available through the NHS or social work departments do much to aid mobility indoors but are more restricted in use out of doors. Transport is frequently a barrier between home and work, shops or recreational facilities for disabled people who find difficulties in using public facilities. The mobility allowance, which also gives exemption from the motor vehicle licence fee, was introduced in the early 1970s with the object of helping those with severe mobility problems to run a car or to pay for taxis or other forms of transport. To those who receive it the mobility allowance is undoubtedly of great assistance, in particular as it is tax-free, payable to the working as well as non-working disabled and is not means-tested. Many disabled people, however, still cannot afford a car, even with assistance from Motability, a voluntary organisation set up with financial support from public funds expressly to help disabled people to lease or purchase a car. Motability has proved very popular but not all disabled people can find the money to cover the lump-sum deposit payable on a car and the cost of any adaptations needed, especially as the mobility allowance has to be surrendered for three or more years.

Mobility concessions, however, will be of limited use if the disabled person is unable to gain access to the facility which he wishes to visit. Access was seen as one of the key issues to be tackled by the Chronically Sick and Disabled Persons legislation. Any public premises built after the act came into force were required to provide access for the disabled to and within the building, together with special parking facilities and toilets 'in so far as it is both practicable and reasonable.' The limitations are obvious; as well as the issue of practicability and reasonableness, older buildings are not covered. Nevertheless, there have been undoubted improvements, notably in the provision of ramps and special parking and toilet facilities and the issue of parking discs. The legislation has been less successful in giving the handicapped access to the decision-making process when their personal interests are involved. It is laid down that they should be represented by handicapped persons, or those with experience of their problems, on various advisory committees dealing with issues affecting the welfare of the disabled. Disabled people themselves, however, have shown disappointingly little interest in taking up this option. The Disabled Persons (Services, Consultation and Representation) Act, 1986 aimed, among other things, at strengthening the role of the disabled and their representatives in the consultative process.

THE VOLUNTARY SERVICES

Voluntary organisations have led the way in providing for the welfare of many sections of the handicapped population and they continue to play a large part in supplementing or standing in for local authority services. In some cases they act as agents for the local authority and are paid on a fee-for-service basis. In other cases the local authority may make a general grant to the organisations' funds. This may be a considerable saving to local authorities, notably in the case of residential accommodation. Conversely, local authority fees and grants enable many voluntary organisations to remain in operation. Of particular interest has been the development of mutual aid organisations for different sections of the disabled population such as the Muscular Dystrophy Group, the Heart and Chest Foundation and the Spina Bifida Society. In many cases the initiative has come from the disabled themselves, a welcome sign of participation and self-help. Some have subsequently developed into highly professional organisations. They provide help with transport, recreational and sometimes residential facilities, as well as advice and mutual support for the disabled and their families. Increasingly they have come to play an important role both in providing funds for research into the causes and possible cures for various disabilities, and as pressure groups pushing for improvements in public services. A more recent development has been the growth of self-help groups among carers of the disabled.

The important contribution which the voluntary organisations already make to the wellbeing of the disabled could, however, be enhanced by closer co-operation among the organisations themselves and some rationalisation of their activities; the very many agencies involved in the welfare of the blind is a good case in point. More effective and more imaginative collaboration between the public and voluntary sectors would also enhance the overall contribution of both sectors to the welfare of their clients, as we saw in the case of services for the elderly.

CONCLUSIONS

It is difficult to draw general conclusions about the contribution of the social services to the welfare of two such large and heterogeneous groups as the elderly and the physically disabled. Often the elderly are stereotyped as frail, dependent and poverty-stricken, a burden on society. Ill-health does increase with advancing age and incomes fall; there are considerable numbers of old people, especially the very old, living at or below the 'official' poverty standard. But the great majority of elderly people enjoy reasonable health, live independent lives in their own homes and have incomes that have increased substantially over the past four decades, largely as a result of improvements in the state pension. The NHS has removed the possible financial burden of ill-health in old age. Housing conditions, however, are often sub-standard and there is a shortage of small, convenient units either to purchase or to rent. For those unable to manage independently, domiciliary services have not kept up with the increase in the numbers of potential clients and there is evidence of considerable strain on the families, in particular daughters and daughters-in-law who do most of the caring. Residential care for the elderly too often provides a regimented, unstimulating regime. The massive growth in private nursing and residential homes since the early 1980s has raised new concern about standards of amenity and quality of care. As the elderly population grows in numbers, and itself ages, less costly ways of caring will need to be sought: boarding-out, improved domiciliary services, greater community involvement and more imaginative use of the potential of the younger elderly.

The disabled have not shared as fully as the elderly in the economic growth of the post-war years nor in the development of the welfare state. The NHS and advances in medical science have kept large numbers of disabled people alive with prospects of normal life spans but rehabilitative medicine has been a low priority. Education and training for employment are often inadequate and job prospects and earnings are poor. For those unable to work, there is a confusing array of state benefits, based in many cases on cause of handicap rather than need, which gives rise to wide inequalities of income. Housing standards are frequently not satisfactory and the disabled have been a low priority for the personal social services. Blaxter's study of a group of disabled adults in Aberdeen illustrates the difficulties often experienced with self-care, employment, income and personal relationships. [19] One of the most encouraging signs has been the strong growth of self-help groups among the disabled which fill some of the gaps in official provision.

Prospects for the elderly and the disabled depend on the extent of future economic growth, on the willingness of the working population to accept higher rates of taxation (or fewer tax reductions) and on the political commitment of government, at central and local level, to the social services. Not least, their prospects will depend on the willingness of people to become personally involved in community care which, if it is to reach its full potential must draw upon the contribution of an increasing number of volunteers from all walks of life.

References

1. Equal Opportunities Commission, *Who Cares for the Carers?: Opportunities for those Caring for the Elderly and Handicapped,* EOC, 1982.
2. G.C. Fiegehen 'Income after Retirement', *Social Trends 16*, HMSO, 1986.
3. *The Government's Expenditure Plans 1985-86 to 1987-88*, Cmnd. 9428, HMSO, 1985.
4. *All our Tomorrows: Growing Old in Britain: Report of the Board of Science and Education*, British Medical Association, 1986.
5. Scottish Home and Health Department and Scottish Education Department, *Changing Patterns of Care: Report on Services for the Elderly in Scotland*, HMSO, 1980.
6. B. Wade, L. Sawyer and J. Bell, *Dependency with Dignity*, Occasional Papers on Social Administration No. 68, Bedford Square Press, 1983.
7. *Housing for the Elderly, Part 5*, Scottish Development Department, 1980.
8. Audit Commission, *Making a Reality of Community Care*, HMSO, 1986.
9. E.M. Goldberg and N. Connelly, *The Effectiveness of Social Care for the Elderly: An Overview of the Research*, Heinemann, 1982.
10. A.J. Norman, *Rights and Risks: Civil Liberty in Old Age*, National Council for the Care of Old People, 1980.
11. See, for example: V. Carstairs and M. Morrison, *The Elderly in Residential Care*, Scottish Health Service Studies, No. 19, Scottish Home and Health Department, 1971; B. Isaacs, M. Livingstone and Y. Neville, *The Survival of the Unfittest*, Routledge and Kegan Paul, 1972; J. Bond and V. Carstairs, *Services for the Elderly*, Scottish Health Services Studies No. 42, Scottish Home and Health Department, 1982.
12. See, for example, K. Judge and M. Knapp, 'Efficiency in the Production of Welfare: The Public and Private Sectors Compared', in R. Klein and M. O'Higgins (eds.), *The Future of Welfare*, Blackwell, 1985.
13. *Staying Put in Scotland: a guide to innovatory projects which help old people remain in their own homes,* Age Concern Scotland, 1986.
14. A.I. Harris, *Handicapped and Impaired in Great Britain*, HMSO, 1971; and J.R. Buckle, *Work and Housing of Impaired Persons in Great Britain*, HMSO, 1971. For a discussion of the difficulies involved in defining and measuring handicap, see D. Duckworth, *The Classification and Measurement of Disablement*, DHSS Research Report No. 10, HMSO, 1982.
15. Scottish Home and Health Department, *Health in Scotland, 1980,* HMSO, 1981; Scottish Home and Health Department, *Scottish Health Authorities' Priorities for the Eighties* (SHAPE Report), HMSO, 1981.
16. Scottish Home and Health Department, *The Health Services in Scotland: The Way Ahead,* HMSO, 1975.
17. *Special Educational Needs: Report of the Committee of Enquiry into the Education of Handicapped Children and Young People* (Warnock Report), Cmnd.7212, HMSO, 1978.

18. M. Blaxter, 'Research on the Employment of Disabled People in Scotland' in *Research Highlights No.2: Normalisation*, University of Aberdeen, Department of Social Work, 1981.
19. M. Blaxter, *The Meaning of Disability: A Sociological Study of Impairment*, Heinemann, 1976.

FURTHER READING

The Elderly

C. Philipson and A. Walker (eds.), *Ageing and Social Policy: A Critical Assessment*, Gower, 1986.
A critical analysis of current policies for the elderly together with proposals for alternative forms of provision. Also contains more theoretical discussions of ageism and social policy and the role of the family in caring for older people.

A. Tinker, *The Elderly in Modern Society*, Longman, 1981.
A comprehensive study of the literature and research on the needs of the elderly. It includes useful synopses of, or extracts from, legislation, surveys and other documentation and extensive bibliographical references.

A. Walker, *The Care Gap: How can Local Authorities meet the Needs of the Elderly?*, Local Government Information Unit, 1985.
A short informative discussion of local authority services for the elderly.

The Physically Handicapped

D.A. Boswell and J. Wingrove (eds.), *The Handicapped Person in the Community*, Tavistock Publications and Open University Press, 1974.
Readings in sociological, psychological and practical aspects of physical and mental handicap.

E. Topliss, *Social Responses to Handicap*, Longman, 1982.
A useful discussion of the problems of, and provisions for, the physically and mentally handicapped, with useful extracts from legislation and official documents and a comprehensive bibliography.

A. Walker with P. Townsend (eds.), *Disability in Britain: A Manifesto of Rights*, Martin Robertson, 1981.
Reviews the progress made in meeting the needs of the disabled and makes policy suggestions for guaranteeing their rights.

A. Shearer, *Disability: Whose Handicap?*, Blackwell, 1981.
This book looks at provisions for the handicapped through personal accounts of living with various disabilities. Suggestions are made for improvements in services.

11

URBAN SOCIAL POLICY

The very phrase *urban* social policy betrays the long-standing assumption of politicians that there is a spatial dimension to social problems and merit in attempting to solve them on an area-by-area basis. This chapter considers why the assumption arose, how valid it is, and what the consequences of an area-based approach to urban policy in Scotland have been. Although urban social policy has not received the resources devoted to other social services, such as health or education, it has attracted a great deal of attention from policy-makers, and it has been the subject of much political debate. As a consequence, urban social policy has achieved a symbolic importance that is out of all proportion to the scale of resources involved.

THE ORIGINS OF URBAN SOCIAL POLICY

The 1960s was a decade of upheaval in the social policy arena when the optimism accompanying Britain's post-war affluence was clouded by a 'rediscovery' of poverty, especially in the older areas of the major cities. Various analyses of the causes of urban poverty were put forward by different political and professional groups. The existence of a cycle of deprivation transmitted from generation to generation was widely accepted, but the transmission mechanisms involved were a matter of dispute. Some commentators held that deprivation could be accounted for by cultural norms which influenced parental attitudes and led to inappropriate parenting behaviour. This encouraged the view that a 'culture of poverty' prevented the poor from enjoying the benefits of 'normal' society, and it fostered the belief that deprivation could be tackled by improving the education of young children and their parents. Others stressed the influence of environmental and social factors on the life chances of individuals, emphasising the need for a more effective welfare state, seeking better co-ordination to prevent people slipping through the welfare net, and calling for enhanced social services to compensate for the disadvantages which the poor experienced.

The late 1960s and early 1970s thus became an era of dispute, investigation and experimentation in urban policy. Britain, and especially England, was beginning to adjust to its status as a multi-racial society, and, aware that urban problems were most acute in the areas to which New Commonwealth immigrants had been drawn, the government sponsored a range of enquiries into the social and economic bases of 'deprivation'. Section

11 of both the Local Government Act, 1966 and the Local Government (Scotland) Act of the same year was designed to assist local authorities with the special needs created by 'the presence within their areas of substantial numbers of immigrants from the Commonwealth'.[1] Because of its small immigrant population, Scotland has effectively been unable to use this assistance. Moreover, it soon became evident that a wholly new approach to urban problems was required. The two official documents which were most influential in determining what this approach would be were the Plowden Report[2] and the Seebohm Report.[3] Both acknowledged the existence of *areas* of special need, and together they emphasised the importance of improving social services, including education, for those living in the poorest parts of cities. In this respect they were the direct forerunners of the earlier phase of the urban programme (often referred to as the urban aid programme and now known as the traditional urban programme), which was to change the face of urban policy in Britain.

Although the different aspects of urban social policy which developed towards the end of the 1960s pursued widely agreed aims, the form such policies took is better understood in terms of constraints rather than ideals. These constraints included: pragmatic constraints on the type and extent of data available to identify and delimit urban problems; political constraints on how those problems were to be defined for policy purposes; and economic constraints that influenced how, once defined, urban problems could be tackled. These are discussed in turn.

Empirical Shortcomings

Because of the costs and complexities of data collection, and because of the short period in which political decisions must be made, only a limited range of information is ever effectively available for policy-makers to consider. In the 1960s and 1970s, attempts to specify the extent of deprivation relied heavily on census data, but these are only available on an area basis (for enumeration districts, wards and so on); Britain, unlike some other countries, does not provide data relating to individual characterstics. As a (supposedly) 100 per cent sample, the census provides the most comprehensive data set available. For many key decision-makers the fact that it is comprehensive also means that it is the most 'reliable' source, and this is seen as outweighing the problem of dealing with areas rather than individuals. The consequence, however, is that it is the spatial dimensions of urban problems (especially those relating to the so-called 'inner city') that have become the most prominent theme of urban social policy. This development is not uncontroversial, and many argue that deprivation is not neatly contained in discrete area units. Holtermann in research on the 1971 census showed that the spatial concentration of deprived individuals is often quite low.[4] According to the Department of the Environment, moreover, the spatial concentration of deprivation may be decreasing: between 1961 and 1971 the difference in levels of deprivation between conurbations as a whole and their 'inner cities' fell.[5] A spatial focus for urban policy therefore excludes many of the poor and deprived, half of whom live in areas with higher than average incomes. However, this area-based approach to policy has also seemed desirable from a political and economic perspective, and it has therefore tended to persist.

The Politics of Urban Problems

The way in which social problems are defined affects the kind of policies adopted, and political conceptions of urban deprivation have tended to encourage the area-based approach to social policy. The idea of a cycle of deprivation (whether perpetuated by the cultural norms of the deprived or by the shortcomings of the welfare state) was popular amongst politicians during the 1960s. Urban disadvantage was therefore defined as a problem of specific residential communities, or as a phenomenon of areas where service co-ordination had failed. In either case, a solution was sought in improving access to social services on an area-by-area basis. This approach was deemed appropriate even when the concept of a cycle of deprivation gave way to theories linking deprivation with wider processes of economic change and industrial restructuring. Politicians favoured strategies encouraging better co-ordination amongst the services and agencies already in place to deal with any adverse social consequences of economic change. The government's insistence on viewing urban deprivation as a distributional rather than structural problem is nowhere better illustrated than in its adoption of the concept of positive discrimination.

Positive discrimination is a contentious and frequently misapplied concept. Its use in social policy dates from the Plowden Report which argued for priority treatment for schools in deprived areas. Such selectivity was justified by the argument that equality of outcome rather than equality of resource input is the principle that should underlie social policy. It was argued, for instance, that extra resources were required by schools in deprived areas to allow them to compensate for the lack of support and stimulus provided for children by home and neighbourhood. One of the major applications of positive discrimination in Britain has been through an emphasis on priority areas which have been used to channel resources for inner city, urban and housing policy. As Edwards observed, 'As long as the benefits distributed were communal goods and so long as the beneficiaries are anonymously identified "areas" the practice remained uncontentious'.[6] Whenever positive discrimination in favour of groups has been mooted, however (for example to tackle racial or gender inequalities), the concept has been unacceptable. For reasons of political expediency, then, the area-based perspective has proved resilient, and currently it is as popular as ever.

The Economics of Public Policy

From an economic perspective, the overall budget for urban policy is constrained by (politically determined) limits on public expenditure. The need this creates to find an equitable and politically acceptable way of using resources to maximum effect is probably the main factor encouraging the development of spatially targeted policy in Britain. Given that some form of selectivity is necessary when resources are limited, area characteristics have proved to be the most acceptable criteria with which to target policy. Spatial discrimination avoids the political dangers of appearing to favour particular social groups, and it also offers the possibility of realising additional gains from the 'neighbourhood effects' of social investment. It is assumed that people will benefit both directly from the financial and welfare benefits of a given policy and indirectly if economic and social conditions in a locality are improved.

Owing to a mix of pragmatic, political and economic influences, by the late 1960s urban policy was becoming oriented to the needs of particular urban neighbourhoods: those which could be defined as disadvantaged in terms of their mix of social, economic and environmental problems. This area-based approach was adopted not because it embraced some practical or theoretical ideal, but because it provided the best compromise in the face of the constraints which have been outlined above. From an ethical as well as a social perspective the area-based approach is, however, of rather dubious validity. It does, of course, avoid the stigma associated with identifying disadvantaged individuals but, on the other hand, the boundaries of 'deprived' areas must be arbitrary and they can be socially divisive. More fundamentally, a spatial focus can easily divert attention from the causes of inequality. It ignores issues such as:

> the reorganization of capital; the control of local intervention by the centre; the reduction in resources to the cities; the legal, political, and financial constraints operating on cities; the political inability of some groups in society to influence decisions.[7]

Nevertheless, place of residence has proved the most acceptable focus for the kinds of 'positive discrimination' upon which British urban policy has relied.

THE EVOLUTION OF URBAN SOCIAL POLICY

Though governments have never identified a distinctive arena of urban *social* policy, 1969 was a milestone in integrating social needs fully into the broader concerns of urban management. It has frequently been suggested that the urban programme was launched in 1969 as a reaction to a race relations 'crisis' in England.[8] This may well be the case, but from the beginning the government denied the primacy of the 'immigrant problem', and for our purposes the significance of the Local Government Grants (Social Need) Act, 1969 (the legislative basis for the financial support provided through the urban programme) is twofold. First, it marks the beginnings of an approach to urban problems that has become increasingly spatially discriminatory, even within cities. Initially the country's most deprived local authorities were asked to submit bids for projects to improve community services but, as will shortly be apparent, a much more complex ranking of special need was soon developed. Second, it placed social concerns at the very heart of solutions to urban problems. This is particularly clear in Scotland where, between 1969 and 1975, the urban programme was administered by the Social Work Services Group. Under its direction financial support was offered for the provision of facilities and services in areas of special social needs, so contributing to the running of nurseries, playgroups, community centres, schemes for the elderly and self-help initiatives.

The urban programme in England had explicitly introduced into policy-making the concept of areas of social and economic stress and 'multiple deprivation'. In Scotland this dimension of policy became increasingly prominent as the Scottish Office began to direct urban programme funds more carefully towards comprehensive rehabilitation schemes in small areas of acute deprivation. The implicit rationale for this was to combine the concern of the 1960s with specifically social aspects of urban deprivation in a more balanced programme which was able to tackle the economic roots of decline. This notion of addressing both social and economic concerns on a small area basis was especially encouraged by the report on the Scottish Educational Priority Area, which stressed the interrelationship of social and economic issues.[9]

The focus was given further impetus by the experience of the Community Development Projects (CDPs). Between 1969 and 1972 twelve CDPs were established in deprived neighbourhoods which, it was supposed, had slipped through the net of an otherwise satisfactory range of social services. Scotland's CDP was located in Ferguslie Park, Paisley. The CDPs combined 'action' teams, employed by local government and 75 per cent funded through the urban programme, with university-based research teams which were intended to monitor the work of the projects. As their title implies, they were concerned with community development and were based on the growing field of community work; considerable emphasis was placed on citizen involvement and self-help. Many local authorities had begun to recruit staff, often with a social work background, to foster the development of local communities and community groups. The role of community workers was, however, usually left vague, and it became subject to conflicting interpretations. In particular, a division occurred between, on the one hand, the adherents of community development and, on the other, of community action. This schism can be illustrated in the difference between the official yardsticks for gauging the success of community development in the CDPs and what happened in practice in many of the projects. The official view was that the objective of community development was to improve individual and community functioning. Lapping argues that the Home Office, which was responsible for the CDPs, was looking for:

> evidence of improved personal care (for example, use of preventative health services, family planning); improved family functioning (increased marriage or cohabition stability); improved child rearing practices; and improved physical conditions in the neighbourhood.[10]

This definition of the role of community development is closely related to a cultural view of deprivation, but many community workers saw their role as being more political and conflictual. They adopted the objective of changing the perceived powerlessness of communities in the face of the power of local bureaucracies and the effects of a capitalist economy.

The CDPs concluded that urban problems were not so much a consequence of poorly co-ordinated services or inappropriate cultural norms as a reflection of the poverty and inequality inherent in a capitalist economy. This view did not result in the kind of co-ordinated approach to community development envisaged by the government, and relations with the more radical of the projects became strained. The CDPs were eclipsed by the setting up of three Inner Area Studies, commissioned by the Department of the Environment in 1972 (none was in Scotland), and by the announcement by the Home Office in 1974 of the Comprehensive Community Programmes (CCPs). Whereas the former were essentially research exercises, the latter were also intended to improve the quality and appropriateness of services in areas of intense urban deprivation. Although the CCP initiative was somewhat abortive (the first programme was launched in Motherwell and there was only one other, in Gateshead), its co-ordinated or unified approach to urban deprivation was a direct forerunner of the so-called 'integrated' neighbourhood regeneration projects of the 1970s and 1980s. The shift of the main responsibility for urban policy south of the border from the Home Office to the Department of the Environment in 1977 (a parallel move in Scotland from the Social Work Services Group to the Scottish Development Department had taken place in 1975) meant, however, that the Inner Area Studies had more influence, as exemplified in the white paper of that year.[11]

It was in furthering the notion of this integrated approach that experience in Scotland gave an impetus to the changes of the late 1970s which involved, amongst other things, the development of more sophisticated criteria for the targeting of urban policy. The 1971 census revealed that Scotland had a disproportionate share of deprived areas and a greater concentration of deprived groups than anywhere else in Britain. Partly in response to this, in 1975, the Scottish Office set up the Urban Renewal Unit as a separate branch within the Scottish Development Department (SDD). The URU was intended to ensure that Scottish Office policies in general would have regard to the needs of deprived areas and to the responsibilities of local authorities where there was a high incidence of social deprivation. Responsibility for administration of the urban programme was transferred to the URU, largely in order to encourage local authorities to adopt an area-based approach to the problems of urban deprivation.

The setting up of the Scottish Development Agency (SDA) in 1975 was to give the notion of an integrated area-based approach to urban policy a major impetus. The agency was a merger of the Scottish Industrial Estates Corporation and the Small Industries Council for the Rural Areas of Scotland, together with that section of the SDD which had been responsible for the administration of grants to local authorities for derelict land clearance. Keating and Boyle[12] suggest that it was only reluctantly that the SDA assumed responsibility for the co-ordination of comprehensive urban development schemes. Nevertheless, with the advent of the Glasgow Eastern Area Renewal

(GEAR) initiative in 1976 (discussed below), the SDA took to its furthest point the notion that carefully co-ordinated policies of area-based positive discrimination could alleviate the adverse effects of both socio-economic and environmental change. It was a model that England and Wales were soon to follow.

In 1977 the Labour government's white paper, *Policy for the Inner Cities*, announced the development of an enhanced urban programme and, as had happened in the case of the GEAR project, the direct involvement of central government in local processes of urban regeneration. Policy-makers in Scotland and England were therefore thinking along the same lines, and the idea of a more precise and spatially constrained targeting of urban policy resources, exemplified in GEAR, was reflected in the tiering of local authorities in England into a hierarchy of eligibility for urban programme support: partnership authorities, programme authorities, other designated districts and, with the lowest eligibility, non-designated districts.

This kind of tiering did not occur in Scotland; instead, the SDA (especially from 1981 via its area programmes development division) became the arbiter of area priority. In theory, it was the agency, rather than central government directly, that was to influence the direction of urban programme funds, the allocation of finance made available under the Inner Urban Areas Act, 1978 and the focusing of 'mainstream' programmes (such as education, housing and social work) into areas for priority treatment. Thus in Scotland the direct intervention of central government in local affairs was cushioned to an extent by the use of the SDA to control policy implementation and to direct public expenditure. This introduces, potentially at least, an important element of local sensitivity to Scottish urban policy that is not built into the more rigid 'tiering' system used in England and Wales. Having sketched the legislative framework in which urban social policy is set, we now consider the trends and changes that have occurred over the last decade.

THE ROLE OF THE ENHANCED URBAN PROGRAMME IN SCOTLAND

The urban programme has retained a major role in Scottish urban policy, although the level of funding and the emphases of the programme have altered considerably since its inception in the late 1960s. The criteria for accepting projects put forward for funding have changed over time, reflecting both the different priorities for urban social policy outlined earlier and the role of the urban programme within public policy more generally. The urban programme provides a good indicator of the shifts in successive governments' definitions of urban problems, and it also reflects changing views on the role of social policy in alleviating urban deprivation.

Urban programme grants are made by central government for approved projects to cover 75 per cent of capital expenditure and running costs for a period of four years, the remaining 25 per cent being met by the local authority. Funding arrangements now vary according to whether the originating agency is a local authority or a voluntary body. In the latter case agencies are eligible for a grant for up to a further three years. Once this period has run out no further grant is available and, therefore, projects either have to obtain funding from other sources (for example, in the case of local authority projects finance from mainstream budgets) or close.

The scale of resources devoted to the urban programme has increased considerably since its inception. In 1969-70 a total of £600,000 was spent and this increased slowly during the early 1970s until there was a dramatic increase in 1977-78 and again in 1980-81. Approved expenditure in 1986-87 was £34.5 million. However, although resources devoted to the urban programme have increased substantially in real terms, they pale into insignificance when compared with rate support grant (RSG), the main central government grant to local authorities. For example, Strathclyde Regional Council received £733.2 million in RSG for 1985-86 – some 20 times the total expenditure on the urban programme for the whole of Scotland.

The impact of the urban programe is greater than might be expected from the small resources devoted to it because funds and policy initiatives are targeted towards a limited number of areas which are considered to need priority treatment. These areas must be urban (that is to have 10,000 or more inhabitants) and they must be 'deprived' (which means they must contain enumeration districts which fall within the worst ten per cent in Scotland according to a range of social indicators, including type of household, housing amenities, unemployment, low incomes and levels of permanent sickness). Since Strathclyde in general and Glasgow in particular contain a disproportionate share of deprived areas (45 per cent of the census enumeration districts in Glasgow fall within the worst ten per cent in Scotland), these areas have attracted the main concentration of urban programme resources. In 1984-85 approximately 83 per cent of the total was devoted to areas within Strathclyde and 49 per cent to areas within Glasgow.

Targeting of resources has been refined even further to favour specific small deprived areas identified by the use of census indicators. For example, in Strathclyde 14 areas have been designated by the regional council as 'special initiative areas' because they are perceived to have the worst problems; these are given top priority for urban programme funding. A further 74 areas have been designated as areas of priority treatment and also receive preference in the allocation of resources. As part of its Social Deprivation Strategy the council aims to discriminate positively in favour of these areas in its mainstream expenditure in addition to the use of urban programme resources. Over time the degree of area targeting and the emphasis on a co-ordinated approach through both urban programme and mainstream policies have grown. This means that increasingly the urban programme is seen as providing extra resources as part of an integrated area-based approach to urban deprivation.

As definitions of the urban problem have changed so have the criteria for urban programme funding. At first the emphasis was on filling gaps in provision by expanding existing services for groups such as the under-fives. This emphasis was consistent with explanations of deprivation based on the concept of a cycle of deprivation. But economic issues have increasingly come to the fore with projects such as community business receiving funding. At the same time extra emphasis has been given to projects which provide facilities for and capitalise on the initiative of local community groups. This shows the importance now being attached to the idea of encouraging self-help by creating confidence amongst residents of deprived areas in their own abilities to overcome their problems. When the Conservative government came to power in 1979 they initiated a review of the urban programme in Scotland and following its completion issued a circular in 1981. This confirmed the continuation of the programme but sought to review projects more frequently and amend the criteria for providing grants. Emphasis was to be given to those schemes, especially from the voluntary sector, which could mobilise private sector resources and so release government money for projects which might not otherwise be funded.

Despite these changed priorities, the targeting of funds has, in practice, adjusted more slowly. A sample survey of 116 projects financed between 1977 and 1980 was carried out by the Scottish Office[13] and the results are given in Table 11.1. There is an obvious emphasis on community development (which accounts for the largest proportion of projects), mainly of a 'traditional' nature and originating from local authorities. Common examples are the funding of community development staff and the provision of community centres and meeting places. Overall, community groups or representatives were only involved in originating the proposal for just over one-quarter of the projects. There is, moreover, no sign that the more political elements of community development activity evident in many CDP projects received much support. Many other projects were extensions of existing forms of social work, recreation or education provision, and only seven per cent were involved with economic initiatives.

As Edwards has stressed,[14] despite its title, the urban programme is essentially a funding mechanism rather than a coherent programme. It has been described as 'too small, badly directed and aimed at the wrong targets'.[15] Nevertheless, while the urban programme is only a minor investment when compared with mainstream budgets, as well as its symbolic role it has assumed considerable importance for urban policy at a time when other sources of public funds are tightly constrained. Since it is easier to manipulate new resources than it is to alter the distribution of existing expenditure, the programme is a much more important source of assistance for deprived areas than its overall size would suggest. But there can be little doubt that the programme is badly directed. The geographical targeting has been tightened up but there appear to be few effective guidelines as to the types of projects to be supported. The guidelines are very wide, merely giving priority to projects which are part of a co-ordinated local strategy. However, there are very few areas where local structures are in place and available to ensure that this co-ordination occurs. For example, few local authorities have decentralised the administration of services to a local level and little use has been made of structures which already exist such as community councils.

Without an efficient system of local prioritisation, it is not surprising that

TABLE 11.1:

Urban Programme Projects by Type, 1977-80

	No. of projects		%	
Community projects	49		42	
Community development		26		22
Information/advice centres		12		10
Community centres		9		8
Community transport		5		4
Community newspapers		3		3
Social work	34		29	
Day-care facilities		12		10
Social work with children/families		9		8
Residential/hostel provision		7		6
Home support/domiciliary services		4		3
Advice/counselling on alcoholism		4		3
Street warden/good neighbour schemes		3		3
After-care for offenders		2		2
Occupational therapy aids		2		2
Intermediate treatment		2		2
Recreation and leisure	26		22	
Play sports facilities		12		10
Youth clubs		10		9
Arts/library facilities		3		3
Pensioners' meeting place/centre		2		2
Adventure playground		1		1
Education	21		18	
Facilities for under-fives		15		13
Family learning units		3		3
Specialist teachers		2		2
Education for ethnic minorities		1		1
Employment and industry	8		18	
Training		4		3
Careers advice		2		2
Factory premises		2		2
Co-operative development		1		1
Environment	7		6	
Administration	1		1	
Total	116			

Note: The categories are not mutually exclusive so that the figures do not sum to 116 projects or 100 per cent.

Source: *The Urban Programme in Scotland: Results of a Monitoring Exercise*, Scottish Office, 1984.

the urban programme in Scotland sometimes appears badly co-ordinated. With the importance of local sensitivity in mind, we now turn to consider the effectiveness of some area initiatives that have relied on both urban programme funding and resources from mainstream budgets which local authorities have been able to 'bend' to favour selected areas.

AREA APPROACHES

The GEAR Project

When the Department of the Environment published an analysis of indicators of urban deprivation from the 1971 census it showed a concentration of deprivation within the West of Scotland and more specifically within Glasgow. Several areas were considered as the focus of an area-based project but parts of the East End of Glasgow were eventually chosen, for a mixture of political and more pragmatic reasons.

The area selected was largely built up during the nineteenth century around newly emerging industries. Economic decline in the twentieth century had left the area with increasing unemployment, industrial dereliction and worsening housing conditions. During the 1960s five areas in the East End were designated comprehensive development areas, leading to the demolition of unfit housing and the movement of population to peripheral council schemes. The outward migration resulted in a substantial reduction in population (from approximately 115,000 in 1961 to 82,000 in 1971) and altered the population balance because it tended to be the younger and more able members of the community who moved out.

The Glasgow Eastern Area Renewal (GEAR) project was set up at a point in urban policy when emphasis was being switched from a concern solely with social policy as the instrument of change in areas of social deprivation. The CDPs and Inner Area Studies had made policy-makers aware of the economic aspects of deprivation that were increasingly seen to be the root cause of urban problems and which therefore should be tackled directly. At the same time, however, there was still felt to be a role for 'traditional' social policy in alleviating urban deprivation. An emphasis on using social policy to discriminate positively in favour of areas of deprivation, ensuring that services were so managed as to be sensitive to their particular needs, had underlain the CDPs and CCPs. The GEAR project also took on board the emphasis, evident in the CCPs and stressed by the Inner Area Studies, on co-ordinating policies between agencies and on 'bending' mainstream programmes rather than merely relying on additional resources. It was the inability of the CDPs to influence these issues of co-ordination and redirecting funds from existing programmes that was a major reason for their failure to tackle urban deprivation effectively. The GEAR project was designed to avoid these failings of the CDP approach. There was to be a twin emphasis on economic and social issues, positive discrimination in favour of the GEAR area in terms of resources, and mainstream programmes were to be co-ordinated and tailored to fit its needs.

The influence of a dual emphasis was apparent in the wide range of bodies which participated in the GEAR project and in the way it was initially organised. The participants were the Scottish Development Agency, Glasgow

District Council, Strathclyde Regional Council, the Scottish Special Housing Association, the Manpower Services Commission, the Housing Corporation and the Greater Glasgow Health Board. They were to retain responsibility in their own fields, but the SDA was to perform an overall co-ordinating role, to be carried out by its urban renewal directorate with a staff of 37 of whom 12 were concerned with social policy issues.[16]

Co-ordination was to be achieved through a number of working groups of officials drawn from the participating bodies. These groups were chaired by a representative from the organisation with primary responsibility for the service. The concerns of the working groups included population, education, community care, leisure and recreation, and health. These working groups were disbanded in 1979 when their findings were incorporated in overall project proposals.

In 1981 the organisational arrangements for GEAR within the SDA were changed, and the large co-ordinating team was reduced in size. Most emphasis was placed on the economic and environmental initiatives being undertaken by the agency, although the team retained its responsibility for overall project co-ordination, community involvement and the running of the GEAR centres. Inevitably, given these changes in structure, the bulk of responsibility for co-ordination and management within the social policy field was handed over to other participating agencies. Social policy issues, therefore, came less to the fore in GEAR and became the responsibility of individual participants working within its formal structure of committees or the informal networks created through the project. Keating and Boyle[17] argue that GEAR began with a commitment to social improvement but, mirroring the shift in government policy, placed increasing emphasis on the economic aspects of renewal, most specifically those aiming to attract new businesses into the area. All the SDA area renewal initiatives since the GEAR project was established have conformed to these concerns. The project thus marked both the beginning and end of attempts in Scotland by central government to intervene in order to integrate social and economic development on an area basis.

The original conception of the GEAR project demanded that existing programmes should be steered towards the area so that the initiative could proceed without undue reliance on new sources of finance. The SDA was to make money available for environmental and economic projects while GEAR was to be given priority for urban programme finance, but any further increase in resources depended on mainstream programmes being flexible enough to pay special attention to the area. At a time of severe financial restrictions this meant taking resources from elsewhere, and there are political and pragmatic reasons why this proved difficult. In the event, even Strathclyde's Social Deprivation Strategy, whose very rationale is to discriminate positively in favour of areas of social deprivation, has had only limited success in redirecting existing resources to the area. Although attempts have been made to assess the amount of extra resources attracted to the East End by the existence of the GEAR project, firm conclusions are impossible because no one knows what would have happened had it not existed.

It is easier, however, to gauge whether the project resulted in social policy in the GEAR area being different than elsewhere. Evaluations suggest that the structure of the project (particularly the way it was largely operated through existing agencies) meant that established forms of social policy provision, such as in education and health care, were merely replicated or extended; they were not redesigned or explicitly integrated with economic policies. Fundamental questions about the relationship between social and economic policy, and about the extent to which social policy could be used to cushion the effect of economic restructuring or to absorb the consequences of inevitable decline, were never resolved. Indeed, as far as it is possible to judge, such questions were never raised.

Nevertheless, major changes have taken place in the GEAR area since the late 1970s, most notably in relation to housebuilding, housing conditions and environmental improvement. Some major new industrial and commercial developments are also planned in an effort to offset the continuing loss of jobs in traditional manufacturing industry. Many of these achievements are undoubtedly due to the existence of the project but it is not clear which and what proportion. The project wound up in 1987 when the SDA ended its formal project co-ordinating commitment, and responsibility has reverted to the district and regional councils which have set up a number of joint committees in an attempt to co-ordinate policies. Central government through the SDA has continued to set up area-based initiatives, but in line with the change of emphasis in GEAR these have concentrated on economic issues, primarily by encouraging business development.

Economic Projects

The first area-based economic initiatives were set up where there were substantial job losses due to plant closures. In 1979 the closure of the Glengarnock steelworks led to the creation of the Garnock Valley Task Force, and in 1980 a task force was set up to develop a business park on the site of the former Singer factory in Clydebank. Further area-based projects have followed. They have no fixed pattern, reflecting rather the individual circumstances of each area and the objectives of the parties involved. In some projects, as in Dundee, the SDA takes a lead role, whereas in others, for example in Port Dundas (Glasgow), it is taken by different agencies such as the district council. More recent projects have given a significant (sometimes leading) role to private sector institutions. In these economic initiatives, emphasis is usually on industrial development through environmental and infrastructural improvements, industrial building and investment, and business promotion.

The other major area-based economic strategy has been the creation of enterprise zones. The first of these to be located in Scotland was set up in Clydebank in 1980, followed by others at Invergordon (following the closure of an aluminium smelter) and on Tayside (split between Arbroath and Dundee). The objective of the enterprise zones is to free business from official controls, but in practice the main differences have been that rate bills are met by the Treasury for ten years and some planning restrictions are lifted.

The emphasis on economic renewal still leaves regional and district councils with the problems both of defining the role of social policy towards deprived areas and of alleviating social disadvantage at a time of limited public resources. Local government has sought to meet these aims in two ways. First, it has attempted a strategy of area-based positive discrimination in the overall allocation of resources. An example of this which has already been mentioned is Strathclyde's Social Deprivation Strategy which aims to redirect existing, and concentrate new, resources on areas of priority treatment within the region. The drawbacks of this approach are that the scope for re-allocation is not great (because of institutional rigidities and the small amount of new resources which are available) and that local structures cannot always be developed to ensure that the resources are effectively directed to meet the needs of an area. Second, the development of an area-based approach to resource allocation has coincided with general moves to decentralise the housing and social work services, providing at least the potential for more locally sensitive policy implementation. For instance, local authorities are being urged by central government to decentralise housing management, particularly in difficult-to-let estates, and to build on the experience of the Priority Estates Project in England. The result has been a number of community-based, local area projects, usually formed around housing issues but broadening out into other social and economic concerns. An example of this kind of approach is the Barrowfield Project.

The Barrowfield Project

Barrowfield is an area of some 600 council houses in the GEAR area, consisting of tenements which were completed just after the second world war. It is a physically distinct estate cut off from surrounding areas by major roads and the Celtic football ground, and the area has a bleak and desolate atmosphere. Barrowfield stood out on a number of deprivation indicators in the 1971 and 1981 censuses, such as the degree of overcrowding, the proportion of the population on low incomes and who were handicapped or permanently sick. Unemployment and the proportion of single-parent families were high. Barrowfield's problems were thus related to housing, social and economic issues.

The Barrowfield Project was set up in 1980 by Glasgow District Council and Strathclyde Regional Council. One aim was to improve housing administration and social services in the area by encouraging residents to participate in their management. At first a co-ordinating group and a steering group were set up, composed of officials from relevant agencies. A series of working groups was organised to cover the environment, housing and employment. In 1983 a full-time co-ordinator was appointed with funds from the urban programme, while changes were made to the project's organisational framework to bring it closer to people on the estate, and to increase local autonomy and resident involvement.

The project has achieved some significant changes. The housing and social work departments increased the number of staff working in the area and opened a joint local office there funded from the urban programme. Together with residents, a credit union has been set up to provide loans to local people, and campaigns have been undertaken to improve the take-up of welfare benefits. A community business has been established with funding from Strathclyde Community Business (an organisation set up by the regional council to use urban programme funding to stimulate enterprises in deprived areas employing local people). This originally paid for a manager and some clerical support but has been expanded to cover other management needs. A repairs co-operative has also been set up, enabling tenants to control housing repairs by employing an administrator to organise repair work which is then carried out by a private contractor.

A phased programme of environmental improvements was also drawn up; funding was agreed through Glasgow District Council for work within the curtilage of the houses and through the SDA for work in open spaces. At one stage the SDA withdrew from its commitment to the first phase of the scheme as part of a reassessment of priorities and thus put the whole project at risk. However, after an outcry they re-instated their support. The SDA and the district council are also funding a number of smaller environmental projects which are designed to employ local labour, either through the local community business or various MSC schemes. Great interest has been expressed by policy-makers in the Barrowfield project. It has proved that a locally managed project run by local people can be flexible, co-ordinated, able to draw on diverse sources of funding, and successful in promoting policies which do something to meet the needs of a neighbourhood.

As a consequence of progress in Barrowfield, the same general approach is being applied in other 'problem' areas in Scotland, although the precise nature of each project is obviously different. The influence of the Barrowfield model has been particularly evident within the rest of the GEAR area where other local communities have seen its relevance for their neighbourhoods. Community workers have been quick to seize on the opportunity provided by these projects to improve the capacity for self-management in local areas, and they have encouraged community groups to press for their own schemes. With responsibility for the GEAR project moving to the local authorities, it seems likely that the Barrowfield model will be more widely adopted and be seen as an important and effective way of co-ordinating policies, at least in the East End of Glasgow.

On the basis of a review of the GEAR project, Donnison[18] has proposed a change of approach towards the welfare state, encompassing both policy-making and the delivery of social services. He characterised existing services as being centralised rather than consumer oriented, and organised on functional, specialist and professional lines. While services of this kind have great strengths, they are relatively powerless, he argued, to deal with the intense social problems generated by the collapse of traditional industries. In the future social policy should, therefore, be flexible enough to adapt to the needs of particular areas rather than emphasising the achievement of uniformity of provision based on nationally defined norms. Policy-making and services should be community-based and founded on organisational structures oriented towards local needs. They should also be organised so as to be both responsive to the demands of local people and democratically controlled. Social policy should take account of economic needs so that the social and economic objectives of urban policy can be integrated. There should be an awareness of the interaction of social and economic policies. The Barrowfield project fulfils all of these criteria and it may well indicate a new direction in which urban social policy is heading.

CONCLUSIONS

The shape of urban policy has changed considerably in the last 20 years, though the approach of area-based priority treatment has been a constant theme. Indeed, it is in Scotland that this theme has found its most complete orchestration through the efforts of the SDA which has guided area-based policy in a way that is potentially more sensitive to local needs than the designation of partnership and programme authorities south of the border. Within this spatial framework, however, the changed emphasis of urban policy has been striking.

The initiatives of the 1960s (epitomised in the traditional urban programme) were based on the premise that a cycle of deprivation, arising from poor and unco-ordinated service delivery or cultures of poverty, lay at the heart of the 'urban crisis'. However, the lessons of the CDPs and Inner Area Studies were that economic difficulties form the root of much social malaise; and in the 1970s a phase of British urban policy, inspired partly by the GEAR initiative, was developed to integrate social and economic strategies to tackle urban decline. But during the 1980s the principle of economic regeneration has come to dominate area-based policy, often at the expense of social priorities. This is clear from the changed emphasis of the enhanced urban programme and the shift of priorities in the second phase of GEAR; it is also apparent in the setting up of new initiatives such as economic regeneration projects, enterprise zones, freeports, and the urban development corporations in Merseyside and London Docklands. During the 1980s, then, the thrust of both area-based and mainstream social and economic policy in Scotland, as elsewhere in Britain, has been to encourage the wealth creating sector in preference to managing the consequences of economic restructuring. Unfortunately, this may, as Keating and Boyle[19] observe, be occurring at the expense of the social fabric of Scottish cities.

Despite the pessimistic prognosis that must be given when the principle of wealth accumulation overrides that of social well-being, there are positive lessons to be drawn from Scotland's experience of urban social policy. First, in terms of the targeting of area initiatives, there is little doubt that the flexibility introduced by setting up a co-ordinating body such as the SDA offers the potential for more sensitive investment strategies than the approach followed in England and Wales. Second, Scotland's experience of a range of scales for area initiatives – from GEAR to the more recent economic projects – suggests that the most effective use of resources will be to channel them into areas small enough to be meaningful to residents though not so small that they discourage investors. Finally, the experience of Barrowfield indicates that the most successful attempts at area regeneration will be those which capitalise on local initiative, deal with problems as they are defined from the 'bottom-up', and combine a multi-agency approach with the provision of sufficient resources to combat the economic hardship that results from industrial change. More than two decades after the first development of urban policy, its initial social focus has been increasingly replaced by an emphasis on wealth creation. Nevertheless, the experience of Barrowfield and similar projects indicates that urban social policy still has a role to play. How prominent this will continue to be in an ideological climate where the emphasis is on attempts to further social aims through the market rather than through the welfare state remains to bc seen.

References

1. M. Fitzgerald, 'Immigration and Race Relations: Political Aspects No 15', *New Community*, Vol.13, No.2, 1986.
2. *Children and Their Primary Schools* (Plowden Report), HMSO, 1967.
3. *Report of the Committee on Local Authority and Allied Personal Social Services* (Seebohm Report), Cmnd. 3703, HMSO, 1968.
4. S. Holtermann, 'Areas of Urban Deprivation in Great Britain: An Analysis of 1971 Census Data', *Social Trends 6*, HMSO, 1975.
5. Department of the Environment, *Study of the Inner Areas of Conurbations*, DOE, 1975
6. J. Edwards, *Positive Discrimination*, Tavistock, 1987.
7. P. Lawless, *The Evolution of Spatial Policy*, Pion, 1986, p.62.
8. J. Edwards and R. Batley, *The Politics of Positive Discrimination: An Evaluation of the Urban Programme 1967-77*, Tavistock, 1978.
9. C. M. Morrison (ed.) *Educational Priority: Vol.5: EPA – A Scottish Study*, HMSO, 1974.
10. A. Lapping (ed.) *Community Action*, Fabian Tract 400, 1970, p.3.
11. *Policy for the Inner Cities*, Cmnd. 6845, HMSO, 1977.
12. M. Keating and R. Boyle, *Re-Making Urban Scotland,*, Edinburgh University Press, 1986.
13. *The Urban Programme in Scotland: Results of a Monitoring Exercise*, Scottish Office, 1984.
14. J. Higgins. N. Deakin, J. Edwards and M. Wicks, *Government and Urban Poverty*, Blackwell, 1983.
15. Keating and Boyle, *Re-Making Urban Scotland.*
16. R. Leclerc and D. Draffan, 'The Glasgow Eastern Area Renewal Project', *Town Planning Review*, Vol.55, No.3, 1984.
17. Keating and Boyle, *Re-Making Urban Scotland.*
18. D. Donnison, *Urban Policies: A New Approach*, Fabian Tract 487, 1983.
19. Keating and Boyle, *Re-Making Urban Scotland.*

FURTHER READING

J. Higgins, N. Deakin, J. Edwards and M. Wicks, *Government and Urban Poverty*, Blackwell, 1983.

A readable account of the evolution of inner city policy.

D. Donnison and A. Middleton (eds.), *Regenerating the Inner City: Glasgow's Experience*, Routledge and Kegan Paul, 1987.
A review of the GEAR project.

D. Donnison, *Urban Policies: A New Approach*, Fabian Tract 487, 1983.
A short critique of existing social service provision and discussion of an alternative community-based approach.

M. Keating and R. Boyle, *Re-Making Urban Scotland*, Edinburgh University Press, 1986.
A discussion of the economic aspects of Scottish urban policy.

P. Lawless, *The Evolution of Spatial Policy*, Pion, 1986.
A chronological outline of the development of area-based approaches to policy-making in Britain.

INDEX